POLYMATH PRODUCER

How to Master the *Language*
of Music Production

POLYMATH PRODUCER

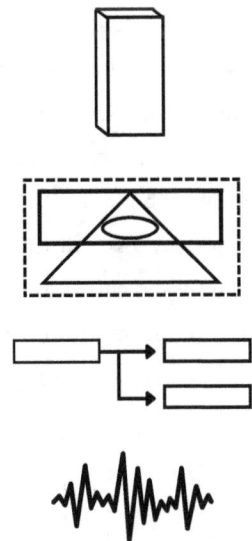

Jonathan William Ferrier

Copyright © 2024 by Jonathan William Ferrier
Published by Deeper than Words Publishing, 1st Edition, 2024
Book Cover by Jonathan William Ferrier
Illustrations by Jonathan William Ferrier
Author Photo by Jason Benson
Editing by Larry Butler

All rights reserved. No part of this book may be reproduced by any mechanical, photographic, or electronic process, or in the form of a phonographic recording; nor may it be stored in a retrieval system, transmitted, or otherwise be copied for public or private use – other than for "fair use" as brief quotations embodied in articles and reviews – without prior written permission of the publisher. Except as permitted by Australian copyright law.

This publication is designed to provide accurate and authoritative information in regard to the subject matter covered. While the publisher and author have used their best efforts in preparing this book, they make no representations or warranties with respect to the accuracy or completeness of the contents of this book. The author of this book does not dispense business advice. Thus, neither the publisher nor the author assume liability for any losses that may be sustained by the use of the methods described in this book, and any such liability is hereby expressly disclaimed. In the event you use any of the information in this book for yourself, the author and the publisher assume no responsibility for your actions.

Hardcover ISBN: 978-1-7637174-2-8

For music creators, past, present and future...
May this be a light when times get dark.

Dedicated to my parents for whom this entire project would not have been made available to the world without your unconditional support.

Contents

Introduction: The Language of Music Production..1

PART I: The Polymath Producer System

Discovering the Language...7
Polymath Producer Philosophy...17
    Mental Models...18
    How Our Influences Shape the Music We Create.............................22
    How to Systematize This Process..23
    Music Production Analysis...24
    Polymath Producer Frameworks...25
    Level One: Technique Framework...26
    Level 1.5: Resource Mining..27
    Level Two: Core Principles of Arranging Framework........................28
    Level Three: Stems Thinking Framework..29
    Level Four: Sonics Framework...30
    Technique Library..31
    Catalog of Music and Original Sound...32
    Feedback Loops and Iteration...33
    How This Creates World-Class Music..34
    The Polymath Producer System – With Frameworks.......................35
    Standing on the Shoulders of Giants...36
    The Lost Art..36
    Original Sound via Cross-Pollination..37
    Talent Hacking...38
    Benefits of Music Production Analysis...39

The Polymath Producer Feedback Loop..41
This Is the Polymath Producer System..42
Action Steps..43

PART II: Techniques [Analysis Level One]

Learning a Language..47
How to Read Songs Like a Book..51
    What Is a Technique?..51
    Music Production Analysis of Techniques................................52
    Level 1.5: Resource Mining Techniques....................................63
    Technique Library and Technique Documents.......................65
    Technique Library Document Examples...................................66
    Music Production Analysis Document.......................................68
    Resource Mining Document..70
    Technique Library Master Document..72
    Faster Approach to Documentation...77
    Build Your Mental Framework...79
    How Does this Technique Make Me Feel?...............................79
    The Importance of Asking: Why?..80
    The Importance of Asking a Diverse Set of Questions..........81
    Difference Between Techniques From Tracks & Resources...........82
    Cultivating The Technique Miner Mindset................................83
    In-Depth Essays versus The System..83
    How Your Brain Will Memorize Techniques............................84
    What to Expect..86
    The Universal Formula..89
    Action Steps...90

Contents

PART III: Core Principles of Arranging [Analysis Level Two]

The Principles Are Everything...95
The Ten Core Principles of Arranging..99
    Number One: Core Structure Principle..101
    Number Two: Core Harmonic Structure Principle.......................105
    Number Three: Core Rhythm Principle..109
    Number Four: Counter Rhythm Principle.....................................134
    Number Five: Spatial Principle..140
    Number Six: Foreground and Background Principle....................144
    Number Seven: Energy Principle...150
    Number Eight: Call and Response Principle.................................160
    Number Nine: Repurposing Principle...164
    Number Ten: Synergy Principle...169
    Keys to The Kingdom..172
    Action Steps...173

PART IV: Stems Thinking [Analysis Level Three]

The Quest To Go Deeper..177
Stems Thinking: Layering..181
    Stems Thinking...182
    What Are Stems?..183
    How to Group Your Stems for Analysis..187
    Layering Types in Stems Thinking..192
    Layering Type One: Individual Stem...193
    Layering Type Two: Groups of Stems...196
    Layering Type Three: Groups and Groups of Stems....................199
    Steps to Analyze Stem Files - Summary...202
    How to Stems Think with Your Own Music..................................211
    Action Steps...215

PART V: Sonics [Analysis Level Four]

Sonics Confession..219
Learning Sonics..223
    What Are Sonics?..223
    The Musical Arrangement versus Sonics...................................223
    Ear Training..224
    The Experiment..225
    The Journey..226
    My Strategy for Golden Ears...230
    Can You Hear the Truth?..234
    The Goal for Polymath Producer with Sonics............................238
Analyzing Sonics...244
    Principles of Sonics...245
    Steps to Industry Standard Sonics Overview.............................250
    Real-Life Example: Mixing and Mastering "Just Like Me"..............255
    Prerequisites..260
    Step One: Analyzing Sonics (Reference Matching)......................264
    Scientific Method of Reference Matching.................................265
    Technique Library: Documentation of Sonic Techniques...............274
    Reference Matching for Each Part of the Production Chain...........278
    Sonics via Stems Thinking..279
    Visual Analysis of Sonics...280
    Sonic Problems Along the Production Chain............................281
    Step Two: Produce Your Sonics..283
    How the Song and Arrangement Impact The Sonics...................284
    Learning Recording and Editing..285
    The Pro Mixing and Mastering Workflow.................................286
    Real-Life Example: Mixing and Mastering "Late to the Party".........289
    Exposing the Problems in Your Production Chain......................292
    Goals, Problems, and Tools...295

Entire Framework Workflow..298
Step Three: Iterate to Industry Standard............................300
Benefits of Knowing the Whole Production Chain............302
Think for Yourself and World Class Standards..................303
Action Steps...306
You've Learned the Four Primary Frameworks..................308

PART VI: Original Sound

Building Blocks..313
Your Catalog of Music...317
    The Framework..317
    Important: Before You Move On...319
    The Goal When Creating Your Music..................................320
    Feedback and Iteration...321
    Example of Original Sound...323
    Musical Taste..324
    The Myth of Genre...325
    Transcending Generations...326
    Trends versus Perennial Sellers..328
    World Class Sonic Standards...329
    Evolution of Sound..329
    Every Decision Counts..330
    Collaboration and Original Sound.......................................330
    The Golden Thread..331
    Songwriting...333
    Cross-Pollination..336
    Aiming the System at a Goal..339
    Action Steps..342

PART VII: Transcendence

Transcending the System..347
Vision and Transcendence..351
    Transcendence..351
    The Paradox of Heart and Mind..351
    Moving Into The Unknown..352
    Find Your Own Truth..352
    Humans Are Born to Speak the Language..353
    How Simple Can You Make It?..353
    Standards and Identity..354
    Be > Do > Have..354
    Think For Yourself, Feel For Yourself..355
    Inner Source..356
    Get Out of Your Own Way..356
    Genius..357
    Action Steps..357

BACK MATTER

    My Gifts to You..359
    The Road Map..360
    Additional Resources For Faster Success..363
    Appendix I: Summary of Action Steps..367
    Appendix II: Polymath Producer Glossary..375
    Notes..385
    Acknowledgments..393
    About the Author..395

POLYMATH PRODUCER

Download all additional resources from this book at www.polymathproducer.com/resources or use the QR code.

polymath
/pah-lee-math/
noun
a person who has in-depth knowledge of a wide range of subjects

producer
/pro-du-cer/
noun
1. short for "Music Producer" in the music industry
2. a person who oversees the music production of a song from start to finish

polymath producer
/pah-lee-math pro-du-cer/
noun
1. a person who can complete the whole production chain themselves
2. a person who transcends genre
3. a person who understands the language of music production

INTRODUCTION:
The Language of Music Production

WHAT IF music production could be turned into a universal language? What if you could then use any building block of that language to form the most beautiful music of your life? That is what this book will show you how to do.

Music production can feel complex. It requires a music producer to create a piece of music from nothing. As well as create that music using what feels like unlimited variables.

Most modern music producers are also polymaths. They're required to know how to complete the entire production chain including:

- Songwriting
- Arranging (track composition)
- Recording
- Editing
- Mixing
- Mastering

When you learn music production, it is like being in a foreign country where you don't know the language and then expected to speak it. It can be challenging. Then naturally, as we all do, we turn to the Internet. We learn from YouTube, books, and programs. We learn to use tools, but don't know why or when we need to use them in context. We learn to copy existing genres, but don't learn how to transcend genre. We power through for years and years until we finally become professional. It is an uphill battle. Trial and error is how we manage to get a track complete. Starting tracks, finishing tracks, and being original are constant struggles. While in this vortex, it feels as if we can only rely on the Internet for answers.

But what if there was a way to understand music production as a language – a universal language that transcends genre? What if there was a way you could sit at your studio and allow your intuition to deliver the answers to the music you are creating, like magic? This book will show you how to do that.

What you're about to learn is powerful. This isn't any normal book about music production. This book is meta - It is the underlying framework of everything you've ever learned and ever will learn about music production. Everything about the language of music production is built on top of what you'll learn in this book. This book is about the fundamentals. The fundamentals are how you master a skill. It is a book on mastery.

This book is for music producers who want to learn how to master the language of music production. You master music production by analyzing the greatest music of all time. Once you learn this "secret language", you will never think about music production the same way again. This secret language has been in front of us our whole lives; we only need to look at it the right way to understand it.

By the end of this book, you will have a step-by-step system to help you:

Learn and master the language of music production, activate your genius, and make your impact on the future of music...

You will become a **Polymath Producer...**

Introduction

You will:

- Learn and master the language of music production through analysis.
- You will then learn how the great music producers of all time have created their music.
- You will then use the building blocks you learn to make the music of your dreams a reality.
- You will then positively impact the world with your music.

To become a Polymath Producer, you will learn:

- How to master the language of music production – the entire step-by-step system.
- The secret mindset shift to view music as building blocks.
- The Ten Core Principles of Arranging in every piece of music ever produced.
- How to master layering in your arrangements.
- How to become industry standard at mixing and mastering.
- How to transcend genre and find your own original sound.
- How to transcend the mind and let creativity and authenticity flow.

Before we move on, I want to thank you for trusting me with your most valuable resource: your time. Your purchase of this book tells me that you are ready for a transformation. You have proven you are humble enough to learn new ideas. You have proven you are motivated to live up to your true potential as a music producer.

Now, it is only a matter of reading the words on these pages and taking action on the steps I show you. It is as simple as that. When we come out the other end of this together, you will have experienced a transformation. You'll have the roadmap to evolve into your ultimate potential as a producer. I believe in you. Let's take the first step.

I'll begin by sharing how I discovered the language of music production...and how you can, too...

PART I:
The Polymath Producer System

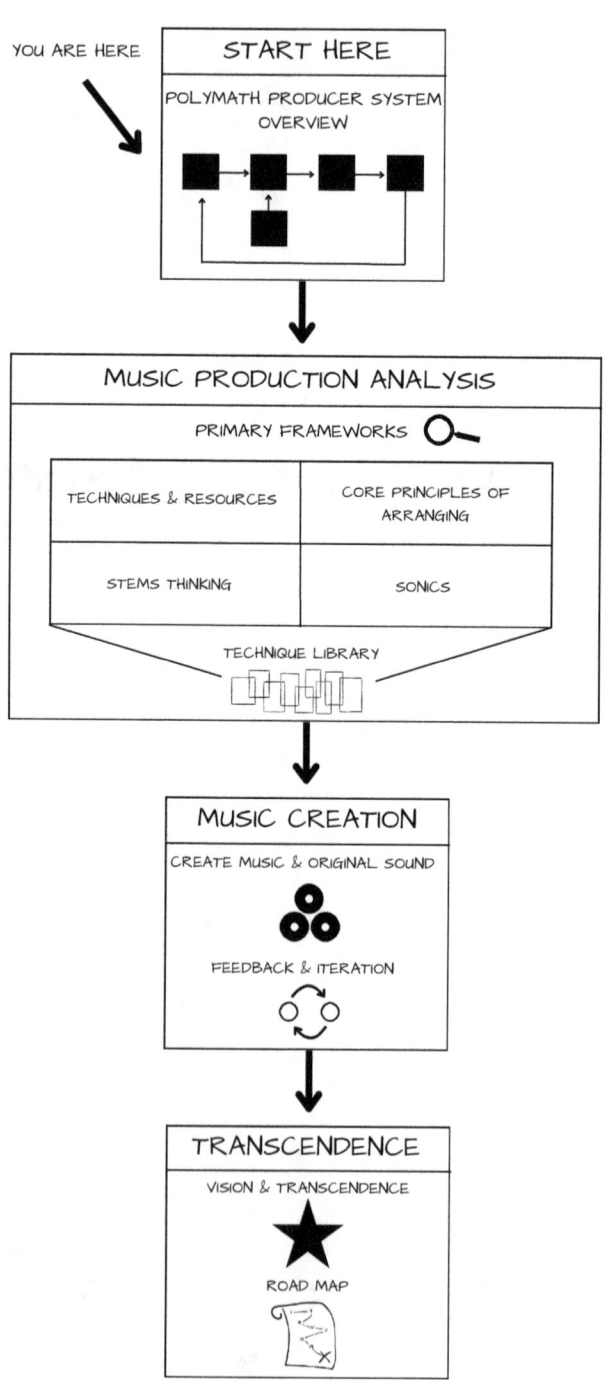

Discovering the Language of Music Production

I SAT AT MY music studio desk. It was my bedroom in my parents' house, but it was a studio nonetheless. The room was dark, like a cave. My parents called it the "Bat Cave" because it would be where I would spend most of my days. In this cave, I was trying to discover the secrets of music production.

On this day, my inspiration and motivation ran high. I had heard music from the top modern hits, which were fresh in my head. I knew what I wanted to achieve: music that sounded as good as theirs. I thought to myself, *How hard could it be?* I was in that phase of my music production skills where I thought I knew way more than I actually did.

I opened my digital audio workstation (DAW) and started tapping away at the keyboard. *Their synths sounded big; let's add a bunch and see what happens.* I tested different things for a few hours. *Why wasn't my music sounding as good as theirs?* I became obsessive, throwing myself into trial and error. I'd look at YouTube tutorials when I would try to find an answer – desperate attempts to find solutions. But every time, my trial and error would fall short.

Soon enough, I came up with something that sounded like a track. I didn't mix it, though. When I'd used mixing plugins in the past, my tracks sounded even worse than before, so I avoided them.

I showed it to my family and friends. My mother loved it. My friends who wanted to be nice said they loved it, too. But I could sense their indifference. Then other friends gave me the harsh truth: I wasn't there yet.

The pain struck me right in the stomach. They were right. I secretly knew it, but I'd been in denial. When I compared my track to the professionals', mine didn't match their quality. A tidal wave of disappointment rushed through me. A mixture of embarrassment and self-hate because my skills weren't where I wanted them to be. Embarrassment turned to anger as I blamed the circumstances I found myself in.

"It was because I didn't have an in-person mentor!"
"It was because I didn't have the fancy equipment!"
"It was because I didn't have the right connections!"
"It was because I didn't live in LA!"
"If only they could see my potential!"

What I wanted was to know the secrets that the professionals knew. I wanted to be artistically fulfilled and create the best tracks I could. I wanted to make music that could stand the test of time. I wanted to impact the world with my music. I wanted people to associate their most incredible memories with my music – a soundtrack for their lives.

But deep down, there were also darker parts of me, too. I wanted the social approval. The status that comes with being able to make a track that is so impressive people can't help but tell you. I was secretly insecure. My self-image was that of a top music producer, but the reality at the time was nothing like that. I had potential, but I was a lot more arrogant back then. If not outwardly, inwardly. I wanted to escape from how I felt. This conflict between who I was and what I believed I could become. The potential I knew I had and wished to fulfil in this lifetime. The feeling of time slipping away, everyone else getting ahead faster than me. My ego ran wild, prime for taming. After this cocktail mix of emotions, I concluded that they knew something I didn't. They had skills I didn't have yet that I wanted access to. There was a gap between me and the top producers. I felt like I wasn't allowed access to these secrets. Or at least it seemed. And that was what was holding me back from getting everything I wanted. That is what I needed to discover. I needed to find out what they were doing differently than me so I could reach the same results.

I got more frantic. *Maybe the answer is in a YouTube video I missed, a program I missed, a book I missed. That is it – more information from people who know what they're doing.* However, most of the information I found from these resources was about mixing. Most of the information was also genre-specific. So I started to think that mixing would solve all my music production problems. *That has to be it. Because that is all anyone is ever talking about. No one is ever talking about arranging, so all my problems are mixing problems.* I tried out the mixing tactics I was learning. *It still doesn't seem to be as good as the top tracks. What am I doing wrong?* Round and round I would go, making minimal progress. But I didn't know what I didn't know. I felt lost.

Around the same time, legendary music producer Rick Rubin had a podcast interview with Tim Ferriss. While listening to the podcast, one line grabbed my attention so much that I had to listen to it multiple times. It was like a lightning bolt through my body. An epiphany. A sense of hope. Here is the quote:

> *"The only way to use the inspiration of other artists is to submerge yourself in the greatest works of all time, which is a great thing to do. If you listen to the greatest music ever made, that would be a better way to work through to find your own voice to matter today, than to listen to what is on the radio and thinking 'I want to compete with this.' It is more stepping back and looking at a bigger picture than what's going on at the moment."* – Rick Rubin[1]

I thought, *I've already been analyzing tracks. I listen to music all the time. Perhaps I wasn't analyzing correctly. Maybe I should take Rick Rubin's advice seriously. I should start immersing myself in the great works of all time again.* So that is what I did. I started listening to the great music of all time. I listened and began analyzing them. I looked for answers. **I read the songs like a book.**

At first, I started writing essays containing information from what I had heard. School teaches you to do things like this. It was a habit. But I noticed that after completing each essay, I didn't remember any of it. I couldn't use any of the information in my tracks. Yet I persisted; I continued to immerse myself in the great music of all time. I analyzed relentlessly.

Around the same time, I was reading non-fiction books from diverse fields of knowledge. That is where I started to open my mind to concepts outside of music. They helped me find the secret. I began to read books on how talent develops and the fastest way to master a skill. I read hundreds of books on various topics. These topics included psychology, business, history, sales, marketing, human nature, mastery, biographies, self-development, spirituality, language learning, and more.

In my research, I stumbled upon an unlikely hero named Charlie Munger. He was a man in his nineties who had nothing to do with the music industry. Munger, instead, was a billionaire master of investing. Munger attributed much of his success to what he called *mental models*.[2] With mental models, he claimed that you could see the world clearly and become wise. As I read his work, I was blown away by how this man thought about life. He said that within each primary discipline there are a few big ideas you can apply to anything in life. Whether that is chemistry, economics, biology, physics, mathematics, statistics, engineering, psychology, human behavior, business, investing, systems, strategy, the list goes on. It all connects. You can use key concepts from any of these disciplines to view other disciplines through.

For example, there is a mental model in economics known as *the sunk cost fallacy*. When you put time and money into something, you don't want to back out. You've already put too much into it. You can use this mental model to view any area of life.

Through mental models you become a polymath by learning the key ideas from many fields of life. People have developed these ideas over thousands of years. Each mental model helps you to see life more clearly. I wondered if I could apply mental models to my music production; perhaps I could "see it".

I was also learning Spanish around the same time. Language learning systems use a very particular set of skills to make it easier. You start with pronunciation, then move to words, grammar, and conversations.

I also analyzed every book I read. At the end of each book, I would always pull out the key information I'd found from the books.

These concepts and many more resulted in a perfect mix of ingredients. As I analyzed music through various mental models, I began to see music as a language.

After completing a five-hundred-word analysis essay on a piece of music I was analyzing, I always found around five to ten music production *techniques*. When I located the techniques and pulled them out of the essay, I could then take action on them while I was creating music.

One of the key concepts of talent growth I'd read about was *chunking*. Chunking is one of the fastest ways to learn a skill. Chunking is when you break a skill into parts so that you can learn each chunk more easily. When you put the chunks back together the whole process becomes easier. I realized that the techniques I found in my essays were the chunks of music production. Techniques were building blocks I was discovering in the music I was analyzing. The essays then became irrelevant to my process. So, I removed the essays from the process to make analysis easier. Instead, I simplified the process and wrote down one technique at a time – this was chunking. So from then on when I analyzed, I was listening out for one technique at a time. When I found it, I would write down what it was, why the producer used it, how to use it, and the reference track I found it in. I wasn't only learning *what* a producer had done; I was learning *why* they had done it.

As I started analyzing this way, producing myself became much easier. I was starting to "think" like the professionals. I began to know what to do when I was creating. These building blocks would come up intuitively while I was creating. My intuition started to become that of a professional. That is because the building blocks I was now using were those I found from the great music of all time. I analyzed for a year and a half like this.

One morning, I woke up, and it felt like clarity had deposited into my brain. I had all core principles of arranging in my head in the exact order. I wrote the diagram down on paper in my notebook to see it. These were in every track I'd ever analyzed...

The Ten Core Principles of Arranging.

- Core structure principle
- Core harmonic structure principle
- Core rhythm principle
- Counter rhythm principle
- Spatial principle
- Foreground and background principle
- Energy principle
- Call and response principle
- Repurposing principle
- Synergy principle

Creating became easier after chunking the skill and finding the core principles of arranging. My tracks were sounding like the top tracks in the world. My confidence grew. My speed of creating became faster than ever. Most importantly, I no longer had to "think" about the art of creating music. It simply happened.

I then stumbled across stem files from some of the great producers of all time, such as Quincy Jones. Stem files are the individual tracks of entire arrangements in their final form. I used the same technique building-block mindset – and saw the stem files through the "lenses" of the core principles. I felt like I could finally "see" and "know" how Quincy Jones thought while creating. I knew why he made the moves he did. This skyrocketed my growth as a producer. I called this process *Stems Thinking*. It helped me learn how to layer arrangements like a top professional. I did come back to mixing and mastering. I developed a framework for that too. But, that's a story for later in the book.

Being an entrepreneur, I wanted to know whether this would work for others too. So, I started a program version of this book, called *the Polymath Producer System*. I showed a few music producers who were initially skeptical about it. But, after using the Polymath Producer System, their results shocked me and them.

They were saying things like:

"I've learned more in four weeks than years prior."
"This should be in universities."
"This is genius."
"This turns music into a universal language."
"This is the secret sauce."
"You deconstructed music production."
"This information is priceless."[3]

I showed them the system you're about to learn in this book, and it worked fast. Amazingly, they achieved this by simply listening to music with their headphones and using the system you're about to learn. It is that simple and fun. Anyone can do it. It only requires the right mindset. I realized that these producers had been experiencing the same problems I had in the past. This system solved those problems for me and them. That is when I knew the content in this book was bigger than just me. It had the power to change lives all around the world.

I saw music production as a learnable language. With these building blocks, I could then create my own original sounds. My music became more unique, and people no longer said, "You sound like this [insert artist]." They started saying, "Your music should be on the charts," and "This production is genius."

When I work with artists, I can see the building blocks they desire and let my intuition create that sound with them. At first, I used my mind to analyze the greatest music of all time. This allowed my mind to stop overthinking by chunking the skill. The building blocks of the great producers of all time now a part of me. Then, my mind relaxed, got out of the way, and I'd let my intuition come through while creating music. Where genius resides. Then, I would let my head come back in to refine what had come through my intuition. As Rick Rubin stated in that same Tim Ferriss interview:

> *"Try not to think too much – the job is more emotion and heart work than it is head work. The head comes in after to look at what the heart has presented and to organize it. But the initial inspiration comes from a different place and it's not the head. Creating art is not an intellectual activity, it is more inspiration."* – Rick Rubin[4]

Part I: The Polymath Producer System

The journey toward this moment came with spiritual growth. I'm not the same person I was when I started. Yes, I still have the same goals as before; I'm still creating music that I aim to stand the test of time. But now I have more of a quiet confidence. The arrogance dissipated as the journey humbled me. The original desires I had are no longer charged with emotional intensity. I've done a lot of letting go and surrendering. I am at a point in my skillset where I can achieve whatever sound I want if I put my mind to it. That, to me, is priceless. The inner freedom. The knowing that my creativity is infinite. I'm ready to impact the world with my music, and I now have the system, the skills, and the confidence to do it.

I have become a Polymath Producer.

I had learned that the secret was there all along. To master the language of music production, analyzing the great music of all time was the way. After this journey, I placed the entire framework into the book you're about to read. I call it the Polymath Producer System.

My mission with this book is to activate this genius within music producers just like you. I want to help your mind understand music production. Then, you can let your heart come through while creating. Then, create your own original sounds and make your own mark on the music industry. You will follow in the same path taken by some of the great Polymath Producers of all time. From classical composers like Beethoven, all the way to modern-day producers like Quincy Jones. Music production analysis was and is the way.

What you're about to learn is the product of decades of work. Thousands of hours analyzing thousands of tracks. Thousands of hours behind the DAW experimenting with my findings. As well as thousands of hours putting this book together - refining the information to its most simple truths. You will get all my key findings inside this book.

So let's start with the foundations of it all. In this first part of the book, you will learn the **Polymath Producer Philosophy.** The philosophy behind the language of music production. You will also learn the overview of the **Polymath Producer System.** This system will help you master the language of music production.

Polymath Producer Philosophy

THE MUSIC PRODUCER oversees the entire music production chain from song to completed master. The music production chain is the following parts in this order: songwriting, arranging (track composition), recording, editing, mixing, and mastering.

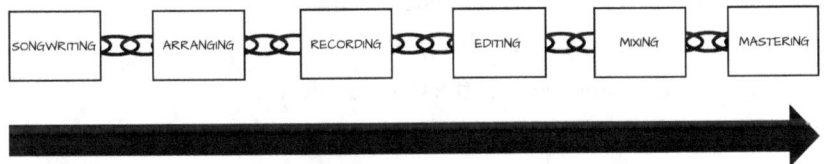

In this book, the definitions of these parts will be as follows:

- **Songwriting:** Creating the song's melody and lyrics. Includes title, harmony (chords), and structure too.
- **Arranging (Track Composition):** The creation of every musical part around the song. This includes all instrumental parts and vocal parts other than the song. Sometimes referred to as "arrangement", or "music production" in the modern day.
- **Recording:** The recording of any vocals and/or instruments for the song and arrangement.
- **Editing:** The process of polishing the parts you have composed and recorded. This includes fades, cuts, comping, timing, tuning, etc.
- **Mixing:** The mixing of the production so that it sounds well balanced in volume, frequencies, dynamics, and space.
- **Mastering:** The process of finalizing the stereo mix so it is ready for distribution.

The further down the production chain you get, the less you need to create something new from nothing. With songwriting, you create everything from nothing. With arranging/composition and recording, you create everything from nothing around the song. With editing, mixing and mastering, you balance and enhance the recording sonically.

This book provides a step-by-step system to master the language of music production. This system will help you become a world-class music producer.

What makes a world-class music producer?

The ability to make *effective decisions*.

What makes someone an effective decision-maker?

Mental models.

MENTAL MODELS

In the last section, I wrote about billionaire Charlie Munger who used what he called mental models.[5] Munger was one of the best investors in the world. He said that mental models played a role in getting him there. Mental models are models within your mind of how you see the world.

A quote attributed to Abraham Maslow says, "Give a man a hammer, and he'll see everything as a nail."[6] That is because when you have one mental model or way of viewing the world, you see everything through that lens. The more mental models you have, the more accurately you see the world. There are a few mental models that are the giant dominoes. These mental models create significant positive shifts in your life. Here are a few of the big ones that I have used to help discover the language of music production. I will teach them to you now, and you will find them throughout this book. These mental models will not only help in music but also in life. You can use them to see any area of your life more clearly.

80/20 Principle: 80% of all outcomes or results will come from 20% of all effort or inputs. It can also be other variations like 90/10, 95/5, etc. A real life example would be: 20% of your financial investments will get you 80% of your wealth. You can apply it to any area of life. I noticed that music production analysis was the 20% of action (input) that gave me 80% of my skill growth (output) as a producer.

Analysis: A detailed examination of something to form an understanding. You will apply analysis to music production in this book to master the language of music production.

Compound effect: When you take consistent action, you will see compounding returns on your investment. Small becomes large over time. When you analyze music productions over time, this compounds your skill level.

Critical thinking: When you objectively question, analyze and make your own judgment about something. You will use critical thinking when analyzing music productions. You will use it to think for yourself.

Divergent and convergent thinking: When you consider many possible paths of a solution to a problem. You then decide on the best single path. You use these thinking types while producing music. Music production analysis makes this thinking easier.

First 20-100 hours: It can only take 20-100 hours of focused practice to become better than ninety percent of the world at a skill. As long as it is learning in the right direction and chunked successfully. In this book, you will learn how to apply this theory to music in practice.

First principles: When you take an idea and break it down into its fundamental parts. You can then build the ideas back up and understand them better. We use first principles thinking throughout this book. We use it to analyze music production and create original sound.

Inversion: Thinking through problems in reverse. Inversion is at the heart of this music production analysis system. By analyzing finished music first, you are learning solutions for problems you will face.

Scientific method: Running tests and changing one variable at a time to find new solutions. You do this within a system. When you produce a track, you do this scientific method: one decision after another.

Skill chunking / talent hacking: Chunking helps you master a skill because the brain loves learning in chunks. The brain then pieces these chunks together. This entire book's system is built around chunking as a talent hacking method.

Systems thinking: A system is: inputs, processes, and outputs within an environment. Everything is a system within the universe. This book teaches you a system of music production analysis. When used, this system will teach you how to master the language of music production.

Visual mapping: The mental visualization of information as objects within your mind. This system uses the mind to visualize music to make mastery easier.

Mental Models as Lenses

I used mental models such as the ones just stated to discover the language of music production. I saw the music through a set of varying magnifying glasses. I then turned the insights I found into actionable frameworks you and I can use: a *language*. Put simply, to master the language of music production, you analyze the great music of all time. But first, to know where we're going, we must learn where we came from. I'll now show you how we all started learning the language of music production without even realizing it...

HOW OUR INFLUENCES SHAPE THE MUSIC WE CREATE

1) YOUR TASTE IN MUSIC DETERMINES WHO INFLUENCES YOU

2) YOUR INFLUENCES DETERMINE WHAT MUSIC PRODUCTION TECHNIQUES YOU LEARN

3) CROSS-POLLINATION OF TECHNIQUES FROM YOUR INFLUENCES AND YOUR MUSICAL INTUITION, BECOMES YOUR SOUND

Circle One: Look at circle one at the top left of this diagram. Your taste in music from when you were born to the present day determines who influenced you in your life. Your taste in music means you listened to/ listen to specific musical influences in your life.

Circle Two: Now, move to circle two at the top right of this diagram. The musical influences you listen to in your life lead to production techniques you know. The production techniques you know become the decisions you make while producing.

Circle Three: Now, move to circle three at the bottom of the diagram. You then cross-pollinate techniques you learn from your influences into your own productions. The techniques you know combine with your intuition while you create. This process creates "your sound". This is why you make the decisions you make while producing. Like any other system in the universe, your inputs have become your outputs.

Part I: The Polymath Producer System

HOW TO SYSTEMATIZE THIS PROCESS

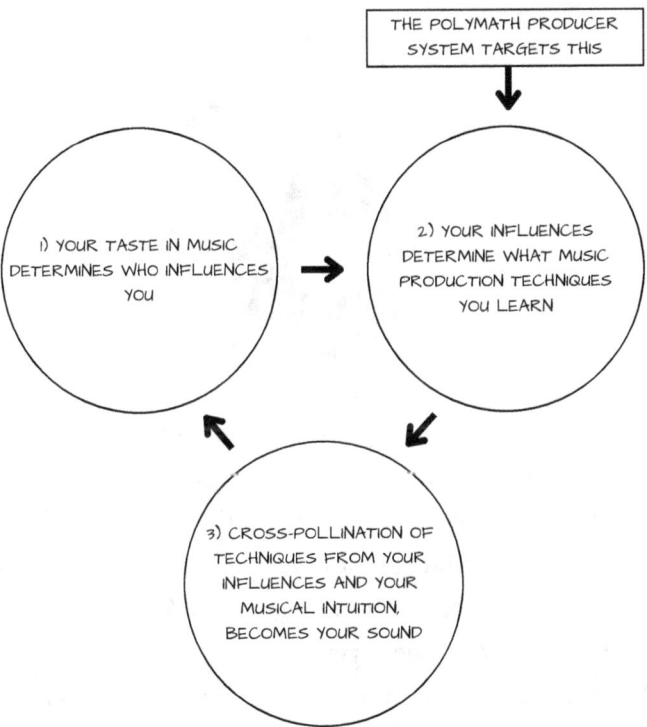

The Polymath Producer System targets circle two of the diagram – *techniques gathered from influences*. In this book, you will analyze your influences, the people you view as masters of the craft. Then you're going to be collecting techniques from their catalog of music.

Important: This does *not* mean copying. It means understanding the fundamental reason why a producer has done something. Then, being able to use the technique building blocks in your own unique way.

MUSIC PRODUCTION ANALYSIS

How do you find techniques through your influences? You do this with *music production analysis*. You can analyze the history of recorded music and discover the techniques they have used. These techniques then become building blocks you can use in your own productions. You can then create new building blocks. You can cross-pollinate building blocks to create new genres. You can create the future of music. Every technique building block is waiting for you to find in the history of recorded music. You have thousands of years of musical evolution at your fingertips from which you can learn.

When you find a technique, you put it in what I call your *Technique Library*. This library of techniques inside your mind is what you draw upon when you create your own music. These techniques are effective decisions in the right context. With the frameworks in this book, you'll choose your influences and gather techniques you want to learn. You'll also make yourself aware of the techniques you have already been using. But you don't leave this to chance. The power comes when you take control of this natural feedback loop.

In the present, you are doing music production analysis. You then learn what has worked in the past. You can then control your future music.[7]

POLYMATH PRODUCER FRAMEWORKS

After years of music production analysis, I discovered four primary frameworks. You can see the language of music production with these frameworks. You will use these frameworks during music production analysis. You will also use these frameworks while you create your own music productions.

They are:
- Level One: Technique Framework
- Level Two: Ten Core Principles of Arranging Framework
- Level Three: Stems Thinking Framework
- Level Four: Sonics Framework

This diagram shows the process: View music through the Polymath Producer frameworks to master the language of music production.

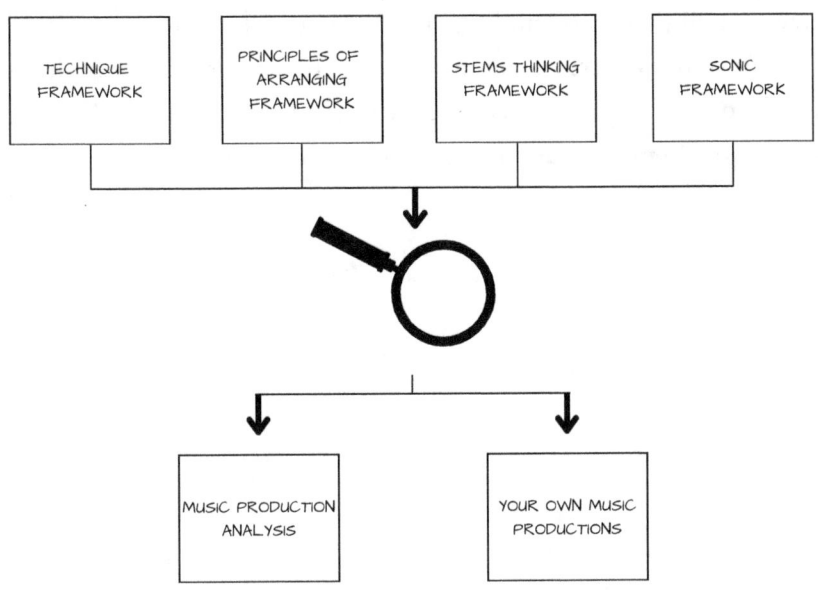

LEVEL ONE: TECHNIQUE FRAMEWORK

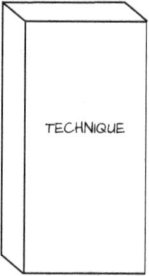

The Technique framework is when you view each decision a producer has made as a building block. This book refers to these building blocks as *Techniques*. You can then analyze music to find one technique the producer has used at a time. This framework chunks the skill in your mind. This framework is the first level of the language of music production and the foundation of it all. You learn to chunk the great tracks of all time into building blocks using analysis. Then, use those building blocks to create your own music. Techniques are the building blocks of the language – like the "words" of the language. We cover techniques in more detail in Part II of this book.

LEVEL 1.5: RESOURCE MINING

Resource Mining is Level 1.5 of the language of music production. You use this framework to find techniques in resources other than music analysis. You do this by analyzing one technique at a time in resources. These resources include YouTube videos, programs, books, articles, mentorship, etc. This framework is where most people start when they first learn production. Resource mining can show you *how* someone did a technique you have found in your music analysis. It is the *how* you use the language inside the DAW. When you do music production analysis, you see what a producer has done: what, why, and how. Resource techniques tie up the loose ends in any knowledge you have found from analysis. You then move everything you learn into your technique library. We cover resource mining in more detail in Part II of this book.

LEVEL TWO:
CORE PRINCIPLES OF ARRANGING FRAMEWORK

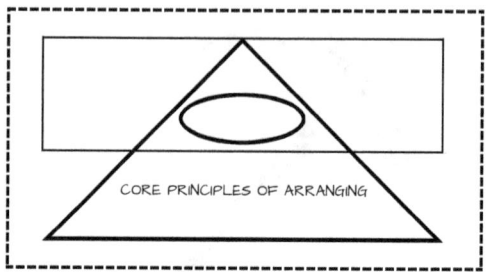

There are ten core principles of arranging. These principles are universal and genre-less. I found these to be in every track I've ever analyzed. You can analyze music through these principles to discover patterns within recorded music. You can also use this framework as a structure to create your arrangements within. This framework is the second level of the language of music production. Principles teach you to visualize the music production in your mind. When it comes to mastery, the most important skills you can master are the principles. You will then understand how the fundamentals of music production work. If technique building blocks are the "words" of this language, principles are the "grammar" of this language. They are the structure in which the words fit. We cover the Ten Core Principles of Arranging in more detail in Part III of this book.

LEVEL THREE: STEMS THINKING FRAMEWORK

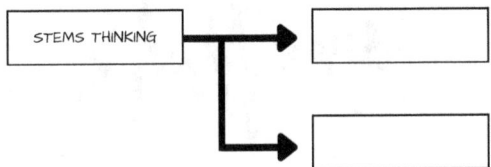

The Stems Thinking Framework is analyzing music as stem files. Stem files are an arrangements tracks in their final form after having been produced and/or mixed. You can use this framework to understand how to layer your tracks. This framework is the third level of the language of music production. Techniques are the words, and principles are the grammar. Stems thinking uses the words and grammar in layers to create complete musical arrangements. Stems thinking is how the music works as individual tracks, sub-groups, and one whole. This framework takes your producing skills to a whole new level. We cover stems thinking in more detail in Part IV of this book.

LEVEL FOUR: SONICS FRAMEWORK

SONICS

The Sonics Framework is mastering sonics with ear training, hearing the truth, and analysis. Sonics is all about how the arrangement sounds when played. Sonics primarily take place during recording, editing, mixing, and mastering. But the song and arrangement choices can also impact sonics too. The sonics framework is the fourth level of the language of music production. Sonics are like the language's "pronunciation": how it sounds when spoken. Through music production analysis, you can become a master of sonics, too. We cover sonics in more detail in Part V of this book.

TECHNIQUE LIBRARY

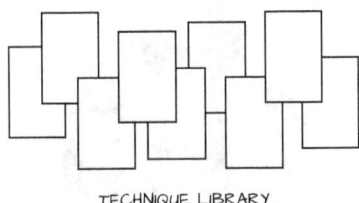

TECHNIQUE LIBRARY

Your Technique Library is all about remembering the language of music production. Everyone has a technique library inside their minds. It is where you store every technique you have ever learned and ever will learn. You then draw upon this technique library whenever you produce music. Think of a library; each book in that library is a music production or resource you have analyzed. Each book contains the techniques you found within that analysis or resource. These techniques are the building blocks you use when creating your own music. We cover the technique library in more detail in Part II of this book.

CATALOG OF MUSIC AND ORIGINAL SOUND

CATALOG OF MUSIC & ORIGINAL SOUND

When you create and finish a track, you add that track to your music catalog. Your music catalog lists all the tracks you have ever created in your lifetime. This part of the system is where you apply all your knowledge from your technique library to create your own music. This step is also where you create your own original sounds. We cover original sound in more detail in Part VI of this book.

FEEDBACK LOOPS AND ITERATION

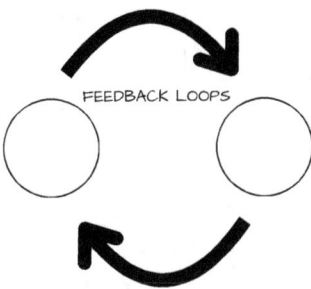

While creating your music, you will have goals. Whatever the goal is, your music will need technique building blocks to create it. While creating your music, there is a constant feedback loop happening. You will iterate until you have the right combination. This loops around as you draw from your technique library until completion.

When you have analyzed tracks from the great music of all time, you form an "invisible checklist". It gives you a benchmark of whether a track is complete to a standard. It is a form of feedback loop you can use. You know when you're on the right track.

You can also use feedback from outside sources such as peers, mentors, and the market. As you loop around the system, you will get less feedback and more praise over time. We cover these concepts of feedback and iteration more in Part VI of this book.

HOW THIS CREATES WORLD-CLASS MUSIC

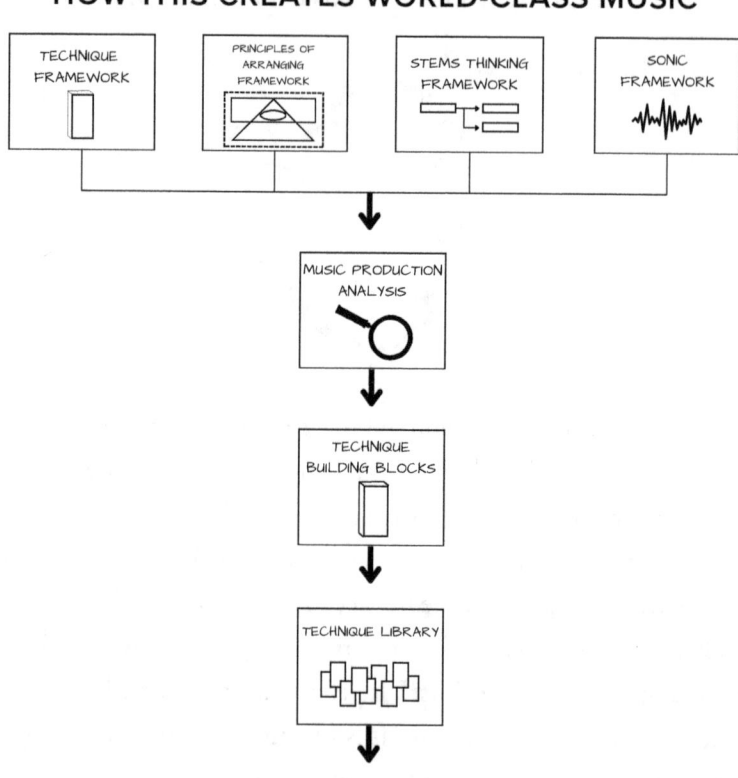

Music production analysis runs parallel with the creation of your music. You gather techniques from the great music of all time into your technique library. You do this in analysis using the four primary frameworks. Once you see music production through these four primary frameworks you can view *your* music through these same frameworks to see the "truth". Then you decide which technique building blocks to use from your technique library on your own music. These educated decisions then make your music world-class. The cross-pollination of techniques can also create an original sound.

THE POLYMATH PRODUCER SYSTEM
– WITH FRAMEWORKS

Here we have the entire system:

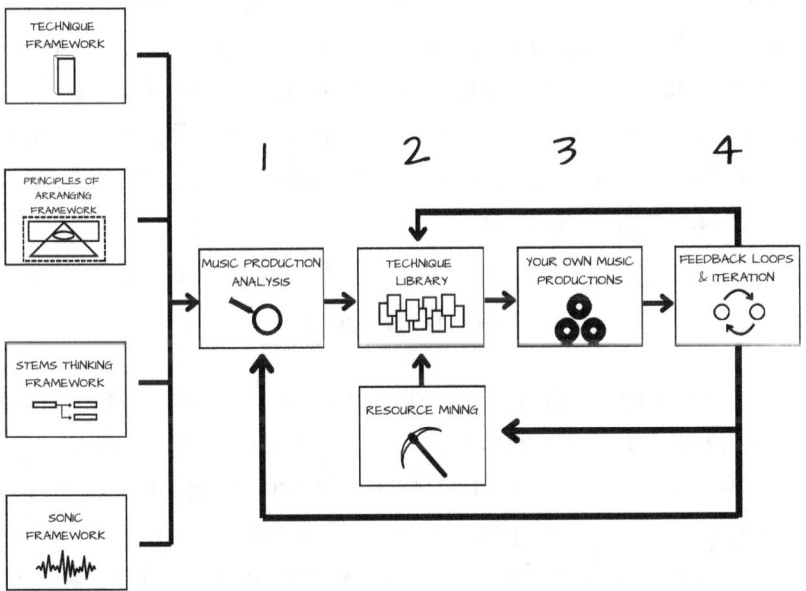

1. **Music Production Analysis.** You do music production analysis using the primary mental frameworks. [Techniques + Resource Mining, Principles of Arranging, Stems Thinking, Sonics]
2. **Technique Library.** You then store all the information you find in your Technique Library.
3. **Produce Music.** You then create your music productions using the same frameworks and technique library.
4. **Feedback & Iteration.** You then get feedback and iterate until you finish each track.

STANDING ON THE SHOULDERS OF GIANTS

Now is the best time in history to use music production analysis. You have access to almost every track ever recorded, and you can repeat-play these tracks as much as you want. That is the advantage you have over the music producers of the past. You can immerse yourself in the language every day with music production analysis. You can understand how music is created from the ground up. When you do it the way I show you in the Polymath Producer System, you will gain a massive advantage over those who don't.

THE LOST ART

When you work with an in-person mentor, you experience them creating entire music productions from scratch. Their mindset gets transferred to you. In modern times, it is becoming rare to have an in-person mentor. Now, you have thousands of mentors at your fingertips on the Internet. But many of these mentors don't know how to explain why they do what they do when they create. You are also not immersed in the language from the ground up daily while they create. So, this way of learning can lack the mindset transfer that comes from an in-person mentor.

The Polymath Producer System is designed to emulate the experience of in-person mentors. Music production analysis teaches you this "lost art". When you use the four primary frameworks, you learn how to think like the original producers. Top producers know how to think like this, but sometimes they don't know how to put it into words.

Analysis opens you up to learn from every composer who has ever lived. If they leave music behind, you can listen to it and learn from them. You can immerse yourself in the language of music production.

It can feel like you were with them creating the music from scratch. As a Polymath Producer you will embody the lost art.

The trap that many producers fall into these days is only focusing on the technical side of production. They often only learn about tools and how to use those tools. Modern producers also often neglect the big picture. The big picture is understanding the entire music production chain from start to finish. The original producers of the 1940s, '50s, and '60s had this big picture mindset. As a Polymath Producer you'll be proficient as a technical and big picture producer. You'll blend both worlds.

ORIGINAL SOUND VIA CROSS-POLLINATION

Music production analysis increases your chances of creating new genres. A genre gets defined after it is created. A genre is created via cross-pollination of genres that have come before it. Cross-pollination is achieved by fusing techniques from multiple genres into a new genre. The core principles of music production are always there. But they are used in different ways by using different techniques. Understanding this allows you to transcend genre. Then, you know the language of music production as a universal language. You can use building blocks to cross-pollinate genres and create your original sound.

TALENT HACKING

In *The Little Book of Talent* by Daniel Coyle, he talks about the most efficient way to master a skill. He found these methods in what he calls "hot beds of talent".[8] These are places where individuals of high talent practice together. He found that the most talented individuals use practice methods to become the best in the world. I've listed some of the strategies from his research next.

These are some of the scientific reasons why the Polymath Producer System speeds up your talent growth.

Watch the best at what they do – Take information from top performers. When you do music production analysis, you watch the best at what they do. You become who you focus your attention on. You stand on the shoulders of giants.

Engrave the skill onto your brain daily – You engrave the skill onto your brain when you do music production analysis. With focus, the decision-making ability of the top producers is engraved onto your mind.

Focus on the principles – Top performers always focus on the principles of their craft. In music production analysis, you will keep reminding yourself of the core principles.

Chunking – Break the skill down into sub-skills. In music production analysis, you are chunking the skill into building blocks. You do this by discovering every technique the producer has used one at a time. These become sub-skills that make up the skill.

Think in images – Visualize the process to imprint the skill on your brain. Music production analysis requires the visualization of music. This process builds neural pathways fast.

Top performers use the R.E.P.S method:

(R) Reaching and repeating – Practice should reach the edge of your ability for the most skill growth. Repeating the skill is also key to skill growth. Each track is a new challenge to hone your ear in music production analysis.

(E) Engagement – To be engaging the practice must be immersive and emotional. Music production analysis is an immersive and engaging practice. It is also fun and uplifting; so the skill engraves onto your brain more easily.

(P) Purposefulness – The task must connect to the skill you are building. Analysis makes you great because a great producer is an effective decision-maker. Decision-making in music comes from wisdom about the craft. This wisdom comes from listening to and creating music. It is a feedback loop.

(S) Strong, speedy feedback – Feedback is important because it immediately corrects your mistakes. It then leads you in the right direction. In music production analysis, your references become your feedback. You can't help but match your standard to the music you admire. It becomes an invisible checklist in your mind. Have you reached the same standard?

Throughout the book you will learn how to apply these in practice using music production analysis.

BENEFITS OF MUSIC PRODUCTION ANALYSIS:

- It gives you a clear mental framework of music production within your mind.

- It lets you listen to music for pleasure but then move to analysis mode. You then find actionable information. You can learn anytime, anywhere.

- It builds momentum by compounding your creativity and output.

- It helps you become a world-class decision-maker in production.

- Trial and error still occurs. But this system allows you to use less trial and error and be wrong fewer times, making you produce faster.

- When you understand the principles of arranging and sonics, you transcend genre. You instead view music as a universal language.

- You begin to create via intuition, creating what is unique to you. You start to see your originality and unique style shine through.

- You can make any vision you or your clients desire a reality. This process compounds over time as you analyze more tracks.

- You choose which tracks you want to analyze. Everyone's technique library will be different. So everyone's sound will be different.

- This system can help you master any part of the music production chain. Your skill level grows.

You achieve these benefits because of the Polymath Producer feedback loop...

THE POLYMATH PRODUCER FEEDBACK LOOP

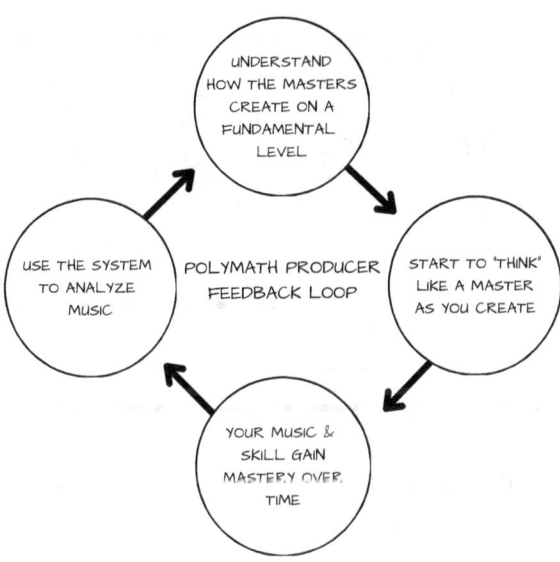

1. You analyze productions from the masters of music production using the Polymath Producer System.
2. You then understand how the masters created their tracks on a fundamental level.
3. Through this process, you develop educated decision-making. You start to "think" like a master as you create your tracks.
4. Your tracks and skill level compound over time as you use this system. You have a huge increase in creativity, originality, and productivity. You develop a masterful, intuitive approach to the craft. You then repeat this to achieve the goals you want.

THIS IS THE POLYMATH PRODUCER SYSTEM

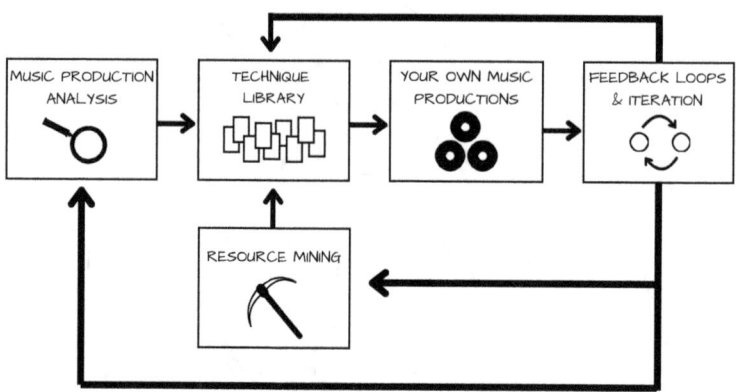

The Polymath Producer System implements these frameworks into a repeatable feedback loop.

Whenever in doubt, these are the only four things that matter. While learning and mastering the language of music production, remember these:

1. Music production analysis.
2. Build your Technique Library.
3. Produce your music.
4. Use feedback and iteration.

With each section of this book, we will go deeper into each primary framework and how to use it. To get the most out of this system, complete the action steps I present at the end of every part. If you follow what I say, you will get results.

ACTION STEPS

	PART I: THE POLYMATH PRODUCER SYSTEM - ACTION STEPS
ACTION STEP ONE	MEMORIZE THE POLYMATH PRODUCER PHILOSOPHY & SYSTEM. FIND A GLOSSARY OF POLYMATH PRODUCER TERMS IN APPENDIX II.
ACTION STEP TWO	DOWNLOAD FREE PRINTABLE PDFs OF THE DIAGRAMS TO PIN UP ON YOUR WALL AT WWW.POLYMATHPRODUCER.COM/RESOURCES
ACTION STEP THREE	JOIN THE POLYMATH PRODUCER COMMUNITY AT WWW.POLYMATHPRODUCER.COM/RESOURCES

By the end of this book you will know a system to master the language of music production by analyzing the great music of all time. In this part, you already learned the overview of that system. You have also learned the theory and philosophy behind the Polymath Producer System. Now we are moving into the practical to get you real life results.

So, let's learn how to use the first framework – Techniques – which is how to chunk music into building blocks. You will now learn the "words" of the language of music production.

COMING UP IN THE BOOK	
PART I: THE POLYMATH PRODUCER SYSTEM	YOU'VE LEARNED THE POLYMATH PRODUCER SYSTEM OVERVIEW
PART II: TECHNIQUES	YOU WILL VIEW MUSIC PRODUCTION AS BUILDING BLOCKS
PART III: CORE PRINCIPLES OF ARRANGING	YOU WILL LEARN HOW TO MASTER ARRANGING
PART IV: STEMS THINKING	YOU WILL LEARN HOW TO MASTER LAYERING YOUR MUSIC
PART V: SONICS	YOU WILL LEARN HOW TO MASTER RECORDING, EDITING, MIXING AND MASTERING
PART VI: ORIGINAL SOUND	YOU WILL LEARN HOW TO CREATE YOUR ORIGINAL SOUND
PART VII: TRANSCENDENCE	YOU WILL LEARN HOW TO TRANSCEND THE MIND

PART II:
Techniques
[Analysis Level One]

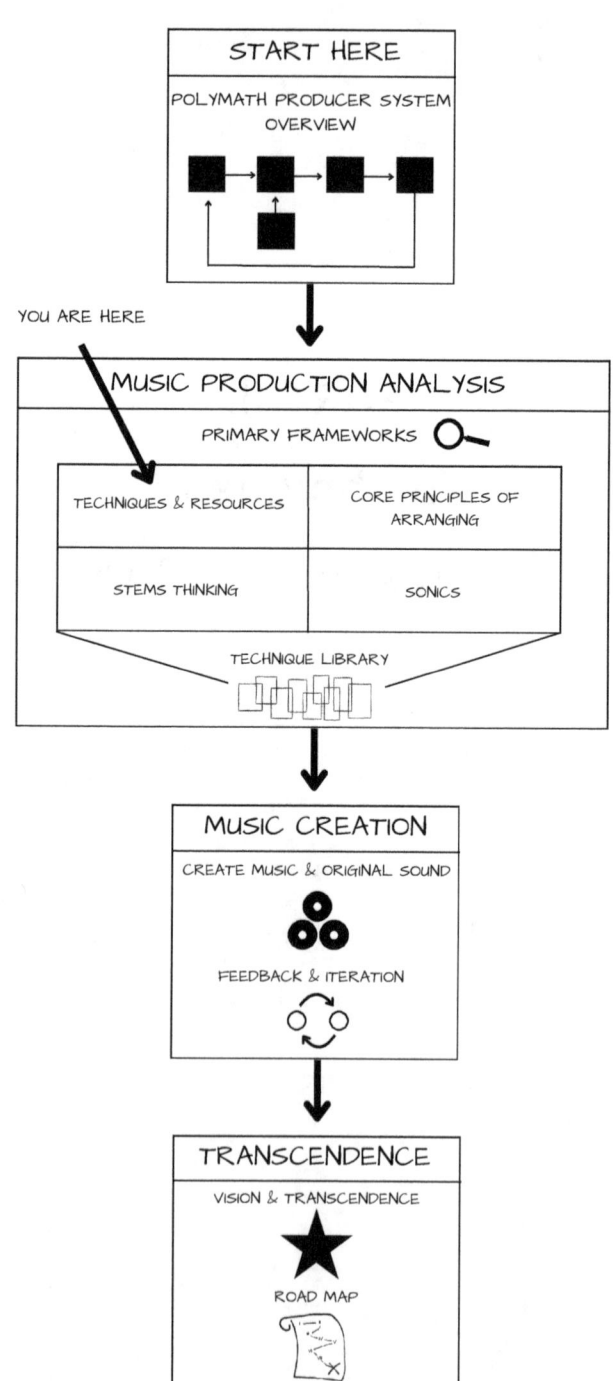

Learning a Language

I REMEMBER WHEN I was learning Spanish, it felt overwhelming. The pronunciation of the words was different from what I used in English. Not to mention thousands of new words to learn. I had the vision in my mind, though. I would be one of those cool, rare types who could speak a second language during a conversation. I could travel to a foreign country and speak the language.

To start, I tried a few language learning apps, but found them difficult to use. I would learn a word but couldn't use it in sentences or pronounce it. It was a mess. For some reason, though, I had this strong desire to learn a new language; I wanted to prove I could. I didn't want to admit defeat to the part of my inner voice telling me it was too hard.

One day, I stumbled across a book called *Fluent Forever* by Gabriel Wyner.[9] This book taught me to take language learning one step at a time. First, I learned the pronunciation of each consonant and vowel. Once I could do this, words became less intimidating because I knew how to pronounce them when I read them. Then, I started to learn the words of the language. To simplify further, I focused on learning the top five hundred words used in conversation by native speakers. The top five hundred words used equate to around seventy-five percent of a spoken language (80/20 principle).

I did this through *spaced repetition learning*. This learning system shows you digital cards at time intervals so that you remember the words. You associate the word with an image in your mind, and it shows you that card again days later. The intervals would vary depending on when I last saw the card and answered correctly or not. This process allowed me to plant the words further in my memory.

As I learned more of these words, I could piece together the grammar and build sentences.

The peak of my Spanish-speaking career was five hundred words. I managed to have a forty-five-minute conversation in Spanish with a native speaker. I did sound like a toddler while doing it, but it was a proud achievement nonetheless.

When I learned Spanish, I did something the brain loves when learning new skills: *chunking*. I took the skill one piece at a time, making it easier. I started with the absolute fundamental part, which was pronunciation. Once I could pronounce the words like a native speaker, I could then read and speak them. After I knew the words, I could create sentences.

It was the same process I used to learn piano. When I learned a Chopin piece, I first learned it one hand at a time. The piece, which appeared complicated, became simplified when I chunked it into one hand at a time. Once I had mastered each hand by themselves, I could place the hands together and play.

Music production includes many skills, but the same process applies. Music production is an art form that involves decision-making. The better quality decisions you can make, the better producer you will become. This process all takes place inside your mind. Music production became simple the moment I started chunking music into techniques. It turned the language into building blocks that I could use in any way. I didn't need to copy anyone. I no longer needed to follow a genre. I could use the building blocks as I wanted to use them.

Just like I did when I learned a spoken language - once I knew how to pronounce each syllable, I could pronounce words. Once I could learn a few words, I could make any variation of sentences using the words I knew. I could make poetry and art.

With music production, the *techniques* are the words. Once I learned the words I could create any variation of them. This chunking process became a superpower.

When you read a book in a foreign language, it can help you learn that language faster. You learn any words or grammar you don't recognize as you read. One word or "chunk" at a time. You see how the word is used in context to the sentence, paragraph, topic, and book.

After applying chunking to music production analysis, I found I was doing the same thing. I was able to "read songs like a book". When I was listening to music for enjoyment purposes, it was like reading a fiction book. I would get lost in the music. But when I analyzed music with chunking, it was like reading a non-fiction book. I was searching for information, for techniques, and finding them.

I'd been searching for answers all along from anything but music. I searched on YouTube, text books, and programs. But, the secret was there the whole time: the music *was* the books I needed to read. When I read the music, I became immersed in the language. Music is where you learn the language of music production. You only need to read it in the right way to find the secrets hidden within. All the holes in your knowledge become filled the more you do this. Soon, you can create music that sounds phenomenal. It is only a matter of time.

In this part: Techniques – Analysis Level One, you will learn how to chunk music into technique building blocks. You will learn how to read songs like a book.

How To Read Songs Like a Book

IN THIS SECTION, we will cover: Level One – Techniques. You will learn how to analyze music as building blocks, which we call *techniques*. This is the first framework to understand the language of music production. You will also learn how to find techniques using Level 1.5: Resource Mining. We'll also be covering how to document the techniques you find into your *Technique Library*. To start, let's learn how to analyze using Level One: the Technique Framework.

WHAT IS A TECHNIQUE?

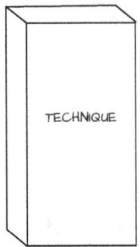

A *technique* is a building block of music that can be anything you find a music producer has done to create a track. When I say "anything" I truly mean anything.

If you hear a guitar in a track, for example, the kinds of techniques you find could be: the part it plays, the part it plays in relation to the rhythm, the part it plays in relation to the harmony and melody, the sound selection choice, how it is recorded, how it is panned, etc. The list could go on and on. It is up to you to ask questions about the instrument, and if you go seeking, you will find. This process is about activating your mind. You become curious. You explore why something works by itself and in relation to the whole. I will mention many more examples later of techniques I have personally discovered so it makes more sense.

Remember the key point: these are building blocks of tracks and you're finding **one technique building block at a time.** You're training your brain to discover one technique at a time. You're learning to compartmentalize the entire craft of music production. This skill will develop the more you do it.

Now that you know what techniques can be, here is how you use this framework to find techniques yourself.

MUSIC PRODUCTION ANALYSIS OF TECHNIQUES:

- Choose a music streaming service and song of choice. A service that doesn't have advertisements works best because you will be repeating the track a lot.

- I recommend listening with your mixing headphones to hear the entire stereo field. Speakers can work, but I've found that headphones allow you to hear finer details.

- Listen to the track on repeat. Start at the introduction and work through the structure section by section. With each section, start with the bass instruments. Then, move up the frequency spectrum. Sometimes starting with the loudest instruments first and then working your way to the quietest helps. You can also think non-linearly and listen to any section or instrument. It is up to you but a structured process can work best.

- Listen to the whole stereo field. With your attention and focus, select one instrument at a time. Then, one technique at a time. Identify and form the technique you find in your mind. The most important thing to remember is to analyze *one instrument* at a time and *one technique* at a time. I will give many examples of techniques soon so this is clearer for you.

- With each technique you find, come up with a memorable name for it. Then, write down *what* it is, *why* you would use it, *how* to use it and the *reference* where you found it. Then, move on to the next technique and do the same.

Other Tips:

- A good way to think about it is to start at the big picture and then select one instrument at a time.

- Another trick is focusing on one section of the structure at a time. Start at the introduction. Do all you can to analyze that. Then, move on to the verse. Do all you can to analyze that. Then move on to the chorus, etc.

- Write out all instruments at the start of your analysis, every single one you hear in the arrangement. It can help to do this at the very start to make the process easier. Then, you won't have to "search" for new instruments as you analyze. Instead, you'll be able to focus on techniques that are used instead.

- Work around the frequency and panning spectrum to find out what is happening. Check the lows, mids, and highs of the frequency spectrum. Check the left, center, and right of the panning spectrum.

- Once you identify something interesting the producer has used, write it down.

- To find more techniques compare how each instrument relates to another. Then compare how each technique relates to techniques found in other tracks you've analyzed.

- It is beneficial (and I highly recommend) to listen to a wide range of genres and influences from the history of recorded music. This diverse mix increases the cross-pollination of ideas. You will notice patterns regardless of genre. When I started, I analyzed one classic track (pre-2010s) and one modern track a day in diverse genres.

- You must focus for this to work; don't multitask. Closing your eyes and visualizing the music can help. It will be worth it.

The following steps is Level One: Techniques, used in a visual example. This example is for the song "Heroes" by David Bowie. Feel free to analyze as you go through these steps.

Technique Analysis Step One: Big Picture

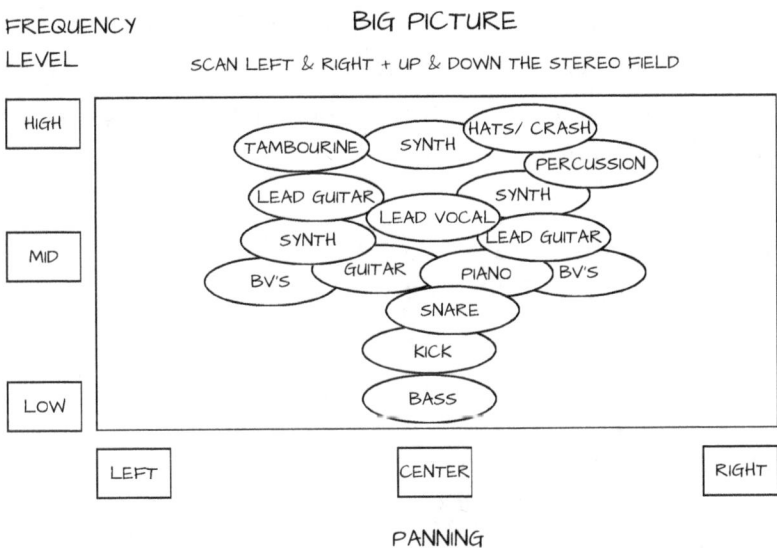

This rectangle visually represents the stereo field or "stage" in your mind. You picture this in your mind as you are analyzing music. Here's the big picture you would hear for this particular example track: "Heroes" by David Bowie. This arrangement has bass, kick, snare, piano, guitar, lead guitars, lead vocals, background vocals, multiple synths, tambourine, percussion, and drum hats/ crashes.

The frequency level is on the left-hand side of the rectangle. Frequency level includes high frequency, mid-frequency, and low frequency. For example, as you can see in this particular track, the synths are higher-frequency. The piano is more mid-level frequency, so it's in the mid-section. The bass and kick are low and in the low-frequency spectrum.

On the bottom of the rectangle is panning. Panning includes left panning, center panning, and right panning. For example in "Heroes", you will perceive instruments such as the lead vocal and kick at the center of your mind. You will perceive instruments like the lead guitars and percussion as coming from the left and right.

When you analyze music, you visualize this rectangle in your mind's eye. When analyzing music for techniques you're scanning this rectangle. You identify each instrument in your mind by going left and right and up and down.

Technique Analysis Step Two: Choose a Specific Instrument

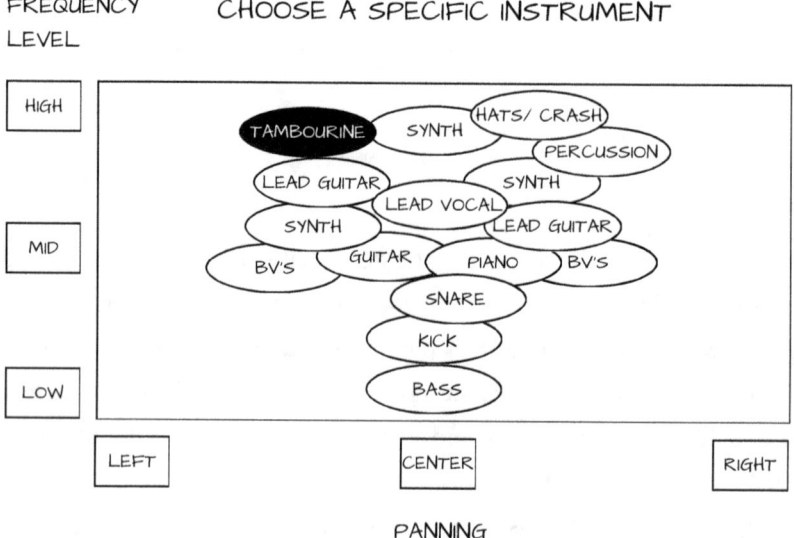

Then, what you do is choose one specific instrument in your mind. In this case, I've used the tambourine as the example you're choosing to focus on. That's the black circle up the top left-hand corner of the rectangle.

Part II: Techniques

Technique Analysis Step Three: Find What Techniques It Is Doing

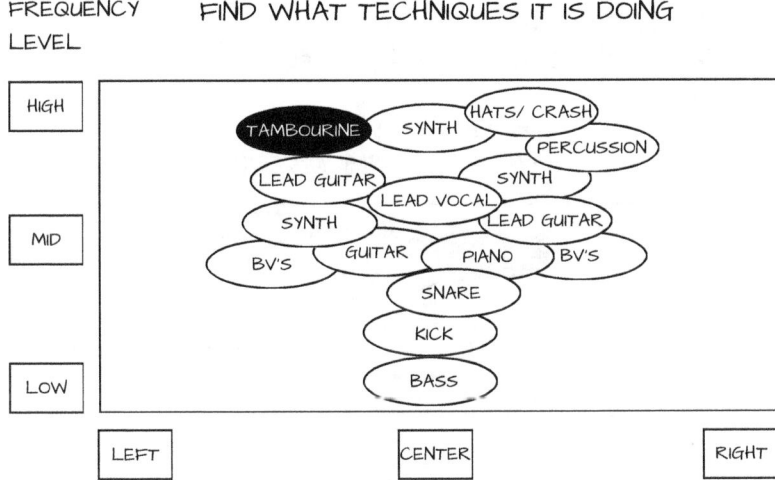

Next step is to find what techniques the instrument is doing. You can do this with creative questioning. Ask yourself, *Is this instrument doing anything I can write down as a technique and use myself one day? What is it doing?* Go as deep as you want to by asking yourself questions.

Creative questioning is key. If you get stuck, continue to ask yourself questions, such as:

- *Why is this working?*
- *How does this instrument relate to the other instruments in the arrangement?*
- *Why did it come in when it did?*
- *What is this instrument playing?*
- *Why are these instruments working well together?*

- *What is the producer doing to create what I'm feeling right now?*
- *What's it doing compared to any other song I've analyzed?*

Technique Analysis Step Four:
Write Down What the Technique Is

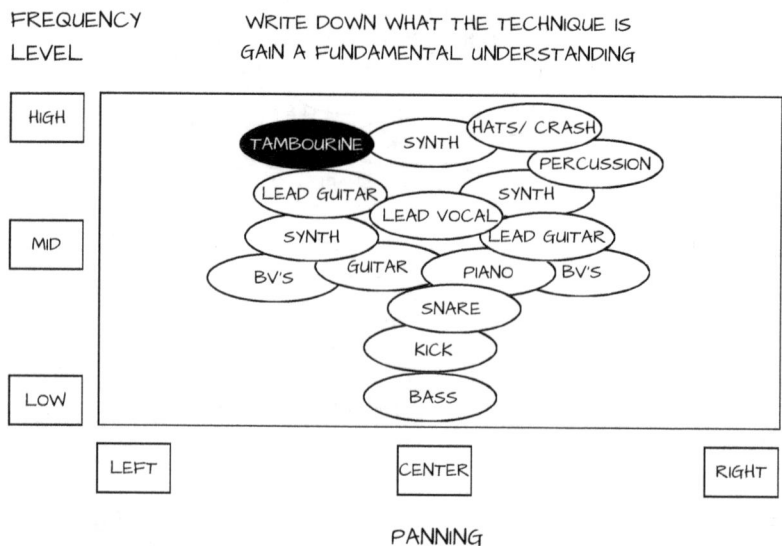

Once you find a technique you want to remember, write it down. Then write down what is happening in the technique you found. For this example from "Heroes" by David Bowie I wrote the following:

> The tambourine is playing an eighth-note rhythm and is also fast. So it is a straight eighth-note rhythm. I noticed it is counteracting with what the kick and snare are doing in this track. The kick and snare are playing a slower, syncopated rhythm. The tambourine is playing a fast, straight eighth-note rhythm. So the tambourine is a counter rhythm. I noticed that the tambourine also pans to the left. This technique worked in the track

"Heroes" because the tambourine was panned slightly left, while the hats and other percussion were panned slightly right. This helped to create space for it and fill out more of the high end. It created a subtle energy development for the second half of the song using an extra counter rhythm. This counter rhythm was the opposite of what the core rhythm was playing.

Bonus Tip

After you find techniques, notice whether you found similar techniques in other music you have analyzed. You'll start noticing patterns in all recorded music, and this is where things get exciting.

Technique Analysis Step Five: Give the Technique a Name

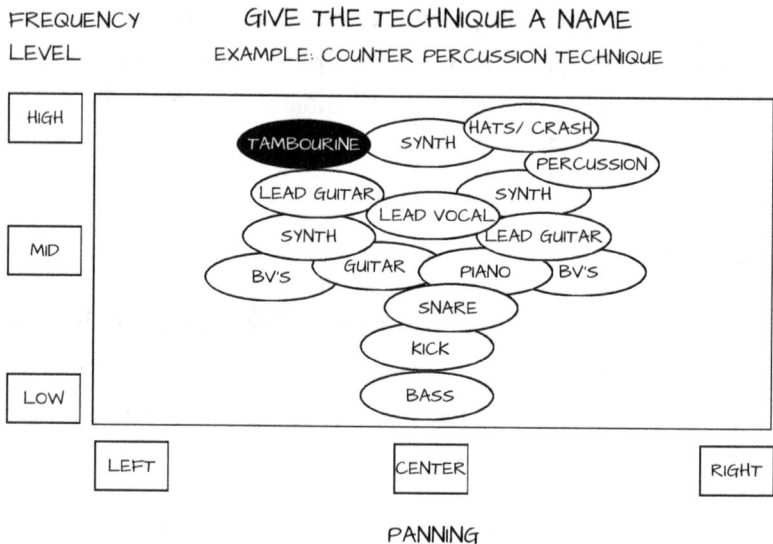

Once you find a technique you want to remember, name it. In this case, I've written *counter percussion technique.* Why did I give it that name? Because the percussion instrument was a counter rhythm to the core rhythm. That is how I remembered it. The techniques you find will be specific to you. So, making your own names will help you remember them.

Technique Analysis Step Six:
Write Down the Technique as - What, Why, How, and Reference

> FOR EACH TECHNIQUE WRITE DOWN:
> WHAT, WHY, HOW, and REFERENCE
>
> WHAT: When you use a percussion panned to the side that acts as a counter rhythm compared with the core rhythm.
> e.g. 8th note straight counter rhythm to syncopated core rhythm.
>
> WHY: Use this when you want to create more energy in the arrangement.
>
> HOW: Create a counter-rhythm to contrast the core rhythm for energy. Opposites can work well.
> Use a percussion instrument like a tambourine, shaker, etc.
> Usually these are panned left or right.
>
> REFERENCE: "Heroes" by David Bowie. In the breakdown section at 1:56 a tambourine comes in on the left-hand side.

For each technique write down: *what* it is, *why* you would use it, *how* to use it, and the *reference* you got it from. This will help you gain a fundamental understanding.

Here's how you lay it out in your *Technique Library document*.

You write the *name*:
In this case it is the counter percussion technique.

You write *what* the technique is:
Using percussion panned to the side that plays a counter rhythm compared with the main rhythm. For example, eighth-note straight counter rhythm compared to the syncopated core rhythm.

You write *why* you would use it:
You use this when you want to create more energy in the arrangement.

You write *how* to use the technique:
Look at what the main rhythm is that you've created. Create a mid-to-high-frequency part with a percussion instrument that can counteract that. It's that simple. Sometimes, the counter rhythm is the opposite of the core rhythm. That is the pattern I've observed.

Then, you write down your *reference*:
I found this technique in "Heroes" by David Bowie around 1:56 of the single version. In the breakdown section, I noticed that the tambourine comes in on the left-hand side. It has that counter rhythm, which creates extra energy. (You can look back at this reference to understand it on a musical level.)

This process is powerful because you understand the fundamental reason *why* it works. When you're creating your own tracks, if you need to create some energy, this is a technique you can use. You know the fundamental reason why it's working, so you can use any variation of this technique. You can also become innovative with techniques you find. Then maybe even invent your own.

Here is a summary of the technique framework you can use while you analyze.

	SUMMARY OF THE TECHNIQUE FRAMEWORK
STEP ONE	LISTEN TO A TRACK SCAN THE STEREO FIELD. • FREQUENCY FIELD: LOWS, MIDS, HIGHS. • PANNING: LEFT, CENTER, RIGHT.
STEP TWO	CHOOSE A SPECIFIC INSTRUMENT.
STEP THREE	FIND OUT WHAT TECHNIQUE(S) THE INSTRUMENT IS DOING. HOW IS THE INSTRUMENT RELATING TO OTHER INSTRUMENTS? WHY DOES IT WORK IN THIS TRACK? HOW IS IT RELATING TO OTHER MUSIC YOU HAVE ANALYZED?
STEP FOUR	WRITE DOWN WHAT THE TECHNIQUE IS.
STEP FIVE	GIVE THE TECHNIQUE A NAME.
STEP SIX	WRITE DOWN THE TECHNIQUE AS - WHAT, WHY, HOW, AND REFERENCE. PLACE THE TECHNIQUE IN YOUR TECHNIQUE LIBRARY MASTER DOCUMENT.

LEVEL 1.5: RESOURCE MINING TECHNIQUES

In resource mining you use the same process as the technique framework. You analyze one technique at a time. But, rather than finding techniques from listening to music productions, you are now analyzing music in *resources* such as books, YouTube videos, mentors, programs, etc.

The same mindset applies as Level One. As you listen to, read, or watch the resource, take note of techniques that are mentioned. You are on the lookout for one technique at a time from producers. When you find a technique you could use one day, write it down. Then you can use it in your own music when it is needed.

For example, I once had a mastering mentor call with Devvon Terrell. He gave me many mastering techniques I could use to make my masters louder.

- **Technique:** Make the clip gain louder to match the loudness of your reference.
- **Technique:** Bring up the side information in volume/EQ to match the loudness of your reference.
- **Technique:** Use multiple limiters to share the load and match the loudness of your reference.

I then documented them into my technique library for use in my own music when needed.

Resource Mining Summary:

SUMMARY OF THE RESOURCE MINING FRAMEWORK	
STEP ONE	ANALYZE MUSIC RESOURCES. THESE CAN INCLUDE YOUTUBE VIDEOS, BOOKS, MENTORS, ARTICLES, AND ANYTHING ELSE WITH VALUABLE TECHNIQUES.
STEP TWO	AS YOU CONSUME THE RESOURCE, LOOK FOR ONE TECHNIQUE AT A TIME THE PRODUCER MENTIONS.
STEP THREE	WRITE A NAME FOR THE TECHNIQUE. THEN WRITE WHAT THE TECHNIQUE IS, WHY YOU WOULD USE IT, HOW TO USE IT, AND THE REFERENCE OF WHERE YOU FOUND IT.
STEP FOUR	THEN PLACE EACH TECHNIQUE INTO YOUR TECHNIQUE LIBRARY.

TECHNIQUE LIBRARY AND TECHNIQUE DOCUMENTS

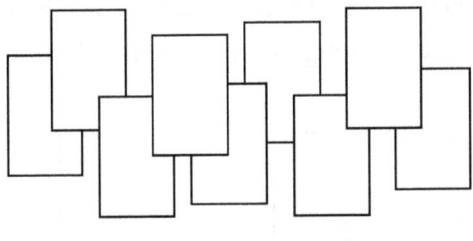

TECHNIQUE LIBRARY

When creating new tracks as a music producer, you draw upon specific knowledge you know in the field. This specified knowledge is inside what I call your *Technique Library*. Picture a vast library with books everywhere around you. I want you to imagine that this library is inside your mind, and every book on the shelves is a track or resource you have analyzed. Within each book are all the techniques you have found from the music and resources.

To make this process easier on the brain, you will create documents. In these documents, you can store the techniques you find. These documents will be a tangible form of your technique library.

There are three documents I recommend you use for your technique library:

1. **The Music Production Analysis Document:** This will be for documentation of any techniques you find from music production analysis using the four frameworks: Techniques, Principles, Stems Thinking, and Sonics.

2. **Resource Mining Technique Document:** Use this to document any techniques you find from resources other than music. These include books, YouTube videos, mentors, programs, etc.

3. **The Technique Library Master Document:** This will contain all techniques you find in a single document. This is where you write the techniques in their *what, why, how,* and *reference* formats. This document is a tangible form of the Technique Library in your mind.

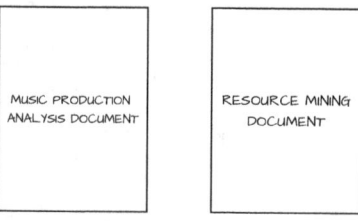

TECHNIQUE LIBRARY DOCUMENT EXAMPLES

The following is the documentation system using the three documents:

1. Find techniques using music production analysis and resource mining.
2. Put the techniques you find from music production analysis and resource mining into documents.
3. Put the techniques into your technique library master document as: *what, why, how,* and *reference.*
4. These naturally move into your technique library in your mind for use in your own music. You can also use the documents to reference the information.

Part II: Techniques

MUSIC PRODUCTION ANALYSIS DOCUMENT

Here is a shortened example of my original document number one. As you can see, I analyzed one modern track and one classic track that day. In the following examples, I analyzed the tracks "Shape of You" by Ed Sheeran and "Be My Baby" by the Ronettes. I then found actionable techniques one by one. I wrote them down in the music production analysis document. Then, I transferred them into my technique library master document.

Music Production Technique Analysis - Level One (Example Document)

"Shape Of You" By Ed Sheeran – Analysis

Principle of core rhythm: One driving rhythm that acts as a grounded center that everything else gravitates around. Most instruments latch onto it with a few exceptions. These exceptions act as counter rhythms to spur continued interest in musical development. Counter rhythms can be both percussion hits and harmonic based.

Real time lyrical narration: Document the story in the verses as the actions and images are happening in real time. Used for story development. Leads into emotion-based choruses.

Simplistic high end: No need to have crashes, hats, cymbals, and white noise if you don't need them. Make sure everything has a purpose; less is more sometimes.

Wall of unison vocal technique: Used in countless Ed Sheeran songs. The lead vocal in the middle on one octave, then a falsetto vocal an octave higher in the middle. Then the left and right sides contain doubles of the original octave. They also have an octave lower than the original octave, and potentially the higher one too.

Momentum building: Each section of the form gains two-to-three instruments with each change of section – this builds energy.

"Be My Baby" By The Ronettes – Analysis

Core rhythm as a hook: Core rhythm loops with the arrangement but is used as a hook. It is used at particular moments alone to emphasize the hook.

Chorus kick flip technique: Changing the loop pattern of the kick into a different pattern in the chorus. Used to create more intensity in the chorus if more are added.

Counter rhythm principle: Making sure the core rhythm and counter rhythm parts are musically different so they combine beautifully, e.g., syncopated/slow core rhythm with straight/fast counter rhythm combination.

Lyrics as confessional: Encompassing the core emotion into the lyric not with sense-provoking words but confessional style words.

Call and response: Lead sings a melody (call), group repeats (response) (as a chord sometimes). In this case the group "calls" first and the lead "responds" in the chorus.

Wall of sound technique: Arrangements with large ensembles, doubling and tripling parts to create a fuller, richer sound. Mixed well enough the listener will perceive each of the different combinations of instruments as one sound. Musically each part is simple; the key is in the combinations.

Snare fills as hooks: Using fills in between vocal phrases as catchy hooks. In this case it is the triplet snare fill.

Third verse instrumental version of vocal melody: Using similar backing, choose a lead instrument to play the vocal melody (in this case strings).

Vocal pads: Chordal sustained vowel backing vocals used as a pad. Used best to build energy.

RESOURCE MINING DOCUMENT

Here is a shortened example of my original document number two – the resource mining document. This is for Level 1.5: Resource Mining techniques. As you can see, I analyzed a YouTube video resource for techniques.[10] I watched the video and wrote the techniques I found one at a time. Then I transferred them into my technique library master document.

Resource Mining Techniques - Level 1.5 (Example Document)

YouTube Video: Alan Walker & Mood Melodies – Alone (In The Studio)

>**Attack transient lead tap technique:** Adding a tap as a lead layer for attack transients.
>
>**Reverse chords technique:** Making a copy of a track in reverse so the chords fall into each other.
>
>**Iconic patch technique:** Creating a unique patch or two with your unique "sound" and then layering it with other presets for thickness.
>
>**Loop layering technique:** Layering multiple loops for a thicker sound.
>
>**Real and computer stack technique:** Layering real and computer instruments for a humanized feel.
>
>**Bass hit technique:** Using a bass drop to enter a section or establish a section.
>
>**Sound layering technique:** Layering of sounds to make them sound thicker.

Strategic FX placement technique: Using FX, repurposed samples, vocal stacks, and glitches in particular places to build tension.

Whisper vocal track technique: Used to give greater character of "air" to the performance. Whispering moves a lot of air without a lot of body to the sound (best to filter everything below 1-2kHz out of whisper track). This can be a way to get a very large sense of size to the vocal performance without that size becoming a burden to fit into a mix.

Repurposing principle: Using sounds, melodies, and ideas you've already used.

Vocal harmonies technique #1: Record each section four times, pan two left and two right.

Side chain compression technique: Sidechaining the bass with the kick. You do this so the bass moves out of the way for the kick when the kick plays.

Filter automation technique: Using EQ automation to open and close a sound.

TECHNIQUE LIBRARY MASTER DOCUMENT

After analyzing the music and resources, I moved all my techniques to document number three: the Technique Library Master Document. The technique library master document is where you put every technique you find from any track or resource.

Important: Writing down and receiving techniques from "credible" sources is usually best. Credible means that you trust where it came from. However, no matter where or from whom you get a technique, you must be the one to know why you are using it in context. **Your skill is a system. In a system, quality inputs = quality outputs.**

The following is a shortened version of what my original Technique Library Master Document looked like:

Technique Library Master Document (Example Document)

Scattered Randomized Loop Technique

What:
A technique used mainly in modern production by grabbing seemingly random samples, and throwing them into the DAW and arranging them in a particular way to create a loop. Samples can include anything that adds to the rhythm, feel, and vibe of the track.

Why:
This technique is great if you want to create a vamp like loop section that repeats but sounds unique and original – and "expensive".

How:
To do this is quite simple. What you are looking for are samples with "potential". Grab your collection of samples that you think could match the vibe you are going for. Go through the samples one by one and

pick out the ones you feel could have potential. Don't think logically; if it feels right then throw it on the DAW into separate tracks. Remember if a sample doesn't work you can always scrap it. Keep doing that until you have a bunch to use. Then all you have to do is arrange them in a way that you think sounds cool and matches the vibe you are going for. The key is to not judge the sound of the sample on its own. Think big picture and consider how it could support the arrangement as a whole. You can also create samples and "expensive" sounds to make your loop sound even more original using your sound design skillset.

References:
Listen to the verse sections of "Roses" by the Chainsmokers or the verses of "Starboy" by the Weeknd and Daft Punk. Listen to the random samples interacting with each other and how it creates movement, vibe, and originality.

Vocal FX Form Technique

What:
As each section of the song form progresses – example: verse, chorus, verse, chorus, bridge, chorus, etc. – so does the wetness of the vocals' FX. This applies mainly to reverb and delay. So the song has a structure: verse, chorus, verse, chorus, etc. Think of the FX carrying that same structural development.

Why:
There are many reasons why this is effective: You'll be able to differentiate between sections of the track. You can make chosen sections more impactful by using this technique. You can create energy development and spike interest.

How:
Start by asking questions. You need to have a clear big picture vision of how you want the vocal FX to go in terms of their journey in the track. Think in terms of energy development. Then automate or mult the FX processing to be more wet or dry depending on the structure.

References:
Listen to "Starboy" by the Weeknd and Daft Punk for a clear example of the Vox FX changing as the song moves from section to section. Driest FX in the verse and most wet FX in the chorus.

Chorus Kick Flip Technique

What:
Changing the loop pattern of the kick of the verses into a different pattern in the chorus.

Why:
The kick holds a lot of energy. So if you have a kick pattern through the verse, and are looking for a way to differentiate the chorus from the verse, think about

adding a few extra kicks in the section you want more energy in.

How:
Add more or less kick pattern placements depending on the section of the song.

References:
Listen to "Be My Baby" by the Ronettes. Listen to how the kick stays the same during the verses, then more get added during the chorus to create more energy.

Live and Computer Stack Technique

What:
Layering real and computer instruments for a humanized feel.

Why:
Use this technique to make your computerized instruments feel more human and real. If you only use computerized instruments, having a real instrument layered with it can make it feel more humanized.

How:
For example, you have recorded a string section as midi, then you record a real string section to layer on top of the midi. This will give you the thickness of the midi, but with the humanized feel of real players.

References:
Alan Walker & Mood Melodies – In the Studio – YouTube Video[11]

That is how I put all the techniques into my Technique Library Master Document.

FASTER APPROACH TO DOCUMENTATION

If you want to simplify the process, only use the technique library master document. Move all techniques you find directly into that alone.

- Find techniques using music production analysis and resource mining.
- Put the techniques into your technique library master document as: *What*, *Why*, *How*, and *Reference*.
- These naturally move into your technique library in your mind for use in your own music.

Faster Approach to Documentation:

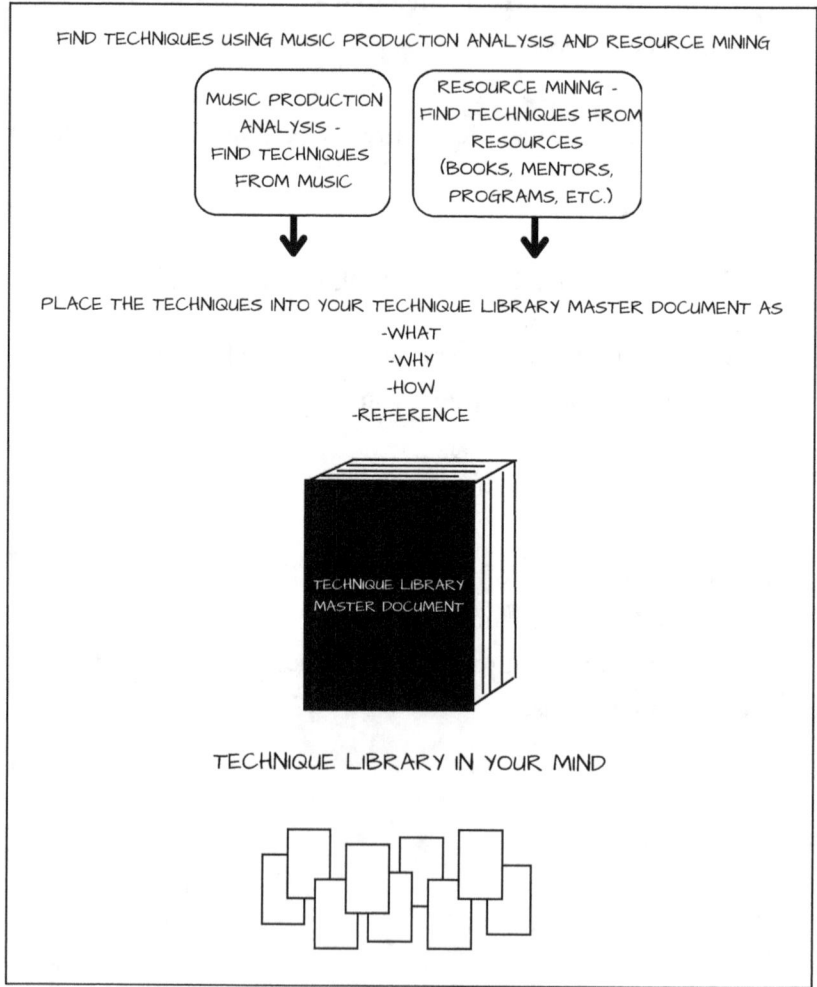

BUILD YOUR MENTAL FRAMEWORK

Remember, the key is to always learn the fundamental skills behind techniques you find – otherwise known as the "why".

Here are examples of how powerful this can get for your creativity:

- Any instrument can use the *vocal FX form technique* in theory and practice. It doesn't have to be the vocals. You could change the FX form for any instrument, for example, guitar FX form, piano FX form, etc.

- Any instrument can use the *chorus kickflip technique* in theory and practice. You could use extra snares in the chorus rather than kicks to have a similar effect.

Over time, you build your framework of how music production works. It grows more powerful and unique to you as you continue this process.

HOW DOES THIS TECHNIQUE MAKE ME FEEL?

How do you find the *why* behind a technique? How it makes you *feel* is why you would use a technique: to create that same effect on the listener. Over time, you'll have the musical techniques to ignite any emotion within the listener. You do this by molding the musical energy to your will with techniques. This is because emotion is energy in motion. Attach every technique you find to the feeling it creates in you. That will become your superpower. If the music impacts you, you know it will impact the listener too. So always feel into how techniques make you feel.

THE IMPORTANCE OF ASKING: *WHY?*

What if you need help finding the fundamental skillset behind a technique? Say it's a skill set you're not particularly good at yet and want to improve. For example, lyric writing, sound design, mixing, transitions, etc. Sometimes you want to know the deeper reason why a technique works. So how do we do this? We achieve this via *first principles thinking*.

First principles thinking is chunking an idea into its fundamental building blocks. You get the idea down to the point where you can deduce it no further. Then, you can build the building blocks back up in your own way. If you are already finding techniques in tracks as I showed you, then you've already been using it. You can target approach this and go deeper. The key is always to ask *Why?* until you reach the fundamental truth.

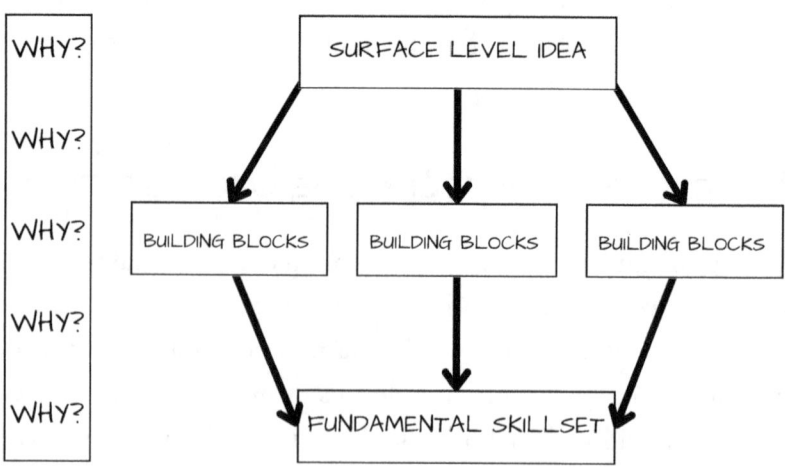

In the above diagram, you have the box at the top, the surface-level idea. You chunk it into its fundamental building blocks by asking *Why?* Why is this skill like this? You then find the technique building blocks involved. Once you find those techniques, you'll find the fundamental skill set that built that surface-level idea. That is the process that you're going through here. Once you have that fundamental skill set, you can use it yourself in your own way.

While you're analyzing, asking *Why?* is the best way to go deeper and deeper into why a technique works. The layers will reveal themselves to you. Eventually you'll hit the fundamental core of a technique or skill set you are looking to learn. This effect happens while using Level One: Techniques.

THE IMPORTANCE OF ASKING A DIVERSE SET OF QUESTIONS

For this to work, you must be creative and curious and let the questions flow as you analyze. I could give you a list of questions, but it works best when you ask them depending on the track you are listening to. Context is everything.

Here are some examples: What is this instrument? Who is playing this? What is it doing? Why is it doing that? How is it playing? Where does it play in the frequency spectrum and panning spectrum? Why? How is it in relation to the other instruments? When does it play that part in relation to the other instruments? How is this in relation to other tracks I've analyzed?

Starting the questions with these words helps to find the right questions to ask:

- What
- Why
- How
- When
- Where
- Who

DIFFERENCE BETWEEN TECHNIQUES FROM TRACKS AND RESOURCES

The techniques you find in Level One of analysis are musical techniques. You will know how to use these in context after you analyze music.

The techniques you find from Level 1.5 of analysis are resource techniques. These are "how to use tools to achieve musical techniques". These techniques show you how to achieve some of the musical techniques. It fills any gaps in your knowledge. You get the fastest skill growth when applying Levels One and 1.5 together.

One of the best ways to find techniques for resource mining is by watching *in the studio* videos of great producers. In these videos, the producer will analyze their own track. They will take you inside their DAW and show you how they used tools to achieve their techniques. These videos will be the closest a lot of us will get to being "in the studio" with the producer. However, combining this with music production analysis lets you know why and when to use what they show you. The "why" and the "when" a producer uses something is, sometimes, what they miss in these videos. We cover every angle by using Levels One and 1.5.

You can also target approach your learning with resource mining. That's when you analyze a track and find a technique but don't know how to do the technique. You can use resources to find that technique even if you don't know what the name of it is. Search online, in books, in programs, and with mentors, and you will find the answer.

CULTIVATING THE TECHNIQUE MINER MINDSET

The human mind has a function called the *Reticular Activating System* or RAS for short. With the RAS, you can program the mind to look for something, and it will find it. You can use this function by training yourself to become a *Technique Miner*. A Technique Miner is always on the lookout for one technique at a time in both music and resources. You are always looking out for technique gold.

One technique at a time adds up daily; eventually, you have a vast and powerful library. The more world-class techniques you find and remember, the more you can take action on. You are taking advantage of the compound effect.

IN-DEPTH ESSAYS VERSUS THE SYSTEM

I used to create "complex in-depth essays" when I analyzed songs. I don't advise you do essays. In-depth essays make the information you find too vague. Essays take too long and don't provide you with actionable information.

When using the technique system, you focus your RAS on selecting one technique at a time. You are then gaining one actionable technique at a time. How I've shown you to analyze makes it much easier for your brain to comprehend what's happening. You're analyzing one technique at a time, and techniques are the building blocks of tracks. So, when your mind understands each technique, it can understand how they interact. Your brain achieves this by itself. You need to trust in this. This process compounds over time and becomes more powerful the more you do it. Overtime, you will notice patterns in all recorded music. All these patterns create a network effect of nodes that link together in your mind.

HOW YOUR BRAIN WILL MEMORIZE TECHNIQUES

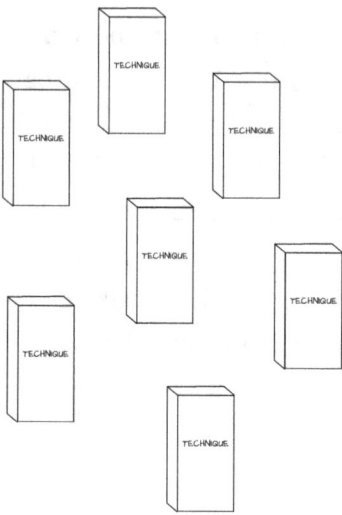

These rectangle building blocks represent *Techniques*. You find and understand individual techniques one at a time.

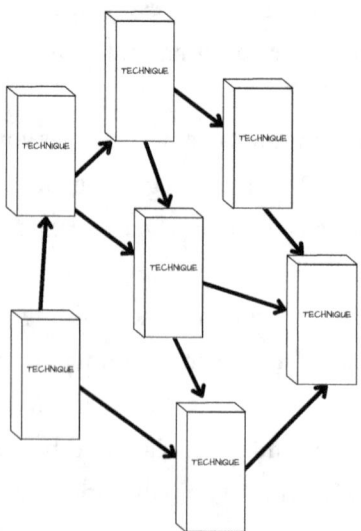

Then, your brain connects the building blocks together within your mind. Your brain does this automatically.

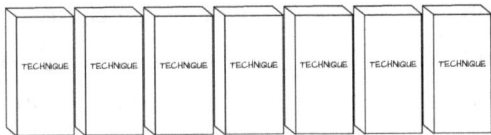

This process builds your mental framework for music production. If there are any "holes" in your framework, they become obvious. You can fill the holes with music production analysis and resource mining.

You might find Technique A from one song, then Technique B from another. Then, when you're creating your own track, your brain will know how to link them. The key here is to make sure you don't forget a technique. If you start to forget techniques, some may fall off the radar until you remember them. You write the techniques down in the technique library master document for this reason.

Why Write Techniques Down?

Writing down techniques helps when learning to ensure the brain connects neural pathways. It helps you to understand and internalize the information deeply. After you write techniques down, you don't have to reference the information like it's a reference book. Yet, you can if you want to.

I developed this process to move the techniques through each document. It ensures you remember what you learn. Some of you may be able to learn without the documents. Others may only need to use the technique library master document. Others may need to use all the documents.

The point is to get into the habit of doing this process in your mind. Eventually, you can drop the writing part if you want to. The habit of doing this process will become automatic in your mind. As long as you remember what you find, that is all that matters. Taking action on the techniques you find in the context of your own music is often the most powerful way to remember a technique.

Although not all techniques will be needed right after you learn them. If you know you won't take action on a technique for some time, writing it down can be beneficial for that reason.

Other Memorization Methods

In Part III – the Ten Core Principles of Arranging – you will begin to use visual drawing techniques. The benefit of drawing is that it connects your memory with visual patterns. Humans evolved to be visual, so drawing activates your primitive brain. This process works best with the core principles of arranging because you discover them as patterns in recorded music. Some members of the Polymath Producer community have used mind maps to gather their information. You can even create your own way of memorizing the techniques that best fit you as an individual. Remember that you can use alternative memorization methods as long as it's always one technique at a time.

As long as you find one technique at a time, then the system should work for you. You must trust that when you use this system, the techniques you find are moving into your subconscious mind. When done properly, you will notice the techniques will come through you intuitively when you produce.

WHAT TO EXPECT

- The Technique Framework is the foundation of all other levels. You can use this thinking to approach all other frameworks in this book.

- You'll always get new insights using this framework. Sometimes, you'll analyze a song, then return to it a few months later when your skills improve. What you'll find are new techniques you may have missed. The techniques are revealed in correlation to the level at which you are ready to receive them. This effect comes from analyzing over time. That's why I teach you the process of analyzing yourself so that you can have the realizations yourself. When you do, it will be life changing.

- It is up to you how "polymath" you want to go. Some may only want to do songwriting and arranging. Others may want to do the whole production chain. Suppose you want to go full polymath by working on songwriting, production, mixing, and mastering. I recommend using music production analysis on all disciplines simultaneously. You'll gain a deep understanding of the record creation process. Do this daily to immerse yourself in the language of music production.

- Analysis from a range of different genres will help you cross-pollinate ideas. I analyzed one classic and one modern track a day when I started. This action allowed me to see what has worked in the past. It also allowed me to see how production and mixing methods have evolved. You can use this on any genre you can possibly think of. Gregorian chants? Yes. Baroque music? Yes. Jazz? Yes. 1960s Pop? Yes. Irish Folk? Yes. You can apply it to anything and everything.

- The more you analyze tracks, the easier it is for your ears to "lock on" to one instrument and technique at a time. After a while, your ears get quick at finding specific techniques in tracks. You may also find your appreciation for the craft becomes deeper. That's why it becomes a fun process.

- Remember: We are not plagiarizing. We are aiming to find the fundamental reason *why* the technique works. We can then use that fundamental knowledge in our own way. For example, I didn't write the "side tambourine technique"; I wrote the "counter percussion technique". Fundamentally, you could use any percussion instrument to create that technique. Not just a tambourine.

- Analysis can be addictive. You get dopamine when you listen to your favorite music. You also get a dopamine hit whenever you find an awesome technique or discovery. This system and this process are fun to do as well. So, if you do get addicted to this process, make sure you don't get stuck in information-getting mode. Always keep your music creation time number one on your schedule.

THE UNIVERSAL FORMULA

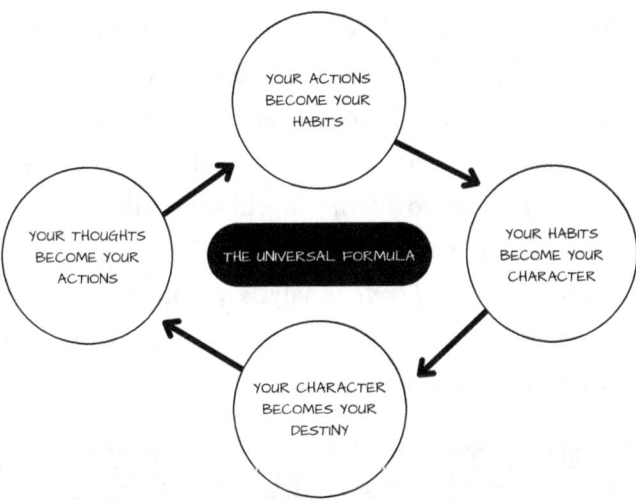

This is the formula that will take place inside you when you use this system:

- Your thoughts become your actions.
- Your actions become your habits.
- Your habits become your character.
- Your character becomes your destiny.

When you analyze music from the great producers of all time, your thoughts (techniques you use) change. Your thoughts (techniques) then become your new actions as you create. If you act on these new thoughts (techniques) enough, they become habits. When your habits are those of a great producer, your character will become that of a great producer. Using the techniques you find within the context of your own creations is the most powerful method for skill growth and memorization. By doing this you're on your way to changing your mind, your skillset, your music, and your life.

ACTION STEPS

Now you know how to chunk music into technique building blocks. You know how to learn the "words" of the language of music production. Congratulations, you have learned the first part of the system and the language. This book is an action-taking program. When you take action on the steps provided, you will get results.

Remember how to master the language of music production? *Analyze the great music of all time.* Analysis requires action. But luckily, this system makes it fun, and it will be easy to do. Here is a full summary of the action steps to get results.

PART II: TECHNIQUES - ACTION STEPS	
ACTION STEP ONE	GATHER YOUR MATERIALS & SET UP THE SYSTEM INCLUDING: • STREAMING SERVICE • MUSIC IN A PLAYLIST YOU WANT TO ANALYZE • LIST OF RESOURCES YOU WANT TO ANALYZE. INCLUDING YOUTUBE VIDEOS, BOOKS, MENTORS, ETC. • GOOD HEADPHONES SO YOU CAN HEAR THE ENTIRE STEREO FIELD • MUSIC PRODUCTION ANALYSIS DOCUMENT • RESOURCE MINING DOCUMENT • TECHNIQUE LIBRARY MASTER DOCUMENT DOWNLOAD PRINT VERSIONS OF THE DOCUMENTS AT WWW.POLYMATHPRODUCER.COM/RESOURCES
ACTION STEP TWO	PLOT THE TASKS TO DO DAILY IN YOUR CALENDAR. SCHEDULE TIME FOR MUSIC PRODUCTION ANALYSIS, RESOURCE MINING AND MUSIC CREATION.
ACTION STEP THREE	TAKE ACTION DAILY, BUILDING YOUR TECHNIQUE LIBRARY. YOU CAN DO THIS IN ONLY AN HOUR A DAY.
ACTION STEP FOUR	WHILE CREATING MUSIC, USE AND IMPLEMENT THE TECHNIQUES YOU ARE LEARNING IN CONTEXT.

Part II: Techniques

	SUMMARY OF THE TECHNIQUE FRAMEWORK
STEP ONE	LISTEN TO A TRACK. SCAN THE STEREO FIELD. • FREQUENCY FIELD: LOWS, MIDS, HIGHS. • PANNING: LEFT, CENTER, RIGHT.
STEP TWO	CHOOSE A SPECIFIC INSTRUMENT.
STEP THREE	FIND OUT WHAT TECHNIQUE(S) THE INSTRUMENT IS DOING. HOW IS THE INSTRUMENT RELATING TO OTHER INSTRUMENTS? WHY DOES IT WORK IN THIS TRACK? HOW IS IT RELATING TO OTHER MUSIC YOU HAVE ANALYZED?
STEP FOUR	WRITE DOWN WHAT THE TECHNIQUE IS.
STEP FIVE	GIVE THE TECHNIQUE A NAME.
STEP SIX	WRITE DOWN THE TECHNIQUE AS - WHAT, WHY, HOW, AND REFERENCE. PLACE THE TECHNIQUE IN YOUR TECHNIQUE LIBRARY MASTER DOCUMENT.

	SUMMARY OF THE RESOURCE MINING FRAMEWORK
STEP ONE	ANALYZE A COLLECTION OF MUSIC RESOURCES. THESE CAN INCLUDE YOUTUBE VIDEOS, BOOKS, MENTORS, ARTICLES, AND ANYTHING ELSE WITH VALUABLE TECHNIQUES.
STEP TWO	AS YOU CONSUME THE RESOURCE, LOOK FOR ONE TECHNIQUE AT A TIME THE PRODUCER MENTIONS.
STEP THREE	WRITE A NAME FOR THE TECHNIQUE. THEN WRITE WHAT THE TECHNIQUE IS, WHY YOU WOULD USE IT, HOW TO USE IT, AND THE REFERENCE OF WHERE YOU FOUND IT.
STEP FOUR	THEN PLACE EACH TECHNIQUE INTO YOUR TECHNIQUE LIBRARY.

After taking action on Levels One and 1.5, you should already see fast skill growth. In the next part, you will learn Level Two: the Ten Core Principles of Arranging. This will be the "grammar" of the language. It is the structure for the technique building blocks. You're doing amazing – let's continue.

PART III:
Core Principles Of Arranging
[Analysis Level Two]

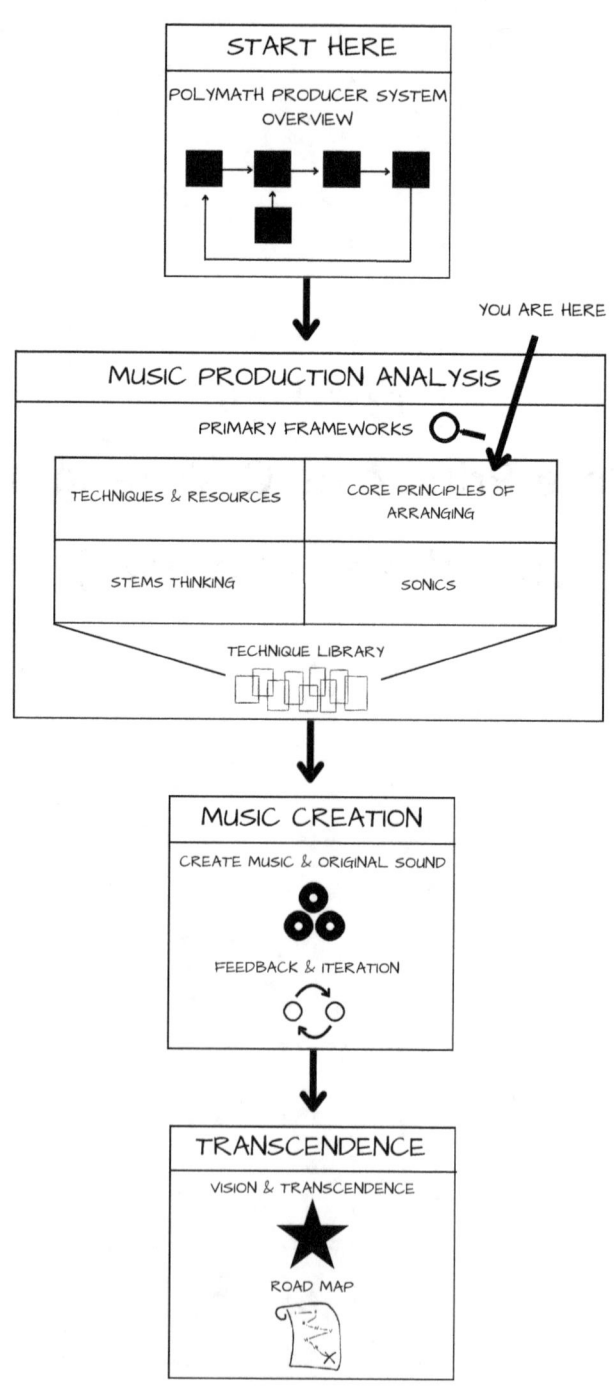

The Principles Are Everything

I'D BEEN analyzing for eighteen months with Level One: Techniques. I started with long-form essays and then moved to finding one technique at a time with chunking. I analyzed hundreds of tracks and found hundreds of techniques from the great producers of all time. After a while, I noticed that certain techniques kept popping up repeatedly. One in particular that kept showing up was the *Core Rhythm*.

Before I learned the language of music production, I always seemed to get blocked by rhythm. I would either put too many rhythms in, or not have a centralized rhythm. I overcomplicated things. I usually felt lost while creating rhythms, so I would throw ideas at the DAW and hope they'd stick.

It wasn't until I started doing music production analysis that things changed. I began to focus on the rhythm as a building block. What I found was that every track had a different pattern for its rhythm; that was obvious.

But over time, I noticed an underlying principle that ran even deeper than the patterns. I called it the *Core Rhythm Principle*. This core rhythm was what the majority of instruments tended to gravitate around. This core rhythm became the central focus. Anything not in line with the core rhythm was a counter rhythm.

I noticed that on a technique level, I was analyzing the *patterns* the track would play. Patterns, for example, were: Does the kick play on beats 1 and 3? Does the kick play on beats 1, 2, 3 and 4? Where does the snare take place? These patterns were technique building blocks I could put in my technique library. However, the underlying principle the technique builds on top of is the core rhythm.

When I found this, everything clicked in my own productions. When I create the core rhythm, I know what all the instruments need to do. That rhythm will be what the majority of the instruments gravitate around. They will play that rhythm or some variation of that rhythm. The rhythm patterns they play within that principle are the techniques.

Although valuable, techniques are all built on top of the core principles. Techniques are the "words" of the language, but they live within the core principles. The core principles are the structure all techniques live within – the language's "grammar".

Techniques can vary depending on genre, but principles are universal. The core principles have existed in every track I've analyzed, in every era of written music.

In life, all skills have a set of principles. These principles are the meta. Principles apply whether learning to play the piano, lifting weights, or learning business. Each area has fundamental principles at play. Once you know those principles, they become the framework you can play in. They are the 20% that, if you focus on them, provide 80% of results. I realized that principles are where significant changes happen. Principles are where I should focus my attention on to master the skill.

After a year and a half of analyzing techniques, it all became so clear in my head. One day, I woke up and wrote in the exact order all Ten Core Principles of Arranging in every track I'd ever analyzed. I saw it in plain sight. It felt like it came from a higher power. Each Principle stacks on top of the other. Each Principle provides the foundation for the next.

Part III: Core Principles Of Arranging

The Ten Core Principles of Arranging:

- Core Structure Principle
- Core Harmonic Structure Principle
- Core Rhythm Principle
- Counter Rhythm Principle
- Spatial Principle
- Foreground and Background Principle
- Energy Principle
- Call and Response Principle
- Repurposing Principle
- Synergy Principle

*

You will learn more about each principle soon. The Polymath Producer community have said that the core principles were the biggest game changer. Once they knew the framework, the production process became easier. The reason is simple: these core principles are what everything else you do builds on top of. Techniques build on top of these core principles.

Whenever I have a problem in my production arrangement, it is usually because I'm not using one of the core principles correctly for that song.

After learning the core principles of arranging, I saw how all music was created. I noticed it as a universal language that transcended genre. I saw genres as a combination of techniques to make that sound. But the principles were the foundation that was in all genres.

Knowing the principles made me feel like one of the original producers from the 1940s and 1950s. These producers knew the craft on such a deep level. They understood the principles of arranging from the ground up.

In the Renaissance era, the renowned polymaths knew this. They would learn the principles of many fields of knowledge. Their genius was when they cross-pollinated those fields of knowledge. Cross-pollination led to new insights, innovation and inventions. By knowing the principles you are following the same path.

In this part, you will learn the Ten Core Principles of Arranging in detail. I will share with you the parts of the principles I've discovered over a decade. If techniques are the words of the language, you're about to learn the grammar. But don't worry, it's not boring. This stuff is fun because it's all visual. It all takes place in your mind. I've made every step of the way easy for you to understand. Are you ready to think like one of the original producers? Are you ready to learn the *lost art?*

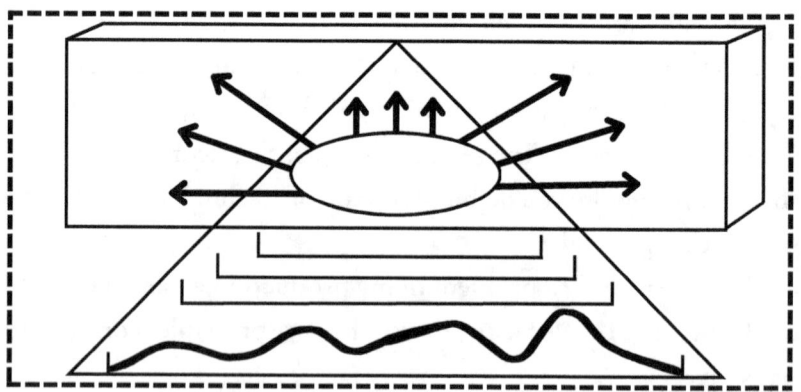

The Ten Core Principles of Arranging

IN THIS SECTION, you will learn the Ten Core Principles of Arranging. You will learn how they work together to form a music production arrangement.

We'll be going through them in chronological order as follows:

1. Core Structure Principle
2. Core Harmonic Structure Principle
3. Core Rhythm Principle
4. Counter Rhythm Principle
5. Spatial Principle
6. Foreground and Background Principle
7. Energy Principle
8. Call and Response Principle
9. Repurposing Principle
10. Synergy Principle

For each principle we will cover the following:

- An overview of what the principle is.
- A deeper explanation of how the principle works.
- How the principle works on a macro- and micro-level (for applicable principles).
- Examples of this principle taking place in music references.

- How to turn the principle information you find in analysis into techniques.

I will give you examples of how famous music productions use each principle. I will make the principles in the examples so obvious they'll be easily recognizable. When you recognize them once, it'll be easier to notice them in your own analysis. During this part, I recommend listening to each reference as you read. You will find a playlist of all music references mentioned in this book at www.polymathproducer.com/resources.

Turning Principle Information Into Techniques

In this section, I will show you how to think about each principle. When you listen to the examples I show you, the principle will then activate in your mind. The principles are the unchanging concepts. The *way* the core principle has been used is what changes. The *way* the core principles have been used is the technique level.

For example: the core structure principle is the form the music follows from start to finish. But there are many different structure combinations you can choose from. Some songs may be verse, chorus, verse, chorus. Other songs may be introduction, verse, pre-chorus, chorus.

As you can see, principles are never changing, techniques change depending on the arrangement. I will show you at the end of each principle how to turn the principles information you find in each analysis into techniques. You will then be able to use these techniques for your own music.

Generally, bringing focused awareness to the principles on an ongoing basis will be enough to learn techniques from them. The process of bringing awareness to the techniques alone will be enough to move them into your subconscious. You will then find that you can automatically use them while creating your own music. This requires a state of utmost concentration while analyzing to work. It also requires a state of trust that you are receiving the information. When the techniques start coming through you while you create, it will feel like magic. The primary aim with this part is to have you understand these principles by bringing continued awareness to them in your music production analysis. Let's begin.

NUMBER ONE: CORE STRUCTURE PRINCIPLE

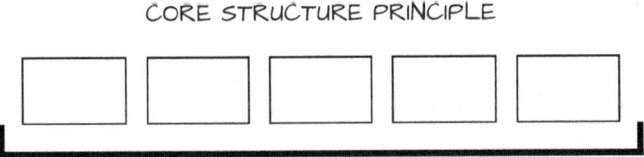

Every track will have a core structure, a form the music follows from start to finish. The core structure principle has two types: macro-level and micro-level structures.

Macro-Level Structure

Macro-level structures are the traditional forms of a track. For example, they include verse, chorus, verse, chorus, bridge, and chorus, etc. Consider them section A, section B, etc.

MACRO LEVEL STRUCTURE

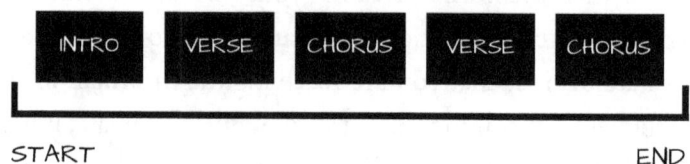

If you look at the diagram, this is an example of a composition and a core structure. The start of the song is on the left. As the track plays it moves through the structure to the end on the right. This particular track has an introduction, verse, chorus, verse, and chorus. Every track will need a different structure to bring out the best in the song. The more combinations of structures you know, the more you can use for your music.

Micro-Level Structure

Micro-level structures are sub-forms within the macro-level structure.

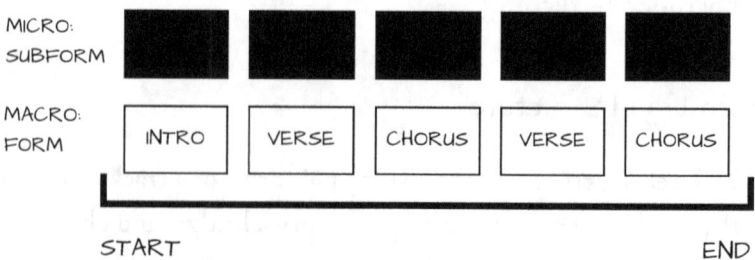

Example: Vocal FX form – When you have more FX on the lead vocal in any given part of the macro structure. Say the lead vocal has less FX in the verse but more in the chorus. That is a sub-form.

You can use sub-forms to create energy movement within the structure (see *energy principle*).

Sub forms are how each instrument develops techniques, core principles and layering through the macro-level structure.

Here are three examples of sub-forms:

1. You only reserve the bass line for the chorus. The bass carries a lot of energy, meaning the verses will feel less impactful than the chorus. You will reserve the biggest impact for the chorus. For example, "Teenage Dream" by Katy Perry.

2. You use more counter rhythms as the structure unfolds. Like, reserving a counter rhythm tambourine for the second half of the song. For example, "Heroes" by David Bowie.

3. You shift core rhythms throughout the song. Using one core rhythm for the verses, and then another core rhythm for the choruses. For example, "The Time of My Life" by Bill Medley and Jennifer Warnes.

Throughout the macro-level structure ask:

- How does the instrument develop in terms of techniques?
- How does the instrument develop in terms of the core principles?
- How does the instrument develop in terms of layering?
- How does the instrument develop in terms of sonics?

Benefits of Knowing the Core Structure Principle

Without structure, nothing else can exist. You need structure so that the other nine principles can exist inside that structure. You learn these structures fast with music production analysis. Then, when you create your composition, you can attach your ideas to a structure that will work best. The act of finding the best structure for your ideas will become intuitive. With analysis, you have already learned structure combinations from other tracks.

The core structure principle is the foundation of the other principles. All other principles build on top of this one. The other nine principles cannot occur without a solid structure. The faster you get your core structure, the quicker the other principles arise.

Sometimes, I'll be halfway through the arrangement of a song, and it won't feel right. A lot of the time, it is because I am not using the proper structure. Structure plays a fundamental role in a track's effectiveness.

Your goal is to know as many of these macro- and micro-level structures that work as possible. Then place them in your technique library. You will find these structures by analyzing the great music of all time. Then, when you create a track, you will have proven structures to work with. This information will save you time by getting you to the best decision faster. You can also cross-pollinate structures for originality.

Core Structure Principle to Techniques

Find macro- and micro-level core structures in your analysis. Write them out or remember them as shown in the below examples. These structure combinations are the techniques. Then move them into your technique library for use in your own music.

Core Structure Principle Examples

Example of the core structure principle on a macro-level:
"Respect" by Aretha Franklin – Introduction, Verse, Chorus, Verse, Chorus, Verse, Chorus, Instrumental, Verse, Chorus, Bridge, Chorus, Chorus.

Part III: Core Principles Of Arranging

Example of the core structure principle on a micro-level: "Starboy" by The Weeknd and Daft Punk – Vocal FX Form

- Verse one: vocal dry with some reverb.
- Pre-chorus one: vocal dry with more reverb and delay throws.
- Chorus one: vocal wettest with reverb and delays.
- Verse two: vocal dry with some reverb and delay throws.
- Pre-chorus two: vocal dry with more reverb and delay throws.
- Chorus two: vocal wettest with reverb and delays.
- Bridge: vocal at its driest.
- Pre-chorus three: vocal dry with more reverb and delay throws.
- Chorus three: vocal wettest with reverb and delays, most of any part of the song.

NUMBER TWO: CORE HARMONIC STRUCTURE PRINCIPLE

Within the core structure is the core harmonic structure principle. The harmony changes as the structure changes. Looped chords are also a possibility. The most straightforward way to understand this principle is chord progression. The core harmonic structure principle has two types: macro-level and micro-level.

Macro Level Harmonic Structure

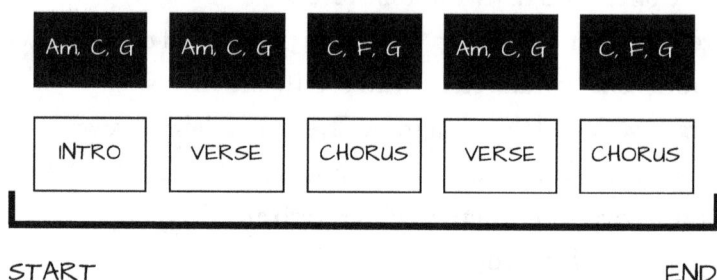

1. The first part to look for in the macro harmonic structure is the key of the track.
2. The second part to look for in the macro harmonic structure are the chord progressions. What is the song's chord progression from the start to the end?

If you look at the diagram, you have the core structure down the bottom. The start of the track is on the left and the end is on the right. On top of each part of the core structure, the chord progressions make up the harmonic structure. In this particular track, there are three chords in the intro and three in the verse. The chords then change in the chorus.

Every track you analyze will be different. The more you learn different chord progressions from analysis, the more you can use.

Part III: Core Principles Of Arranging

Micro Level Harmonic Structure

MICRO LEVEL HARMONIC STRUCTURE

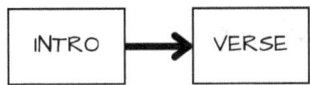

1. The first part to look for in the micro harmonic structure are chord couplets. A chord couplet is two chords. An example of C major to A minor would be a chord couplet. E minor to G major would be a chord couplet. Different chord couplets make you feel different emotions.

2. The second part to look for in the micro harmonic structure is matching harmony with the theme of the song. Use the correct chords to match a certain feeling with a lyric, melody, or instrument parts. For example: If the lyrics are happy, the chords can feel happy to. But, sometimes this can be done with contrasted opposites too. For example, in the song "Big Yellow Taxi" by Joni Mitchell, the chords feel happy, yet the lyrics are somber.

Harmony Can Change in Popularity with the Times

- Many pop music tracks in the 2020s have simpler looped four-chord progressions.
- Pop music had much more complex harmony in the 1940s. You'll even find some diminished chords in there.
- In the 1950s, some pop music harmony became more simplistic with the rise of rock and roll. For example, there's the standard early rock progression. It uses the one, four, and five chords and a turnaround.

- In 1960s pop, chords could be a mixture of complex and simplistic depending on the goal.

How varied your harmonic structure will be is up to you and how deep you want to go with this.

Benefits of Knowing the Core Harmonic Structure Principle:

- You will have the right chord combinations for anything you need when you create.
- You will be able to create the harmony above the core structure quickly.
- You will be able to make the harmony, lyrics, and arrangement congruent. This stack can be powerful for energy development.
- You can also tap into the emotion you want the listener to experience.

This principle holds a strong influence over every instrument and part that you put in the track.

Core Harmonic Structure Principle to Techniques

Find macro- and micro-level core harmonic structures in your analysis. Write them out or remember them as shown in the following example. These chord progression combinations are the techniques. Then move them into your technique library for use in your own music.

Core Harmonic Structure Example

In "Girls Like You" by Maroon Five, the chords are C major to G major to A minor to F major. This progression template for any key would be written as I, V, vi, IV. This chord progression then loops for the whole structure of the song.

Tip: Great books to find chord progressions from are *The Songwriting Secrets of the Beatles* by Dominic Pedler,[12] and anything from the *Great American Songbook*.[13]

NUMBER THREE: CORE RHYTHM PRINCIPLE

CORE RHYTHM PRINCIPLE

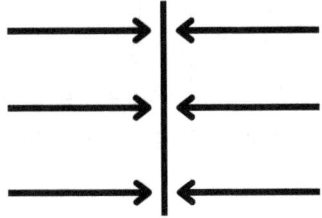

The core rhythm is the primary rhythm in an arrangement. Most instruments in the arrangement gravitate around the core rhythm. By gravitate, this could mean in entirety or as a complement to the core rhythm. It is also the rhythm that the listener generally grasps onto, also known as the groove. It is also the primary rhythm the audience generally moves to.

You can view the core rhythm as two parts in isolation flowing as one unit:

1. *Isolated drumbeat* – primarily the kick and snare/clap pattern. Can sometimes also include the drums/percussion that flow with the kick and snare/clap.

2. *Isolated instrument elements* that flow with that drumbeat. Usually are melodic/harmonic instruments. But can also include drums/percussion that flow with the melodic/harmonic instruments.

The *combination* of isolated drumbeat and isolated instrument elements is the core rhythm.

Example: "Shake It Off" by Taylor Swift. The isolated drumbeat (kick and snare/clap) is introduced from 0:00–0:05. The isolated instrument elements that flow with that drum beat then come in from 0:05 onward in the brass section.

Example: "Locked Out of Heaven" by Bruno Mars. The isolated drum beat (kick and snare/clap) is introduced from 0:00–0:16. The isolated instrument elements that flow with that beat are the bass and the guitars.

The core rhythm epiphany is phenomenal. This epiphany is one of the biggest from a principle you may have in your music production analysis. Hearing it happen in all recorded music will change how you think about music production for life. The core rhythm is essential to understand because it is one of the main blocks to producing quickly. The only way to have this epiphany will be to analyze the great music of all time with this knowledge in mind.

You first analyze the core rhythm by isolating the drum rhythm (the kick and snare/clap beat). Then, look for the instruments that flow with that drum rhythm. The more you learn about these core rhythm patterns from analysis, the more you can use them in your own music. You can even cross-pollinate rhythms for originality. You are harnessing each rhythm pattern as a technique building block.

CORE RHYTHM PRINCIPLE

```
                    HI HATS ──────▶│◀────── GUITAR
ISOLATED
CORE RHYTHM         SNARE ────────▶│◀────── PIANO           INSTRUMENT
DRUM BEAT                                                    ELEMENTS
                                                             FLOWING
                    KICK ──────────▶│◀────── BASS            WITH
                                                             DRUM BEAT
                              =
                         CORE RHYTHM
```

Here is a visual example of what this looks like. If you look at the thick black line in the middle, that represents the core rhythm. If you look at the left-hand side, that is the isolated drum beat. The kick, snare, and hi-hat are playing the core rhythm. If you look at the right, these instruments within the arrangement flow with that drum beat/core rhythm (the guitar, piano and bass).

One of the main workflow problems many producers have is they try to make more than one core rhythm. Learn how to chunk a core rhythm into its parts. Create your isolated drum beat. Then create the instruments that flow with that drum beat. You can also do it in reverse. Start with the instruments - then make the drum beat flow with them. Doing this will connect you with the music's groove, vibe, and feel.

It is up there in modern-day music as one of the most important things, along with lyrics and melody. Core rhythm is essential to making that work. Once you find the right core rhythm, the creation of ideas becomes more effortless. The counter rhythms fall into place. The other principles become a lot easier to create with.

Core Rhythm Considerations

- Core rhythms don't need to be perfect to make sense. Sometimes, the instruments don't flow with the exact isolated drumbeat. Sometimes they flow mostly with the bass line, which flows with the drums. The fundamental truth still applies, and you will notice it.

- *Time signature* can also play a role, though most mainstream music tends to be 4/4 time. Differing time signatures, such as 3/4 time or 6/8 time, can impact the feel of the core rhythm. Examples include: "I Only Have Eyes for You" by the Flamingos in 6/8 time. "What the World Needs Now" by Dionne Warwick in 3/4 time. You can even have songs that switch time signatures like "Hey Ya" by Outkast, which switches from 4/4 to 2/4 on certain turnarounds.

- *Beats per minute* can also play a role in core rhythm. Different BPMs offer different possibilities for rhythm patterns. Some patterns work better depending on BPM.

- Drawing from different genres can also influence the core rhythm patterns you find. Mixing core rhythm patterns from one genre into other genres can create original sounds.

- One of the quickest ways to identify the instruments flowing with the beat is the bass line. The bass line usually flows with the core rhythm drums. This can be a main identifying factor of the core rhythm. The bass line is usually the main "instrument" that flows with the core rhythm drums. The next key identifying instrument will be the *core harmonic rhythmic driver*.

Example: "My Sharona" by The Knack shows this core rhythm process in action. In fact, each concept I've spoken about unfolds in consecutive form in this song, so it is a perfect example. Listen to how the core rhythm drums start the song from 0:00-0:07. Then the bass guitar instrument flows with the core rhythm drums from 0:07 onward. Then the core harmonic rhythmic driver played by the guitar riff comes in from 0:13 onwards. These all then flow together as one core rhythm.

Core Harmonic Rhythmic Driver

In most arrangements there is usually a core rhythm instrument that I call a *core harmonic rhythmic driver*. That is because this instrument can play the core rhythm as chords, harmony, or melody. When there are drums, it usually flows with the drums as one unit. This unit is the core rhythm in full power. When there are no drums, it usually provides the core rhythm itself. This differs with drums which can only play the core rhythm as percussive sounds.

I've observed that there is usually one primary core harmonic rhythmic driver per arrangement. This instrument follows the core rhythm. Every other core rhythm instrument that flows with the core harmonic rhythmic driver either layers or complements it.

The core harmonic rhythmic driver is part of the "core rhythm instruments that flow with the core rhythm drums". But the core harmonic rhythmic driver holds a special focus in the track when there is one.

There is a core harmonic rhythmic driver in most arrangements, which happens in two ways:

1. The core harmonic rhythmic driver will flow with the core rhythm drums if there are drums.
2. The core harmonic rhythmic driver will "drive" the arrangement rhythmically. It will do so even if there are no drums.

Here are some examples from hit songs:

- "American Woman" by The Guess Who. Listen to the lead guitar riff in the intro. It drives the rhythm before the drums come in. When the drums come in at 0:11 seconds, this forms the full core rhythm.

- "Smells Like Teen Spirit" by Nirvana. Listen to the primary guitar riff from 0:00 – 0:24. The guitar riff is the core harmonic rhythmic driver. The bassline, kick, and snare flow together as one with the guitar riff to create the core rhythm.

- "Wannabe" by Spice Girls. Listen to the primary synth keyboard riff from 0:04 – 0:17, that is the core harmonic rhythmic driver.

- "Dynamite" by Taio Cruz. At 0:32 you'll hear that the core harmonic rhythmic driver is obvious. Then when the beat comes in at 0:48, the core rhythm instruments flow with the core rhythm drums. This combination creates the core rhythm at full power.

If There Is No Core Harmonic Rhythmic Driver

Usually, a core harmonic rhythmic driver will combine with the vocal or drums at some point in a track. But if there is no core harmonic rhythmic driver at any given point in the track it can be:

Mainly the core rhythm drums. Example: "We Will Rock You" by Queen, the iconic stomp, stomp, clap. The vocal in this one acts as a core harmonic rhythmic driver as it flows with the beat to create the core rhythm.

A cappella vocal. Example: "Tom's Diner" by Suzanne Vega. In the DNA remix, you can hear that the vocal becomes the core harmonic rhythmic driver.

Counter rhythms. Example: "Eye of the Tiger" by Survivor. Listen to the introduction, the guitar line is a counter rhythm. But then the core harmonic rhythmic driver comes in at 0:10 seconds played by the other guitar riff.

Pads. Example: "Can't Feel My Face" by The Weeknd. The start of the song is only pads and vocals, but the core rhythm drums and bass come in at 0:44.

Instrument that flows with the song. This often happens in minimalistic arrangements. It is when a solo instrument (like piano or guitar) drives the song rhythmically while accompanying a vocal. This instrument is usually a core harmonic rhythmic driver. Examples: "Endless Love" by Lionel Richie and Diana Ross, "Bridge Over Troubled Water" by Simon and Garfunkel, "When I Was Your Man" by Bruno Mars, and "Yesterday" by The Beatles.

Core Harmonic Rhythmic Driver Considerations

- The core harmonic rhythmic driver will be the acting core rhythm until the drum beat combines with it.

- The core harmonic rhythmic driver is usually a secondary hook and mainly focused on rhythm. It can have harmonic and sometimes melodic identity. But it is usually not so catchy that it overtakes the focus of the primary hook. (See *foreground and background principle*)

Core Harmonic Rhythmic Driver Examples

If you listen to "Girls Like You" by Maroon Five, there is a clear example of a core harmonic rhythmic driver in the guitar riff. That riff plays through the whole track; you'll notice it has harmonic and melodic elements. It's catchy and stands out, so it is a secondary hook, but it's not so catchy that it overpowers the lead vocal. That is a clear example of a core harmonic rhythmic driver because it drives the song without active drums in certain sections. Then, when the drums come in, the core harmonic rhythmic driver flows with the drum beat and bass, uniting as one to create the full core rhythm.

Here are even more core harmonic rhythmic driver examples from hit songs. Listen to how each track has a primary core harmonic rhythmic driver. Then listen to how that flows with the drum beat. I will label a short time stamp so you can hear an obvious example in each song:

- "Million Dollar Baby" by Tommy Richman. The core harmonic rhythmic driver is the keyboard/synth stabs, which flow with the bassline and drums. 0:13–0:40

- "Mood" by 24K Golden feat. Iann Dior. The core harmonic rhythmic driver is the main guitar riff, which flows with the bass line. 0:00–0:30

- "Lean On" by Major Lazar, DJ Snake, and Mø. The core harmonic rhythmic driver is the synth stabs that play throughout the whole track. They flow with the bass line. 0:00–1:07

- "Cheap Thrills" by Sia. The core harmonic rhythmic driver is the marimba/synth stabs that play throughout. The bass line then flows with them. 0:00–0:11

- "Shake it Off" by Taylor Swift. The core harmonic rhythmic driver is the brass/sax section hook that plays throughout the song in the mid-range. 0:06–0:30

- "Moves like Jagger" by Maroon 5. The core harmonic rhythmic driver is the electric rhythm guitar that plays throughout the whole song. 0:00–0:15

- "Just the Way You Are" by Bruno Mars. The core harmonic rhythmic driver is the piano riff that plays throughout the whole song. 0:00–0:17

- "Tik Tok" by Kesha. The core harmonic rhythmic driver is the synth stabs that play throughout. 0:00–0:15

- "Just Dance" by Lady Gaga feat. Colby O'Donis. The core harmonic rhythmic driver is the synth stabs. 0:08–0:31

- "Hot in Herre" by Nelly. The core harmonic rhythmic driver is the electric keyboard rhythm riff in the mid-range that plays throughout. 0:12–0:30

- "In da Club" by 50 Cent. The core harmonic rhythmic driver is the synth stabs that flow with the bass. 0:00–0:37

- "Smooth" by Santana and Rob Thomas. The core harmonic rhythmic driver is the rhythmic piano riff that plays throughout the whole song. 0:18–1:36

- "Jump Around" by House of Pain. The core harmonic rhythmic driver is the keyboard/piano sound that repeats in the background. The bass flows with that. 0:07–0:25

- "Another One Bites the Dust" by Queen. The core harmonic rhythmic driver is the bass line and guitar line that flows with that bass line an octave higher. 0:00–0:21

- "Moondance" by Van Morrison. The core harmonic rhythmic driver is the piano riff that plays throughout the whole song. 0:00–0:07

- "Sunshine of Your Love" by Cream. The core harmonic rhythmic driver is the bass line and the lead guitar riff that play throughout. 0:00–0:16

- "I Can't Get No Satisfaction" by the Rolling Stones. The core harmonic rhythmic driver is the lead guitar riff and acoustic guitar, which flows with the bass line – 0:00–0:15 – you can hear the lead guitar riff and the acoustic guitar flowing together.

- "I've Got You Under My Skin" by Frank Sinatra. The core harmonic rhythmic driver is the brass section riff – 0:00–1:30 – which is similar to the "Shake it Off" by Taylor Swift example.

- "Concerto No. 4 Op 8. Rv297 Winter 1. Allegro" by Vivaldi. The core harmonic rhythmic driver is the harpsichord stabs. 0:00–0:37

Difference Between the Core Harmonic Rhythmic Driver and Other Instruments that Flow with the Core Rhythm

Here are some differences between a core harmonic rhythmic driver and other core rhythm instruments in an arrangement.

Core harmonic rhythmic driver:
1. Usually, this instrument is a mid-to-low, mid-frequency range instrument.
2. This instrument can usually play music and rhythm (e.g. piano, guitars, synths, etc.).
3. Usually it carries the isolated core rhythm instrument section as its full rhythm.
4. It is usually more in the foreground than other core rhythm instruments.

Example: "Shape of You" by Ed Sheeran. The instrumental plucks that play from 0:00 onwards is the core harmonic rhythmic driver. When the drums and bass aren't playing, these plucks act as the core rhythm. When the drums and bass come in at 1:09 you'll hear they all flow with the instrumental plucks as one unit. That unit then becomes the full core rhythm.

Other instruments that flow with the core rhythm:
1. Can be the core harmonic rhythmic driver itself.

2. Can layer the core harmonic rhythmic driver. Example: "Treasure" by Bruno Mars. There are moments in that track where a piano and synth play the same rhythm as the core harmonic rhythmic driver guitar.

3. Can complement the core harmonic rhythmic driver. Example: "Lose Yourself" by Eminem. Listen to the chorus synth strings from 1:39-2:00. These synth strings complement the guitar core harmonic rhythmic driver. They come in to highlight it, then come off to let it breathe. (See *core rhythm highlighters* and *energy principle* in this Part.)

4. Plays similar core rhythm drums or instruments but in higher octaves. Example: "Walk On By" by Dionne Warwick. Listen from 0:00-0:34. The high percussion instruments play similar rhythms to the core rhythm drums and core harmonic rhythmic driver in the piano.

An example of all four of these taking place at once is in "Smooth" by Santana and Rob Thomas. In the introduction from 0:00–0:18, the piano core harmonic rhythmic driver is layered and complemented an octave higher by the brass section.

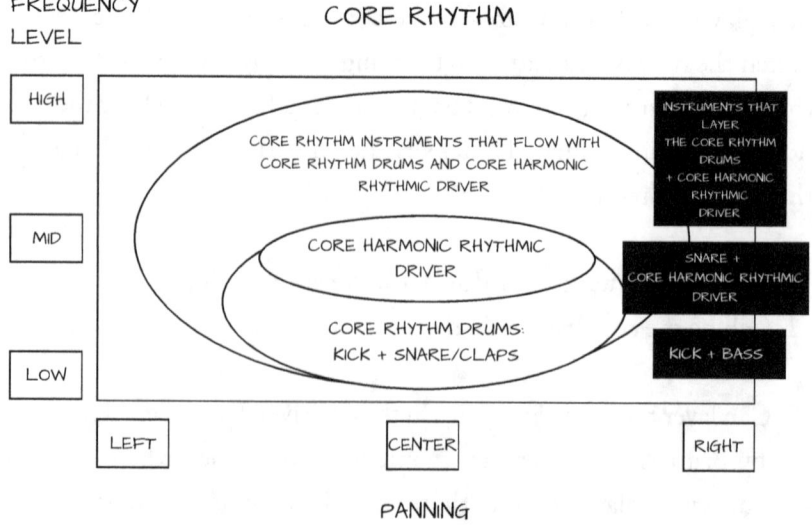

Core Rhythm Changes

The most common core rhythm method is to use the same core rhythm throughout most of the track. Michael Jackson did this in "Wanna Be Startin' Something".

But sometimes, core rhythms can change at different parts of the structure. You may have one core rhythm in the verse, but then the core rhythm changes in the chorus. You can change core rhythms throughout the arrangement, if the song needs it. Changing core rhythms in the arrangement can create interest in the development of a track. But, use this approach wisely, it must make sense for the song.

- Example: "Driver's License" by Olivia Rodrigo. From 1:27-2:19 you can hear the kick on every beat in the track, four-to-the-floor. Then the bridge from 2:25-3:17 moves to a different core rhythm.

- Example: "Fly As Me" by Silk Sonic. You'll notice that the core rhythm is consistent throughout the arrangement. But before the chorus starts at 1:02, they change the core rhythm temporarily. The primary core rhythm falls off, and the entire arrangement plays a rhythm that sounds like an announcement saying: "Something is about to happen." Then, in comes the chorus. It trains the listener to know that the chorus is about to happen when that core rhythm change appears. This repeats every time the chorus is about to happen throughout the whole track.

Here are some more ways you can make core rhythm changes throughout your track:

1. You can change the core harmonic rhythmic driver but keep the drums the same. An example of this is in "About Damn Time"

by Lizzo. You can hear from 0:00–0:28 that the core harmonic rhythmic driver is the electric guitar riff. From 0:29–0:43, however, the piano becomes the core harmonic rhythmic driver. The bass line changes between them to flow with the core harmonic rhythmic driver. But the drum beat remains the same.

2. You can change the core rhythm drums but keep the core harmonic rhythmic driver the same. An example of this is in "Just the Way You Are" by Bruno Mars. The piano core harmonic rhythmic driver remains the same throughout. The drum beat changes from the verse (0:17–0:52) to the chorus (0:52–1:28).

3. Sometimes the core rhythm changes by changing the core harmonic rhythmic driver *and* the drum beat. For example in "Firework" by Katy Perry, the core harmonic rhythmic driver and drum beat are different in the verses (0:00–0:38) compared to the choruses (0:38–1:25).

Another example of the whole core rhythm changing throughout is "The Time of My Life" by Bill Medley and Jennifer Warnes. The verse from 0:33–1:17 has its own core rhythm. The pre-chorus from 1:18–1:34 has its own core rhythm. The chorus from 1:35–1:52 has its own core rhythm.

Part III: Core Principles Of Arranging

Flowing the Core Rhythm with the Song

While producing for music with a song, there are usually three ways this happens:

1. Producing for a song that is already written.
2. Writing a song on a pre-made production (also known as *toplining*).
3. Writing a song and a production arrangement at the same time.

In all of these cases, the core rhythm sometimes works best when flowing *with* the song. When you analyze, you'll notice that some of the best productions in the world flow with the song as one unit. The song's melody has a certain rhythm; which you can complement with the arrangement's core rhythm – and vice versa.

- Example: "Driver's License" by Olivia Rodrigo. In the bridge section from 2:25-3:17, you can hear how the beat flows with the vocal melody.

- Example: "My Sharona" by The Knack. From 0:19 onward, when the lead vocal sings the song's melody, all instruments flow together as one unit. That is the core rhythm in play with the vocal melody.

- Example: "Hey Ya" by Outkast. Listen to how the lead vocal flows with the acoustic guitar rhythm and the drum beat as one unit. 0:00–0:35

- Example: "To Be With You" by Mr. Big. Listen to how the lead vocal flows with the acoustic guitar rhythm and the drum beat as one unit. 0:30–0:52

What is interesting however, is that you can also play with the core rhythm by using more counter rhythms in the lead vocal. The voice is a rhythmic instrument. So you can choose to flow with the core rhythm, or use your voice as a counter rhythm at any given moment.

Example: "I'm Slim Shady" by Eminem. Listen to how Eminem uses counter rhythmic rapping in the verses, this creates healthy tension with the core rhythm of the beat: 0:18–1:21. Then he moves into flowing with the core rhythm beat during the sung chorus: 1:22–1:40. This creates a smoother feeling. This contrast makes the payoff of the chorus more satisfying.

*

Within an arrangement, the song holds the central focus. Everything in the arrangement is designed to accompany the lead vocal singing the song. The lead vocal has its own gravitational center. It has free reign to be flexible in notes and rhythm. The key is in how the lead vocal and core rhythm arrangement work as one unit, creating a feeling of synergy between the two.

Think of the sun and the earth. They each have a gravitational center, but they complement each other. In this case, if the sun is the song, the earth is the arrangement that circles around the song. Each has its own gravitational pull; each complements the other. As humans we groove and gravitate to the earths (the arrangement) core rhythm in our bodies. The sun (song) though, gives the earth (arrangement) life. Everything revolves around the sun (song).

In simple terms: it's because the core rhythm and core harmonic rhythmic driver usually take place from the low-frequency to mid-frequency spectrum. Our bodies as humans gravitate to the core rhythm of the arrangement (earth). But we focus our attention usually on the song (sun). That is because the song usually takes place in the frequencies we've evolved to focus attention on, the human voice.

Key: the best arrangements serve the song.

Part III: Core Principles Of Arranging

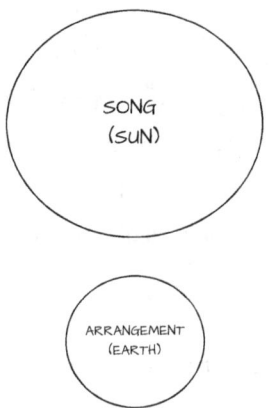

THE ARRANGEMENT SERVES THE SONG

This same principle applies to instrumental music. But the song is replaced by the lead instrumental melody.

Example: "14 Romances, Op: 34: No. 14, Vocalize in C-Sharp Minor (Version for Orchestra)" by Sergei Rachmaninoff. The lead melody of this piece was originally written to be sung by a lead vocal. The instrumental version replaces the lead vocal with violin lines. Listen to 0:00–0:38, where the lower strings provide the core rhythm movement. The lead strings provide the melody.

Point of Difference

How do you make an isolated drumbeat typical to a genre sound interesting? The key is in how you use the core rhythm instruments. Most notably how you use the core harmonic rhythmic driver. You can make the isolated instruments a *point of difference*. Often, this is how specific arrangements stand out.

A good example of this in practice is producer Calvin Harris. Listen to how he uses a similar "four-to-the-floor" house beat in many of his tracks. (Kick on beats 1, 2, 3 and 4 and snare/clap hits on beats 2 and 4.) He then uses points of difference in the core harmonic rhythmic driver instruments. This point of difference makes each track more unique.

Examples: Compare "One Kiss", "We Found Love", and "This is What You Came For" – all produced by Calvin Harris. See how he has used a similar four-to-the-floor beat in each track. But the point of difference in each track is how he has used the core harmonic rhythmic driver. That is what makes each track congruent with the dance genre, but sound unique.

You have two choices with the core harmonic rhythmic driver:

1. The isolated instruments can gravitate strongly toward the drum beat and bass. Example: like the acoustic guitar in "Raindrops Keep Falling on My Head" by B.J. Thomas.

2. You can make a point of difference rhythmically with the instruments. Once you have your isolated drum beat, think about how the harmonic instruments in the middle-frequency range will groove rhythmically in the arrangement. Will they follow the core rhythm drums exactly, or will there be a point of difference?

Example: Another interesting example of the point of difference is in the track "Latch" by Disclosure and Sam Smith. This track's kick and snare pattern gives the illusion it is in 4/4 time, but it is actually subdivided into 6/8 time. So the point of difference you hear in the bass line is actually in 6/8 time. The drums sound like they are in 4/4 time. That is what makes this track sound so unique.

Part III: Core Principles Of Arranging

Core Rhythm Highlighters

Sometimes, instruments within the arrangement accent certain parts of the core rhythm. I call these *core rhythm highlighters*. Core rhythm highlighters accentuate certain parts of the core rhythm. They do this by layering different parts of the core rhythm at strategic times. Sometimes layered in the same frequency range. Other times layered lower or higher in frequency range. This is quite common when the bassline is flowing with the core rhythm. Then the core harmonic rhythmic driver only highlights certain notes of the bassline rhythm. Then does its own thing outside of the bassline. This can also happen with other instruments that flow with the core rhythm drums and bass. As well as other instruments that highlight the core harmonic rhythmic driver.

- Example: "Locked Out of Heaven" by Bruno Mars. Listen to how the background vocals highlight the core harmonic rhythmic driver guitar. 0:06–0:09, 0:13–0:15

- Example: "Hotel California" by The Eagles. The guitar motifs on 2:38, 2:42, 2:45, 2:48, 2:52, 2:55, 2:58 seconds – these all "highlight" the bass line with a similar core rhythm but in a higher range.

In many Motown classics from the 1960s and 1970s, you'll find a guitar chord played simultaneously as the snare/clap hits. It's a guitar that plays rhythmically and harmonically but accents parts of the core rhythm. An example of this is "My Girl" by the Temptations.

In modern arrangements this method is often used in drums. In the Dua Lipa track "Don't Start Now", you will find extra snare and clap hits on chosen beats. These extra sample placements accent the chosen beats they are layered with, creating more energy.

You can also use these to accent certain beats of a bar in other ways. If you analyze Max Martin's projects, he often uses this technique. You will find it in the track "Bang Bang" by Jessie J. The first beat of every eight bars is accented and highlighted with more instruments than any of the other beats in the bars. Listen to 0:27–0:40 to hear this take place.

It's *pressure on* with many instruments playing, but other beats vary in the bar with *pressure off*. The arrangement is breathing; you can do this with the core rhythm. You can accent specific beats and then have the rhythm flow and breathe in and out. We cover this more in the *energy principle*. You are accentuating parts of the core rhythm for more impact with layering. You will learn how to do this layering in more detail in Part IV – Stems Thinking.

Cross-Pollinate Rhythms

Cross-pollinating core rhythms with different genres is a way that new genres can be created. A clear example of this at play is the group Major Lazar. They have been known to cross-pollinate core rhythms from many different genres to create original sounds.

You can be intentional and seek out core rhythms from diverse genres and eras. Each rhythm pattern is a technique. For example, you could grab a kick and snare pattern from a 1960s rock song, and combine it with a hi-hat pattern from a 2020s trap song. You can also cross-pollinate core harmonic rhythmic drivers.

Use your imagination and make exciting core rhythm combinations.

Benefits of Knowing the Core Rhythm Principle:

- You will have patterns in your technique library of any core rhythm imaginable.
- You will be able to produce faster and more effectively.
- You will be able to cross-pollinate core rhythms from any genre for originality.

To Get the Most Out of This section on Core Rhythm:

1. Reread this section until you learn this principle. Listen to all the examples I gave you to get clear on the concepts in practice.

2. Analyze the great music of all time to find what core rhythms they have used. Keep all the concepts I spoke about in mind and bring awareness to them. Once you find core rhythm patterns you like, turn them into techniques.

3. Find core rhythms within multiple different genres to explore diverse core rhythms.

4. While creating, find the right core rhythm that flows with your song. This is key and sometimes the fastest way to find the core rhythm of your arrangement.

5. Look into cross-pollinating core rhythms for originality – mixing genres. Find core rhythms from different genres and time eras and cross-pollinate them into your own sound.

Core Rhythm Principle to Techniques

Find core rhythm patterns in your analysis. Write them out or, remember them in your mind visually, or remember them by feeling. To write them out, you can draw the patterns visually on a diagram. These rhythm patterns are the techniques. Then move them into your technique library for use in your own music. Take note of time signatures and BPMs, too. Write down as many core rhythm drum patterns as there are per arrangement. Some may only need the kick and snare/clap pattern written down. For others you may want to remember the hi-hats and/or percussion patterns. It is up to you how deep you go per track and what technique patterns you wish to remember.

Do the same for core harmonic rhythmic drivers too (and core rhythm instruments that flow with core rhythm drums). Sometimes remembering core harmonic rhythmic drivers through awareness and feeling works best. That is because core harmonic rhythmic drivers are harder to write down as patterns.

Part III: Core Principles Of Arranging

CORE RHYTHM PATTERNS = TECHNIQUES

THE ROLLING STONES - "SATISFACTION": KICK AND SNARE PATTERN = TECHNIQUE

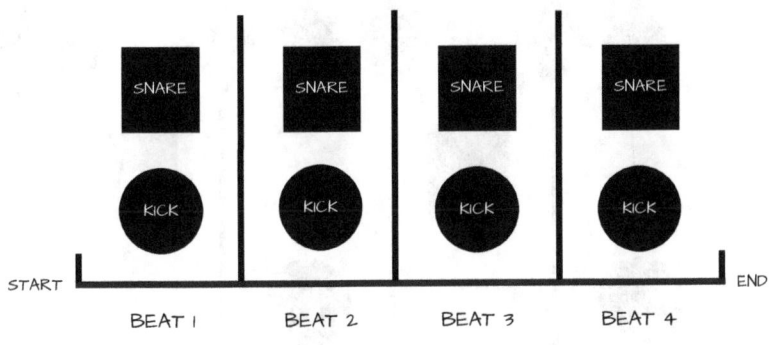

In this example, the kick and snare pattern from "Satisfaction" by the Rolling Stones is a technique.

CORE RHYTHM PATTERNS = TECHNIQUES

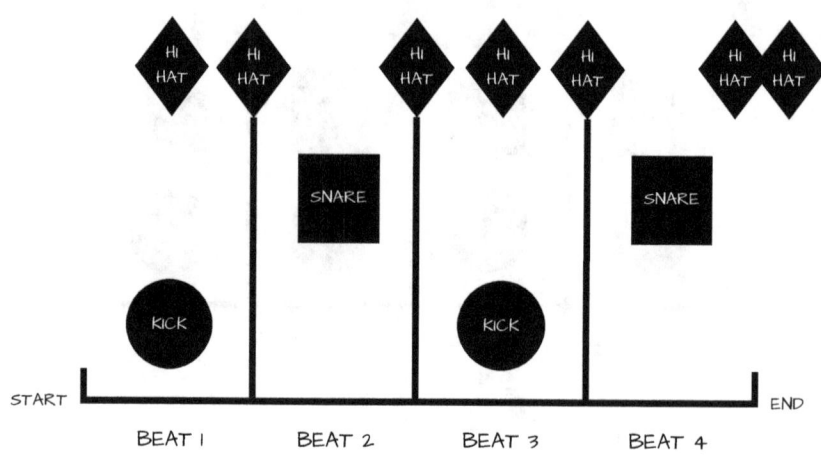

In this example, the kick, snare, and hi-hat drum pattern from "Wannabe" by the Spice Girls is a technique.

If I cross-pollinated these two techniques together it would look like this:

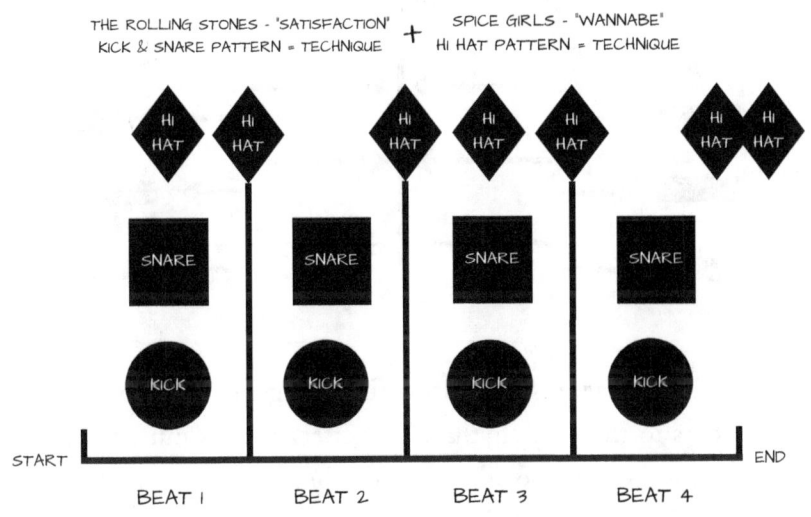

Cross-pollination can become even more unique when using core harmonic rhythmic drivers, core rhythm drums, and genre-style mixtures. We cover this more in Part VI on *cross-pollination*.

NUMBER FOUR: COUNTER RHYTHM PRINCIPLE

COUNTER RHYTHM PRINCIPLE

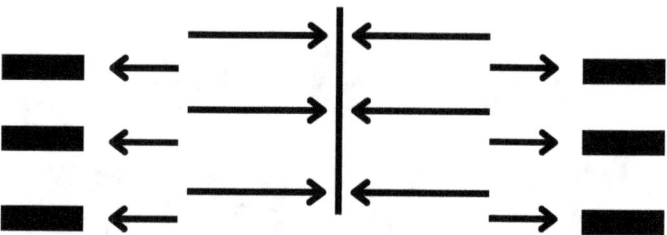

Counter rhythms are instruments in the arrangement that play opposing rhythms to the core rhythm. This effect creates musical interest and energy – the purpose of counter rhythms.

COUNTER RHYTHM PRINCIPLE

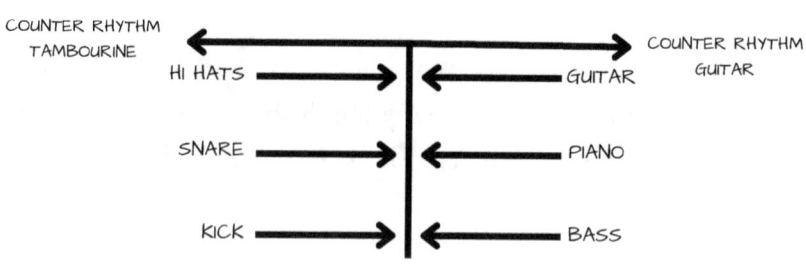

COUNTER RHYTHMS CREATE CONTRAST
TO THE CORE RHYTHM

In this diagram, the core rhythm is the thick black line in the middle. The core rhythm drumbeat is on the left of the line. The core rhythm instruments are on the right of the line. Both of which make up the core rhythm. Any instrument you hear in the arrangement opposing that core rhythm is usually a counter rhythm. In the diagram the example shows that the tambourine and the counter rhythm guitar are counter rhythms.

The more counter rhythms you add, the more conflict you add to the arrangement. The more dense with energy you make it. Figure out the core rhythm, and then the counter rhythms will be easier to create.

Your goal in analysis is to find the core rhythm. Then find what instruments are counter-rhythmic to that core rhythm. From my analysis, counter rhythms are sometimes the opposite of the core rhythm. For example, a slow syncopated core rhythm mixed with a fast straight-note counter rhythm. This polarity can enhance the energy.

Listening to "Eye of the Tiger" by Survivor will give you a clear example of counter rhythm. Listen to the straight counter rhythm guitar from 0:00-0:09. Then listen to how it combines with the syncopated core rhythm guitar line from 00:10 onward.

Counter Rhythm Principle Examples

Here are more examples of counter rhythms from hit songs:

- "Is This Love" by Bob Marley and the Wailers. The core rhythm is the guitar and bass line that flow together. The off-beat synth stab is the counter rhythm. 0:00–0:16

- "Teenage Dream" by Katy Perry. The straight rhythm electric guitar riff that plays throughout the whole track is the counter rhythm. 0:00–0:49. The core rhythm doesn't enter until the chorus at 0:52–1:23 played by the syncopated electric guitar chords. The core rhythm guitar flows with the bass.

- "All That She Wants" by Ace of Base. The core rhythm is in the synth bass: 0:51–1:11. The counter rhythm is in the piano offbeat stabs.

- "Need You Tonight" by INXS. The core rhythm is in the bassline and the electric guitar that flows with that bassline. The electric guitar that's an octave higher is the counter rhythm. 0:17– 0:39.

- "Superstition" by Stevie Wonder. The bassline has more in common with the brass section in this track which tells me that is the core rhythm. The famous clav riff acts more like a counter rhythm in this track. The off-beat hits create the funk in contrast with the straight bass line.

- "Hot in Herre" by Nelly. The off-beat electric guitar hits are a counter rhythm. 0:11–0:28.

Pads as Glue

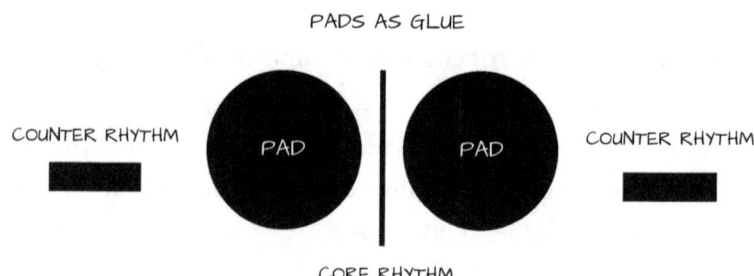

Is a *pad* a core rhythm or a counter rhythm? It depends. Any instrument that can play sustained chords can be a pad. It could be a synth pad, vocal pad, string pad, etc.

Sometimes a pad can be a core rhythm instrument if it flows with the core rhythm. This is when pads play more attack-based parts.

Example: "Bette Davis Eyes" by Kim Carnes. The pads throughout generally flow with the core rhythm.

Part III: Core Principles Of Arranging

But if the pad is in the background, you could view this as a counter rhythm. That is because it runs counter to the core rhythm.

Example: "Stayin' Alive" by the Bee Gees. Listen to the strings pad from 1:12 to 1:21.

However, sometimes, pads are different to the core and counter rhythms. In this case, pads act as a bridge between the core and counter rhythms. They act as a glue. Even with core and counter rhythm parts playing, arrangements can sometimes feel sparse. A pad can be a glue bridge between the two rhythms. Although subtle, this can fill out holes in the arrangement. What I've found in my analysis is that using pads as glue between the core and counter rhythms is its most common use.

Example: "Every Breath You Take" by The Police. Listen to how the core rhythm drives the song from 0:00 to 0:49. When the pad enters from 0:49 to 1:22, it "glues" the rhythms together that you've already heard for the first 0:49 seconds.

While acting as a pad, sometimes pads can play call and response and repurposed parts simultaneously. In "What Goes Around... Comes Around" by Justin Timberlake. From 0:31–0:56 it is mostly core rhythm. From 1:08–2:00, the strings act as a pad. But from 1:34–1:59 the strings play call and response hooks. You could almost view the call and response hooks played as a separate part.

Sometimes pads can move between multiple forms simply by the function of the instrument. Like the brass section in "Superstition" by Stevie Wonder. The brass moves between acting as pad swells from 1:09–1:15, to staccato counter rhythms from 1:15–1:17, and then to call and response hooks from 1:18–1:23.

Pads as Glue Examples

Here are some more examples of pads as glue in hit songs:

- "I Will Always Love You" by Whitney Houston. From 0:43–1:05 the string pads act as glue.

- "Baby One More Time" by Britney Spears. From 0:00 0:31 is mostly core rhythm. From 0:32–1:03, you can hear synth pad glue in the background.

- "Shake It Off" by Taylor Swift. From 0:00–0:41 the track is mostly core rhythm. From 0:42–1:06 the synth pads act as glue.

- "The Time of My Life" by Bill Medley and Jennifer Warnes. You can hear the string pads from 0:42–1:17. They also start playing call and response hooks at 1:04.

- "Sweet Caroline" by Neil Diamond. From 0:00–0:44 is mostly core rhythm. From 0:45–1:24 the string pads act as glue.

Benefits of Knowing the Counter Rhythm Principle

- From analysis, you will have a list of counter rhythms you can use for any track.
- You will understand the fundamental feeling of counter rhythms.
- You will intuitively know how to create counter rhythms that complement your core rhythm.
- You will understand how to use pads.
- You will know how to build energy with counter rhythms. You will do this using layering and micro-level structures.

Counter Rhythm Principle to Techniques

Find counter rhythm patterns in your analysis. Write them out or remember them. To write them out you can draw the patterns visually on a diagram. These rhythm patterns are the techniques. Then move them into your technique library for use in your own music. Sometimes, simply bringing awareness to counter rhythms in analysis can be enough to remember them.

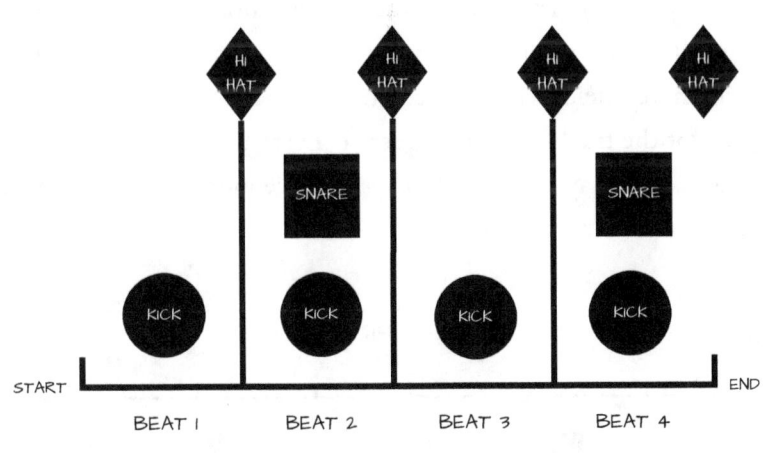

NUMBER FIVE: SPATIAL PRINCIPLE

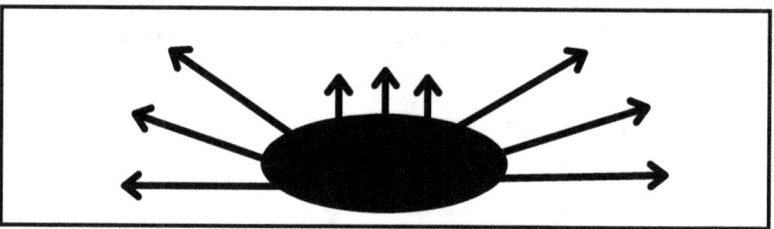

The spatial principle is the instruments you choose and what they play. As well as where you position the instruments and music played within the stereo field. An arrangement must have a mixture of music and space for the track to sound effective. Every track is different. For some tracks, you may need to fill out the space more; for others, you may be able to use minimalism.

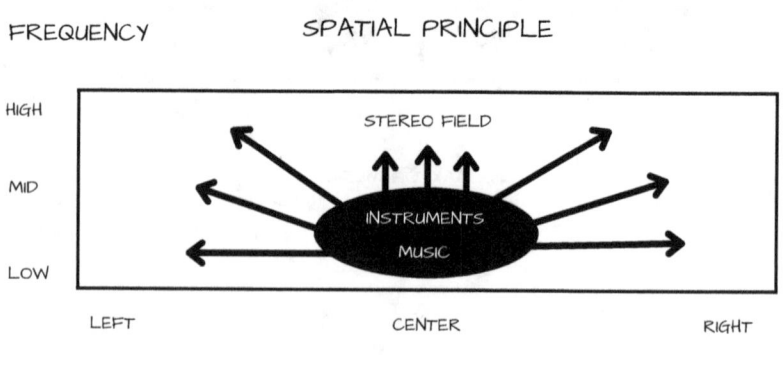

The diagram above is a visual representation of the spatial principle. You will be familiar with this rectangle from Part II: Techniques. On the left, you have high, mid, and low frequencies. On the bottom you'll see the left, center, and right panning. You also have depth, which we'll discuss soon in the *foreground and background principle*.

Inside the rectangle, you place the instruments. The instruments play music made up of musical notes and/or rhythmic patterns. These instruments can be anything: drums, harmonic and melodic instruments, samples, voices, etc. Anything that can be recorded as a sound can be placed in the stereo field as part of an arrangement. The key to a successful arrangement is in *how* you arrange these instruments and music together.

The spatial principle is visual-based. You can visualize and draw diagrams of what you hear in your mind. The brain loves these visual patterns to learn faster.

Recall the diagram we used earlier with the arrangement of "Heroes" by David Bowie:

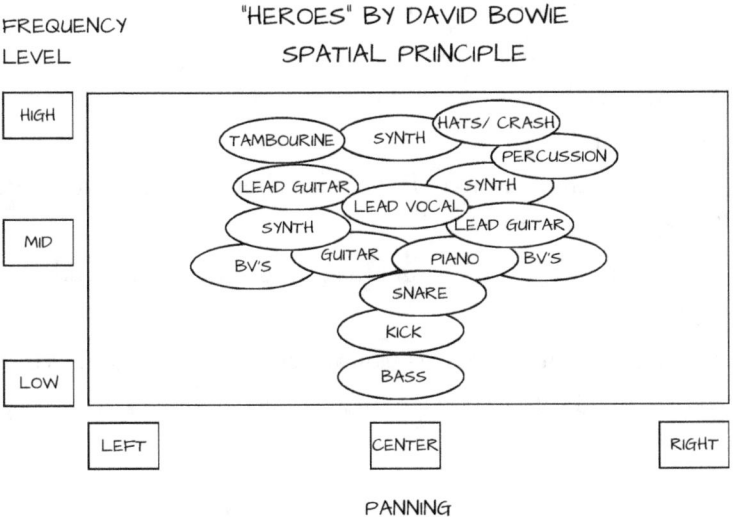

Whenever you analyze a track, you can picture these visual arrangements in your mind. You can even write them down so your mind has visual representations of the great music of all time.

For the spatial principle ask yourself the following while analyzing music:

- Where are the instruments within the stereo field? Visualize the rectangle in your mind of where they are placed.
- What was their sound selection choice? Usually, top producers make key parts of their tracks sound unique to the track.
- When do the instruments come in?
- What musical parts are the instruments playing? (More on this in the *foreground and background principle*).
- Keep in mind that mixing decisions change over time. If you listen to a 1960s track, the panning choices differ from a modern track.

Benefits of Knowing the Spatial Principle

- You will have a visual representation of arrangements from the great music of all time in your head.
- You will have a visual representation of the audio you are arranging in your mind.
- Knowing combinations of instrument choices can help you produce faster.
- You'll know why certain combinations of instruments and patterns work.
- You'll know top producers' sound selection choices, moving you to that standard.

Example of the Spatial Principle in Visual Form: "Tiny Dancer" by Elton John

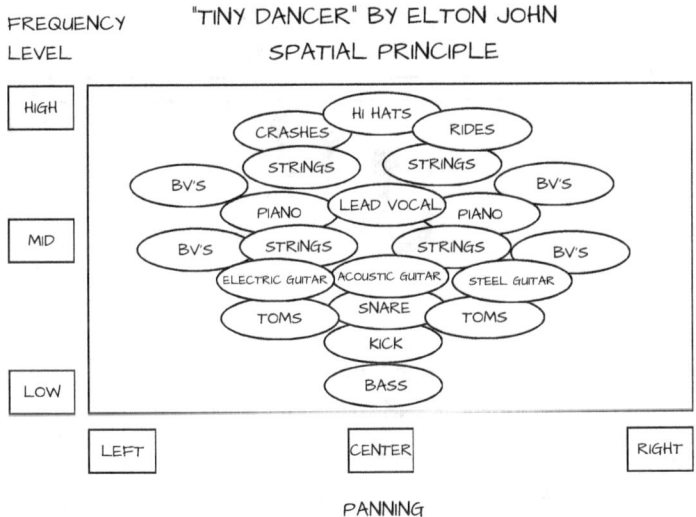

Listen to "Tiny Dancer" by Elton John. While you listen, look at this diagram and see if you can visualize the instruments in your mind. See if the instruments are in the same positions in the rectangle as in your mind. As you analyze other music and create your own diagrams, you will find different patterns of how the producer has arranged. Use these patterns as techniques in your mind.

Spatial Principle to Techniques

Analyze music productions and visualize the above rectangle in your mind of the arrangement. Write out the arrangement like the example above of "Tiny Dancer". Or, remember the arrangements visually in your mind. These visual diagrams of arrangement placements are the techniques. Then move them into your technique library for use in your own music.

NUMBER SIX:
FOREGROUND AND BACKGROUND PRINCIPLE

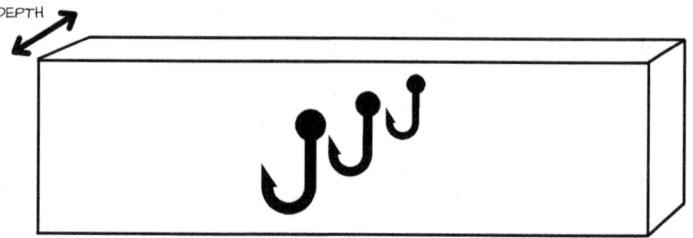

If the Spatial Principle is where you place the instruments in the rectangle, think of the Foreground and Background Principle as a 3D rectangle prism or "stage". Some instruments you put on the stage will be more in front of the others. The instruments in the foreground you can hear more. The instruments in the background, you can hear less. You can achieve this by the musical parts played (macro level). Or you can do this with depth using sonics (micro level).

The musical parts the instruments play are hooks, patterns, notes, or motifs. For this book, we will call all musical parts played *Hooks*.

Macro Level Foreground and Background

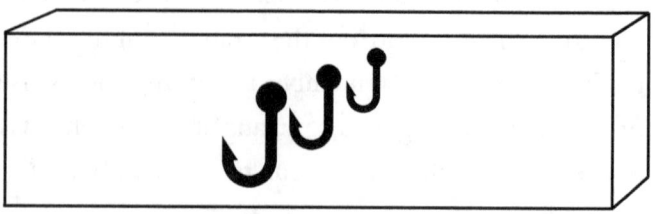

The human mind can only focus on one thing at a time. So every great arrangement has a primary focal point at any given time. One instrument hook will always be the most foreground focus at a time. The most foreground focus is the *primary hook*. The background instruments will support the primary hook with *secondary* and *hidden hooks*. Everything is a hook in your arrangement. At the heart of it all, music consists of individual hooks organized together in a pleasing way.

You will notice three hooks in all arrangements: primary, secondary, and hidden hooks. These hooks consist of rhythm patterns and melodies. The three hook levels are the macro level of the foreground and background principle.

Example: "Treasure" by Bruno Mars

- **Primary Hook:** Lead Vocal

- **Secondary Hooks:** Bass guitar, adlibs and vocal responses, claps, guitar core harmonic rhythmic driver, guitar fill before chorus, kick, snare, synth fills.

- **Hidden Hooks:** Bells, BV harmonies, crashes, hats, synth horns, piano, stick, synth FX, vocal FX.

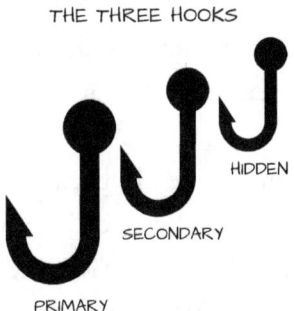

Primary Hooks

There will be a primary hook at any given time during the arrangement. This primary hook is what the listener focuses on. It is the focal point for their attention. This hook could be, for example, a lead vocal or lead synth, etc. It is often the most audible part to the listener at any given time. It can often be the catchiest part of the track. The primary hook is usually what you remember most from the track. Very rarely is there nothing playing in the stereo field. During an arrangement, there is always some focal point the listener gravitates to. There can only be one primary hook at any given time. That is because the listener can only grasp one primary hook in the arrangement at any given time.

Secondary Hooks

The secondary hooks support the primary hooks. They are usually noticed by the average listener but they are more in the background. An example would be a core harmonic rhythmic driver instrument in an arrangement; like the guitar riff in "Girls Like You" by Maroon 5. That is a secondary hook because it's catchy but not so catchy that it's overpowering the vocal.

Now, there can be multiple secondary hooks. But there will most likely be a hierarchy of which secondary hooks are most in the foreground. I'll use the "Girls Like You" example to explain. The kick drum is a secondary hook. It's not as in the foreground as, say, the core harmonic rhythmic driver guitar. But, it's still a secondary hook. You can hear it clearly.

Secondary hooks can also be fills between the primary hook material. Suppose I use the "Girls Like You" example again. In that case, you hear the guitar core harmonic rhythmic driver as a secondary hook. Sometimes it plays in between vocal phrases and the melodic part of that guitar acts as a temporary primary hook. Then, when the vocal comes back in, the guitar returns to its secondary hook role.

Secondary hooks are usually catchy but don't overpower the primary hook. They only temporarily take on the role of a primary hook as fills.

Hidden Hooks

Hidden hooks are the instruments in an arrangement that aren't obvious to the average listener. You only notice them if you focus. For example, this could be white noise, pads, or background vocal glitches.

They can also be instruments that add more to the vibe and feeling and less to being the focal point. So that's what hidden hooks are about: the track's vibe.

You could get away with only having the primary and secondary hooks in an arrangement. But it could sound sparse. Hidden hooks are the hooks that can add that professional polish.

Sometimes I'll call these parts *advanced arrangement subtleties*. I do this because they're subtle and the average listener can't hear them. But they can make an arrangement sound professional. Hidden hooks are often parts the audience can feel, but don't know are happening. For example, like vocal harmonies. Or like pads layered underneath the arrangement that add to the vibe.

In analysis, you'll find these hidden hooks. You'll start to see that they're a key part of making your tracks sound professional. This is especially true today. Even back in the 1940s, in the orchestral arrangements, you would hear these hidden hooks in play.

Secondary and hidden hooks can also be repurposed primary or secondary hooks. We'll cover repurposing later when we cover the *repurposing principle*.

When you create your music, the power comes when you know

whether an instrument part should be a primary, secondary, or hidden hook. Once you've categorized it, arranging becomes much easier. That is because you'll know what purpose each part plays in the arrangement. What do you want the listener to focus on? Are you putting in too many hooks for your listener to handle at once?

Micro Level Foreground and Background

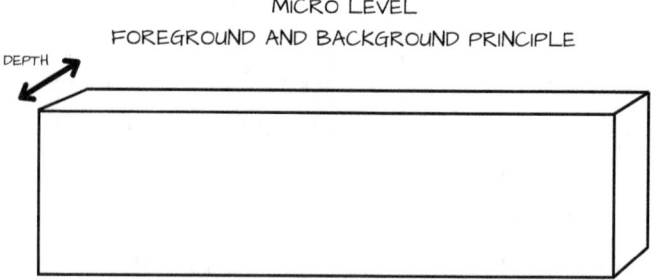

The micro level foreground and background is how the individual hook is then processed to be perceived front or back. How deep is the instrument in the rectangular prism? You can change this with *sonics processing*. Which we cover in more depth in Part V of this book.

Examples: If there's more reverb on a track, it'll be toward the background. If the volume is down, it'll be toward the background. If you cut off the high-end frequencies of the instrument, it will feel further back. If the volume is louder, then it will be more foreground. It'll be more foreground if you've got a very dry sound.

As you train your ear, you can identify the hidden background hooks within your analysis.

Example: "Kiss" by Prince. Listen to how dry all the sounds are. By using strategic sound selection and volume, he made the instruments sound close and further back. The dry sound makes everything sound up front and close. It also helps it become funkier because there is no "washiness". Compare that with "Don't Dream It's Over" by Crowded House. This track sounds like all the instruments have some reverb and/ or delay on them. This makes the whole track feel "further away" than the Prince track. It all depends on the "vibe" you are looking to achieve.

Benefits of Knowing the Foreground and Background Principle

- You'll be able to create your primary, secondary, and hidden hooks and know where they are placed. As well as calculate how many you'll need for an effective arrangement.
- You'll know whether a hook is a primary, secondary, or hidden hook.
- You'll be able to know whether you are using too much of any one hook.
- You'll have a clear primary focal point at any time during the arrangement.
- You'll know what sonic depth each hook requires on a micro level.

Foreground and Background Principle to Techniques

Find the three hook levels in your analysis. Write out which hook level each instrument is like I did with the "Treasure" by Bruno Mars example. Primary, secondary, or hidden hooks. You can also just bring awareness to them and remember them that way. Also discover how the arrangement has used sonics processing for depth. These hook levels and sonic processing choices are the techniques. Then move them into your technique library for use in your own music. I will show you how to find sonic techniques in more depth in Part V of this book.

NUMBER SEVEN: ENERGY PRINCIPLE

ENERGY PRINCIPLE

The most effective arrangements feel like they are breathing. There are many instruments playing at the same time (pressure on). Then, there are fewer instruments playing at a time (pressure off). This movement creates a motion of energy, which creates *emotion* in the listener.

The key point is simple: with motion, comes emotion in the listener. Mastering the flow of ups and downs is important, both on a macro level and a micro level.

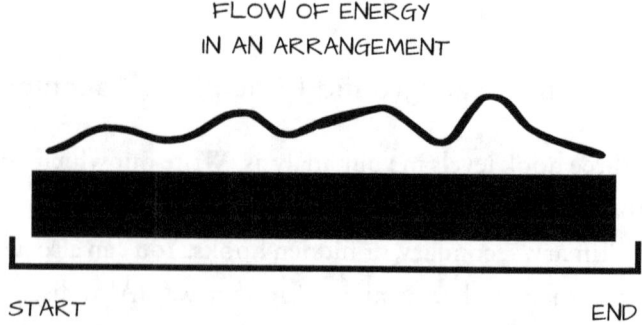

FLOW OF ENERGY IN AN ARRANGEMENT

START — END

If you have a look at the arrangement diagram above, you'll see in the core structure principle, there is energy flow. You can see the flow of energy from the start to the end of the arrangement. That is what the energy principle is. It is all core principles moving in a way where you're creating energy.

You can take your listener through an emotional journey with the energy principle. *How does what I'm creating make me feel? How does what I'm creating make the listener feel?* You must decide what emotions you want to activate in the listener. You must also choose how you develop that energy over the entire core structure. Having the ability to do this, you will know if the track is getting boring, which is very important to avoid.

You can think of your track as a mini-drama. There are ups and downs, and you take your listener through a journey, through a story. An arrangement should be enjoyable from start to finish. Every part of your track is like a mini-song in the song itself. With each section, there's a beginning, middle, and end, and then a transition for every section you have. The audience never gets bored.

The energy principle has a macro level and a micro level.

Macro Level Energy

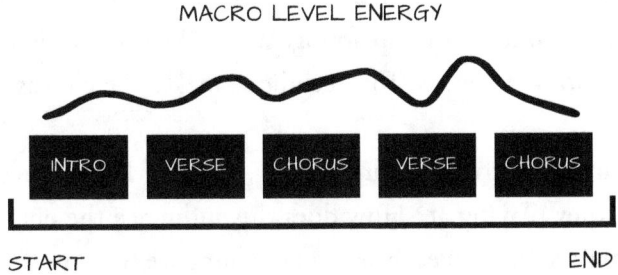

The energy on a macro level can come in three ways:

1. How many instruments are playing at the same time.
2. What frequency levels those instruments are playing on.

3. The use of micro-level structure techniques introduced at strategic moments. Example: how all techniques, core principles and layering develop throughout the arrangement.

How many instruments are playing around the same time:
A certain number of instruments will play within each section of the core structure. For example, in the verse, there may be three instruments. In the pre-chorus, five instruments. In the chorus, seven instruments. More instruments mean more energy. Fewer instruments mean less energy.

Note: Sometimes fewer instruments in an arrangement can create a *vacuum effect*. This vacuum effect can be powerful because it creates focus. So although you have fewer instruments, it can sometimes magnify the effect. It depends on what emotion you're trying to evoke in the listener and why. You can hear this vacuum effect in the track "When I Was Your Man" by Bruno Mars. The vacuum effect also takes place in the track "Royals" by Lorde.

What frequency levels the instruments are playing on:
Using the frequency range, you can introduce low, mid and high instruments to create more energy. For example, the sub-bass holds a lot of energy. In modern pop arrangements, the sub-bass is sometimes withheld until the chorus. This technique makes the chorus feel more impactful.

How many instruments are playing, and at what frequency spectrum are they playing at? How does this influence the energy as the listener moves through each section of your core structure?

Example: "Don't Stop Believing" by Journey. Listen to how each part of the core structure has more instruments. They are introduced as the song goes from start to end. As more instruments get introduced, the sections get more and more energetic. As more instruments are introduced, the frequency spectrum widens.

Micro-level core structure techniques introduced as form progresses:

As first seen in the core structure principle, the micro level is all about sub-forms. Sub-forms are techniques used at particular parts of the core structure to develop energy. For example, you can withhold the sub bass from the verse sections and only use it on the choruses. You could withhold a counter rhythm tambourine until the final chorus. You could use more reverb on the vocal in the choruses and keep the verses more dry.

As the core structure progresses in form, you can stack techniques and layers over time in strategic places. This technique stacking builds energy. Techniques are built on core principles. Therefore, each core principle plays a part in energy development over the core structure.

An example of a track with core structure sub-form techniques is "The Time of My Life" by Bill Medley and Jennifer Warnes. 0:00–2:00

This track develops energy by:

- Shifting core rhythms throughout the core structure.
- Widening the frequency range as the core structure unfolds.
- Adding in more instruments as the core structure unfolds.
- Adding in counter rhythms as the core structure unfolds.

Macro Level Energy Examples

Here are some more examples of macro-level energy in hit songs:

- "You've Lost That Lovin' Feeling" by The Righteous Brothers. Listen to the energy progression from 1:50–3:20. The core harmonic rhythmic driver remains the same, but the core rhythm drums and counter rhythm drums build over time. The frequency spectrum widens as the track progresses. Listen to how high the strings get at 2:41.

- "I Will Always Love You" by Whitney Houston. Starting as a single a cappella vocal, the arrangement adds more and more instruments over time. This both widens the frequency spectrum and adds more energy. Coming to a climax, when the key of the harmony changes at 3:07.

- "Teenage Dream" by Katy Perry. This track develops energy by holding back the core harmonic rhythmic driver until the chorus. The drums hit harder in the chorus with layering techniques. Adding higher and lower frequency instruments creates contrast between verses and choruses. More counter rhythms are added by the final chorus.

- "In da Club" by 50 Cent. Uses the addition of higher octave instruments and counter rhythm instruments to develop energy. From 1:19–1:40, high octave strings double the core rhythm. There is also the addition of a straight note counter rhythm guitar.

Micro Level Energy

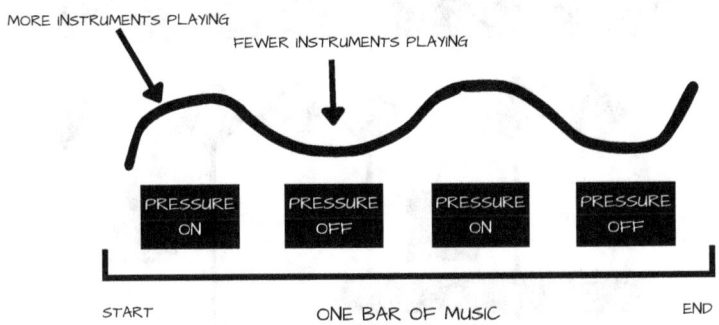

Instrument clusters will play all at once (a pressure-on moment). Then some instruments will fall off (pressure off moment). The cycle continues over and over again throughout the whole arrangement. Some instruments coming in, some coming out. It feels like the arrangement breathes on a bar-to-bar basis. Pressure on = more energy at any given time. Pressure off = less energy at any given time. This is micro-level energy.

In the core rhythm, there will often be core rhythm highlighters. Core rhythm highlighters are instruments only playing on certain parts of the core rhythm. These highlighters can create that breathing effect. The layering decisions are making that breathing effect. Some instruments play at the same time. Some fall off. Others keep going. Pressure on can be emphasized by the use of widening the frequency spectrum too.

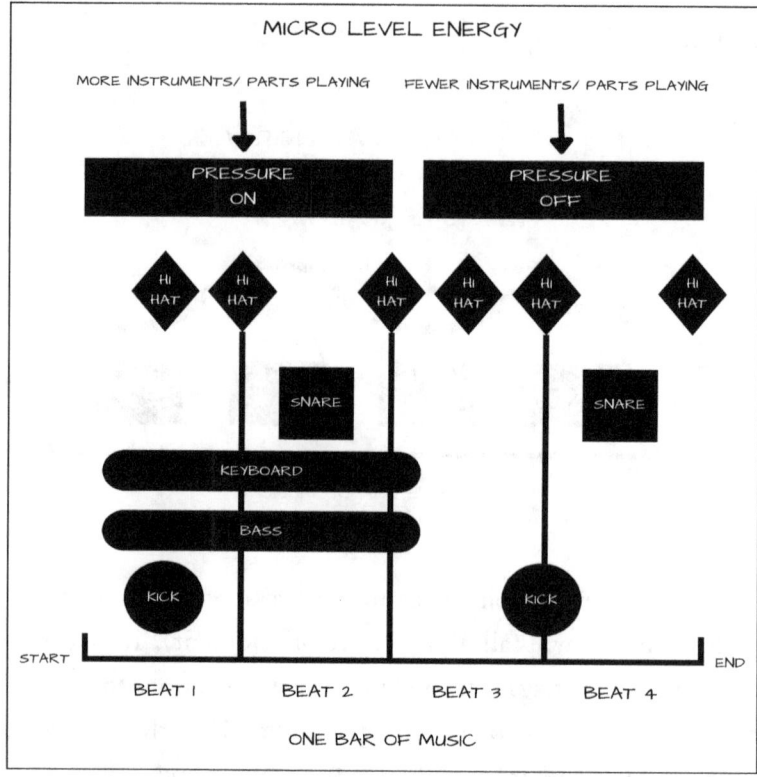

This breathing effect will be in some of the best arrangements you listen to. It can happen to the micro detail. We cover this layering process more in Part IV: Stems Thinking.

To create the breathing effect further, the instruments create call and response with each other within each bar of music. We will cover call and response deeper in the next principle.

Example: "Lady Marmalade" by Patti LaBelle and LaBelle. Listen to how the arrangement breathes in and out in energy with each bar. The breathing effect cycles as more instruments play, then fewer instruments play. Although it happens throughout the whole track, listen from 1:28-1:36 – this is a clear example of this breathing effect taking place. Listen to how the instruments aren't playing all the time, they use space effectively.

Micro Level Energy Examples

Here are some more examples of micro-level energy in hit songs:

- "One Dance" by Drake, Wizkid, and Kyla. Listen to the piano from 0:07–1:34. Every time it plays it creates a pressure-on moment. When it isn't playing, it is a pressure-off moment.

- "Baby One More Time" by Britney Spears. Listen to the entrance hits at 0:10, 0:20, 0:30. These create pressure on moments. Then the beat by itself is pressure off.

- "Easy" by The Commodores. Listen to how the pressure on moments take place when the kick and snare hit. Pressure-off moments happen in between those.

- "Crazy in Love" by Beyonce and Jay-Z. From 0:30–0:49, you can hear the pressure on moments with the brass hits. The pressure off moments are the moments between the kick drums.

Contrast

The energy principle comes down to one fundamental concept: *contrast*. With contrast on a macro and micro level comes interest. With contrast over the course of the core structure, comes interest.

Energy Principle Summary

The energy on a macro level (full core structure) can come in three ways:

1. How many instruments play during the arrangement at any given time.
2. What frequency levels those instruments are playing on.
3. The use of micro-level core structure techniques at strategic moments. How the techniques, core principles and layering develop over the macro structure.

This process happens over the course of the macro level core structure.

The energy on a micro level (bar-to-bar basis) can come in three ways:

1. The more instrument clusters playing at a time, the more pressure is felt.
2. The fewer instrument clusters playing at a time, the less pressure is felt.
3. The instruments hooks will play call and response with each other. (We will cover this in the next principle on *call and response*).

This process happens on a bar-to-bar and beat-to-beat basis. This process usually happens through strategic layering (*Stems Thinking*). It also happens through core rhythm highlighters (see *core rhythm*).

Note: All core principles of arranging impact the energy of your arrangement. All techniques impact the energy of your arrangement. How you use the core principles and techniques becomes the energy.

Benefits of Knowing the Energy Principle

- You'll know how to develop energy within your arrangements by how many instruments are used.
- You will know how to use frequency levels to build energy.
- You'll know energy techniques used by the great music of all time.
- You'll know how to use energy to activate emotions in the listener.
- You'll know how to use micro-level core structure techniques to develop the energy of each instrument and the whole arrangement.
- Your arrangement will breathe in and out on a micro level and sound world-class.
- You'll know how to use each core principle of arranging and sonics to build energy in your arrangement. As well as layering.

Energy Principle to Techniques

Find macro- and micro-level energy in your analysis.

For macro-level energy, write down how many instruments take place in each section of the core structure. For example, three instruments in verse one, five instruments in chorus one, etc. Write down what frequency levels these instruments are on. Write down any core structure micro-level techniques used to create energy development. Also bring awareness to how each core principle has been used to build energy throughout the arrangements. Place these in your technique library. It can also be enough to bring awareness to the macro-level energy.

For micro-level energy, it will be enough to keep bringing awareness to it in your analysis. Soon you will find that you'll naturally create this breathing effect in your music.

NUMBER EIGHT: CALL AND RESPONSE PRINCIPLE

CALL AND RESPONSE PRINCIPLE

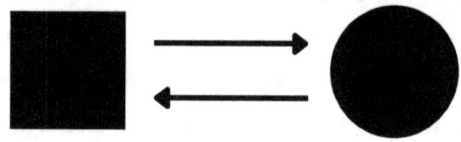

The most effective arrangements usually have hooks that the instruments play that relate to each other – like cause and effect. The sounds are interacting with each other in call and response. One instrument plays a hook – which is the call. Then, the next instrument plays a hook – the response to that call. Having them relate is key. To do this, the response to the call is sometimes a variation on the call.

The simple way to understand this principle is that everything begins and ends in a cycle. For every call that begins and ends, there is a response that begins and ends. There is a domino effect from the start of the track to the end – a continuous line of call and response hooks working together as a team.

For example, a kick will play, and then the response will be a snare. The bass will play phrase one, and then the bass will play phrase two on a different root note. Even the notes it plays rhythmically will have a call and response.

Everything is call and response. When you think of it this way, everything starts to connect. This principle is one of the foundations of having *synergy* in your arrangement. Each instrument plays an independent hook. But they work together as a team to create synergy.

This principle works with hook levels – primary hooks, secondary hooks, and hidden hooks. Your primary hook will connect to your secondary hooks and hidden hooks. Your secondary hooks will connect to your primary hook and hidden hooks. Your hidden hooks will connect to your primary hook and secondary hooks. Everything connects with call and response.

On a micro-energy level, your arrangement will "breathe" (as described in the *energy principle*). You will also know how to take what you already have and repurpose it into responses to calls (as described later in the *repurposing principle*).

You must know: *What is the purpose of this instrument? What is the purpose of the musical part that it is playing right now? How does it connect with the other instruments?*

You will begin to think of how each instrument connects to the others in the arrangement. The instruments are dancing or breathing with each other in and out.

In your music production analysis, notice the following:

- One instrument hook will call.
- Another instrument with the same, different or variation of musical material (hook) will respond.
- The instruments sound like they're dancing or breathing with each other.

Listen to "Billie Jean" by Michael Jackson. Listen to the instrument fills between vocal passages. Also, listen to the lead primary hook in the vocal – "Oh oh, Oh oh" – The first two "Oh oh" play one motif, the call. The second "Oh oh" is the same rhythm moving down, not up.

Everything has a call and response, and it is a domino effect from the start to the end of the arrangement.

Call and Response Principle Examples

Example of this principle: "Dancing Queen" by ABBA. Listen to how every instrument is in a constant dance of call and response. The vocals make calls; then the rest of the instruments respond. Responses from piano fills, to the string fills, to the bass line fills, to the guitar fills, to the synth fills.

Here are some more examples of the call and response principle in hit songs:

- "Uptown Funk" by Mark Ronson and Bruno Mars. Listen to the call and response between every instrument from 0:33–0:50.

- "Fire" by Ohio Players. Listen to the call and response between every instrument from 0:24–1:29.

- "Fly Me to the Moon" by Frank Sinatra. From 0:07–0:38, listen to how the flute plays responses to the lead vocal calls.

- "Dreams" by Fleetwood Mac. From 0:16–1:11, the call and response between the lead vocal and the electric guitar hooks that play between phrases.

- "Sweet Caroline" by Neil Diamond. From 1:03–1:25, the call and response between the lead vocal melody and the brass hooks.

- "What Do You Mean?" by Justin Bieber. From 0:30–0:45, the call and response between the lead vocal melody and the flute hooks.

- "Shake It Off" by Taylor Swift. From 1:42–2:18, the call and response between the lead vocal melody and the brass hooks.

- "I Want To Know What Love Is" by Foreigner. From 1:34–2:00, the call and response between the lead vocal melody and the synth hook that plays between phrases.

Benefits of Knowing the Call and Response Principle

- You will be able to create hooks that interact with each other within your arrangement with ease.
- Each instrument will communicate effectively with the other instruments in your arrangement.
- You will set the foundation for the synergy principle to take effect.

Call and Response Principle to Techniques

In your analysis, find how the producer has used call and response. Bringing awareness to this principle will be enough. You will start to use this principle as you understand it from analysis.

NUMBER NINE: REPURPOSING PRINCIPLE

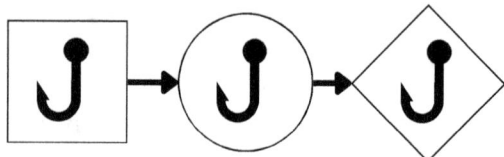

Usually, the most effective arrangements have some sort of repurposing. Simple hooks play throughout, and the instruments play variations on those hooks. The simplest way to understand this principle is to *use what you already have*. You invent the parts during your main creative phase. These parts are: primary hooks, secondary hooks, and hidden hooks. Then, you can build the rest of the arrangement by repurposing what you already have. Only create entirely new parts when needed.

A king of repurposing is Beethoven. The example I like is "Symphony Number Five: Movement One". Listen to that symphony's first iconic eight notes: *Dun, Dun, Dun, Dun... Dun, Dun, Dun, Dun.* If you continue to listen to the rest of the piece, you'll notice that Beethoven grabbed those eight notes and repurposed them to create the entire arrangement. He's repurposed the rhythms and the melody to create the whole movement. You can hear this in play, and it's phenomenal.

In modern-day music, the same thing is happening. When analyzing, you'll notice this principle is everywhere. Now, you'll be able to consciously use this principle, making arranging much more effortless. It also makes your arrangements sound much more professional to the listener. They may not know it's happening, but it sounds genius.

Here is the process:

- The instruments are playing the three primary hooks in the form of notes and patterns.

- The initial hooks then become call and response and repurposed parts to fill out the arrangement.

That's what you're doing for most of the arrangement.

This principle makes the creation of the hooks that your instruments play easier to do. You can use what you've already created, creating variations in melody, harmony, rhythms, and instruments. In the first creation phase, you usually create your main hooks. The whole arrangement is primary, secondary, and hidden hooks. Create your hooks first. Instead of creating new hooks, you can then do what Beethoven did; you can repurpose what you already have. You could vary the primary hook and make it a hidden hook in your arrangement. You could do the same thing with secondary and hidden hooks.

Repurposing is a way to develop the whole track from start to finish. This principle also makes the whole arrangement have more synergy.

The Primary Ways of Repurposing Are:

1. Melodic/harmonic.
2. Rhythmic patterns.
3. You can also repurpose all prior principle techniques/patterns you have already created including:
- Core structures. (Forms and sub-forms)
- Core harmonic structures. (Chord progressions)
- Core rhythm patterns.

- Counter rhythm patterns.
- Spatial instruments. (Instrument choices)
- Foreground and background hook parts played. (Three hook levels + sonics processing)
- Energy techniques.
- Call and response techniques.

For example, you could have a percussion instrument play a part that is the same as the melody rhythm sung by the vocal. It wouldn't have the same melody, but the same rhythm. The untrained audience would feel it's familiar but not know why. You can also repurpose these in variations; they don't have to be the same part. By variations, I mean it could be something similar but different.

While analyzing tracks, look for how the producer has repurposed what they've already created. Usually, if you find the hooks of their track, you will find the repurposing principle used from start to finish.

An obvious example is the Beatles track "She Loves You". From 0:00–0:10 listen to the melodic line in the primary hook of the lead vocal. While the Beatles sing the verse melody, listen to the guitar fill played between vocal phrases, 0:29–0:31. The top melody of the guitar chords is playing the primary hook of the chorus repurposed as a secondary hook fill. It's the same top melody and the same rhythm, repurposed. Genius.

You can do this repurposing when you know the principle deeply. You can place genius-sounding repurposed hooks within your arrangements. Whether they know it or not, the great producers of all time use the repurposing principle.

Repurposing Principle Examples

Here are some more examples of the repurposing principle in hit songs:

- "Sunshine of your Love" by Cream. Listen to how the guitar riff, bass line and lead vocal all use a similar hook melody. From 0:00–0:41.

- "Just Dance" by Lady Gaga. Listen to how Akon doubles the core harmonic rhythmic driver synth at 0:18–0:19 and 0:30–0:31 with his vocal. From 0:48–1:04, the synth hook is playing a similar melody to the lead vocal.

- "Waterfalls" by TLC. Listen to how the bass line is playing a similar rhythm to the lead vocal in the chorus from 1:18–1:38.

- "Kiss from a Rose" by Seal. The lead vocal hook from 0:00–0:22 is played also by other instruments too.

- "The Tide Is High" by Blondie. The bassline flows with the same rhythm as the lead vocal: 0:30–1:27.

- "Another One Bites the Dust" by Queen. The bass line, guitar line, and lead vocal all repurpose the same melody and rhythm. 0:00–0:56

- "Say a Little Prayer for You" by Aretha Franklin. From 0:00–0:12, the piano in the introduction plays a variation on the lead vocal melody of the song.

- "Sittin' on the Dock of the Bay" by Otis Redding. The bass line rhythm flows with the lead vocal throughout the song. The guitar in the chorus from 0:27–0:45, plays a similar rhythm to the lead vocal.

- "I've Got You Under My Skin" by Frank Sinatra. From 2:16 to 2:45, the instrumental bridge repurposes the lead vocal melody.

Benefits of Knowing the Repurposing Principle

- You'll only have to create your initial primary, secondary, and hidden hooks once. You can then use what you already have, to repurpose in creative ways.
- You can also repurpose all prior principle techniques/patterns you've already created.
- Your arrangement will become a mixture of your three hook levels, call and response, and repurposing. This makes arranging faster and more effective.

Repurposing Principle to Techniques

Find the three hook levels of each instrument first – primary, secondary and hidden hooks. Then, in your analysis, find how the producer has repurposed those hooks.

The three ways of repurposing to look for are melodic/harmonic patterns, rhythm patterns, and/or repurposing of the core principle patterns. Write them out or remember them by feel. To write them out, list the interaction between the instruments. For example, the shaker plays the same rhythm as the kick drum. These repurposing interactions are the techniques. Then move them into your technique library for use in your own music.

Bringing awareness to this principle will also be enough. The more you bring awareness to this principle in analysis, the more you will naturally do this in your own music.

NUMBER TEN: SYNERGY PRINCIPLE

The most effective arrangements sound like every instrument has an independent purpose. But each instrument works as a team with the other instruments to create a greater whole. The arrangement creates *synergy*. By doing this, the whole arrangement starts to become a single unit. It starts to sound like it is one element. That is when you know you have an effective arrangement. When you analyze the great arrangements of all time, you'll hear them sound like one sound, one system. This synergy is your north star as a professional arranger.

Example: "Bohemian Rhapsody" by Queen is a masterclass in the synergy principle. Listen to how each instrument in the arrangement consistently flows as one unit.

The easiest way to understand this principle is:

Everything within your arrangement should have a purpose.

Everything should be contributing to a single system. If you find something in your arrangement that doesn't have a purpose, it probably doesn't need to be there. Whenever you create a new part, think,

Is this contributing to the whole arrangement? Does this have a purpose?

The synergy principle links all the core principles together. The synergy principle should naturally take effect when all prior nine principles are used correctly. You will view the big picture more clearly once you understand the synergy principle through analysis.

The synergy principle is also the foundation of systems thinking in music production; what I call in this book *Stems Thinking*. As you move into Stems Thinking, you start to think of every instrument as an individual, a group, and a whole. You will see the relation between each instrument in your track and its purpose.

Knowing this principle will make every decision during the arrangement process more effective. Remember this: *Does this decision I'm making contribute to the arrangement as a whole? Does this have a purpose?* The most successful arrangements of all time have synergy. Everything within them has a purpose; there is no wasted space. Top producers make sure that the entire music production chain has this synergy.

For example, you can make the harmony match the feeling of the melody and lyrics. You can make the sound selection choices match the lyrical themes. You can make your arrangement flow all principles together. You can make your sonics choices match the atmosphere you wish to create. Then as a unit, you create contrast to create energy development throughout the core structure. The song, arrangement, recording, mixing, and mastering all connect as one.

This is your vision.

Part III: Core Principles Of Arranging

Synergy Principle Examples

Here are some obvious examples of the synergy principle in hit songs. Listen out to all the instruments flowing as one unit:

- "Oh, Pretty Woman" by Roy Orbison.
- "Sittin' on the Dock of the Bay" by Otis Redding.
- "December 1963" by The Four Seasons.
- "MMMBop" by Hanson.
- "Locked Out of Heaven" by Bruno Mars.
- "About Damn Time" by Lizzo.
- "Time" by Hans Zimmer.

Benefits of Knowing the Synergy Principle

- You will notice how the great arrangements of all time work together in synergy.
- You will then be able to aim toward this north star in your own music and know when it is happening or not.

Synergy Principle to Techniques

In your analysis, find how the producer has used synergy in their arrangement. Bringing awareness to this principle will be enough. The more you bring awareness to it in analysis, the more you will understand it - the more you will naturally use it in your own music.

KEYS TO THE KINGDOM

THE TEN CORE PRINCIPLES OF ARRANGING

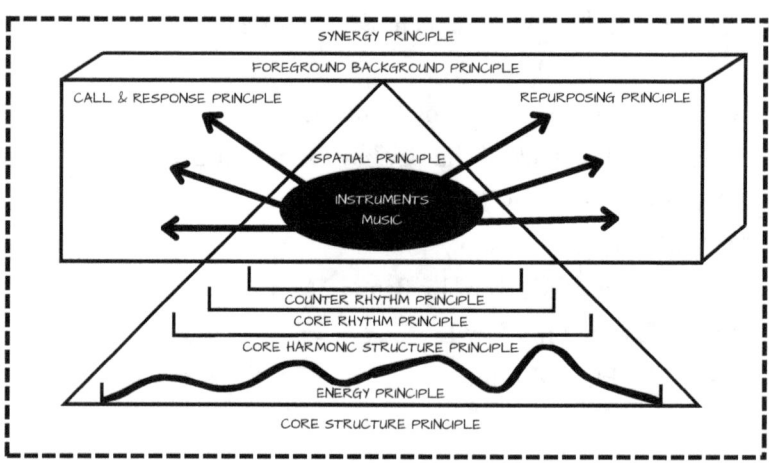

I created this diagram when I woke up that day with the Ten Core Principles of Arranging in my head. Whenever I have a problem with my arrangement, I ask, *Which of these core principles am I NOT using correctly?* Sometimes, my structure is wrong. Sometimes, my harmony is off. Sometimes, my core rhythm isn't the right choice. Sometimes, I try to put in too many primary hooks at any given time. Maybe my energy is off. Whenever you have a problem, you can think about what principle is not working.

In all disciplines, understanding the principles is how you master a skill. It's a commitment to the principles. Basketball players practice dribbling and free throws a thousand times. The piano player practices the scales a thousand times. You practice the principles of arranging until you grasp the keys to the kingdom.

When you analyze now, look for these Ten Core Principles of Arranging in the history of recorded music. Once you notice them, you'll see them everywhere. Then they will become deeply embedded into your subconscious, ready for you to use.

Part III: Core Principles Of Arranging

ACTION STEPS

PART III: CORE PRINCIPLES OF ARRANGING - ACTION STEPS	
ACTION STEP ONE	PRINT OUT THE CORE PRINCIPLES OF ARRANGING DIAGRAM. STICK IT IN YOUR STUDIO WHERE YOU CAN SEE IT. THESE PRINCIPLES ARE EVERYTHING.
ACTION STEP TWO	RESTUDY THIS PART UNTIL YOU HAVE MEMORIZED AND UNDERSTAND THE TEN CORE PRINCIPLES OF ARRANGING. LISTEN TO ALL THE REFERENCES PROVIDED. FULL PLAYLIST OF MUSIC REFERENCES AVAILABLE AT WWW.POLYMATHPRODUCER.COM/RESOURCES
ACTION STEP THREE	WHILE DOING YOUR REGULAR MUSIC PRODUCTION ANALYSIS, BRING ATTENTION TO EACH CORE PRINCIPLE OF ARRANGING USING THE INFORMATION WITHIN THIS BOOK. FIND ONE TECHNIQUE AT A TIME WITHIN THE CORE PRINCIPLES.
ACTION STEP FOUR	USE THE TEN CORE PRINCIPLES OF ARRANGING FRAMEWORK WHILE CREATING YOUR OWN MUSIC

CORE PRINCIPLES OF ARRANGING
CORE STRUCTURE PRINCIPLE
CORE HARMONIC STRUCTURE PRINCIPLE
CORE RHYTHM PRINCIPLE
COUNTER RHYTHM PRINCIPLE
SPATIAL PRINCIPLE
FOREGROUND AND BACKGROUND PRINCIPLE
ENERGY PRINCIPLE
CALL AND RESPONSE PRINCIPLE
REPURPOSING PRINCIPLE
SYNERGY PRINCIPLE

Congratulations, you have now learned the Ten Core Principles of Arranging. You have now learned the grammar of the language. Next up you will be mastering layering with Stems Thinking. This is when you combine the techniques (words) and the principles (grammar) to create full musical works.

PART IV:
Stems Thinking
[Analysis Level Three]

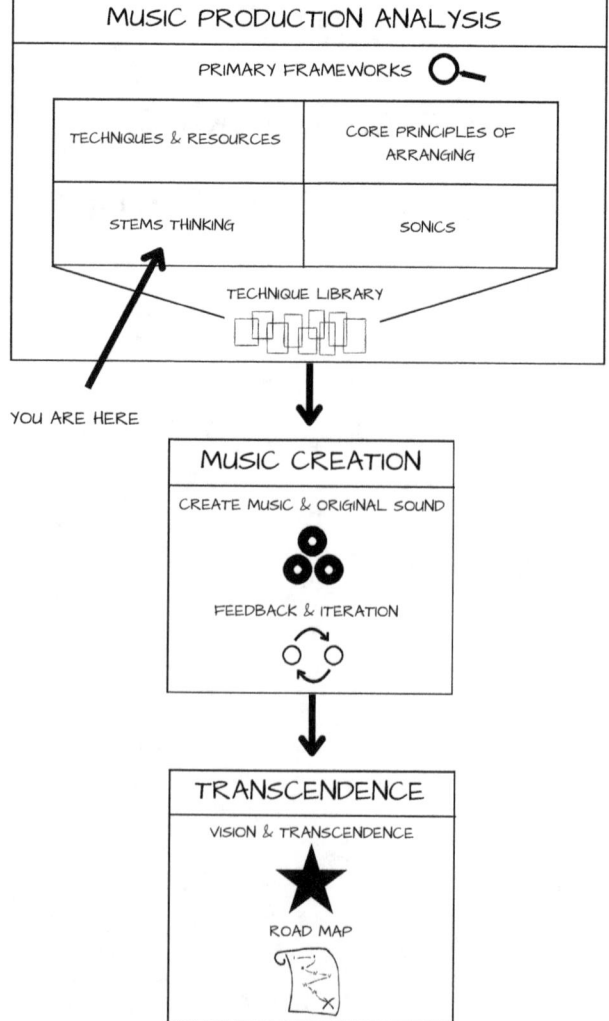

The Quest To Go Deeper

IN MY QUEST to find the "truth", I wanted to hear the greatest music of all time in more detail. Listening to stereo masters on streaming services was getting tiresome. I desired to analyze each instrument in an arrangement on a track-by-track basis. The only way to do that was to find the original stem files of the productions I wanted to analyze.

One day, I stumbled across a website. This website had thousands of stem files from some of the greatest producers ever. There were stem files from the original projects of big hits. Hits from Michael Jackson, Queen, Elton John, Katy Perry, Taylor Swift, Ariana Grande, and so on. I knew that if I applied the Polymath Producer System to these stem files, I'd have access to the minds of producers like Max Martin and Quincy Jones.

I placed the stem files of a track that Quincy Jones produced from the *Thriller* album onto my DAW. My eyes lit up; I saw the inner workings of one of the best-selling tracks ever. I muted all the stems and then organized them into groupings based on their instrument type. I would put the vocals in one group, the instruments in another, the drums in another, and the basses in another. I would unmute the stems one by one, listening to them in isolation and then with the other stems.

I applied the technique and core principles frameworks to the stems. With these "lenses" on, the stem files revealed information fast. Faster than I had ever experienced. I could see what they did with individual instruments to the micro detail. I could see how the individual instruments related to the whole. The core principles revealed themselves in an even clearer light. I noticed that everything in the arrangements had a purpose. I could see how each note related to another note. I could see how each instrument related to another instrument. I discovered how the great music producers of all time layered their tracks. The music started to look like one organic system.

Everything in the universe is a system. The solar system. Our bodies are a system. A business is a system. Everything contains inputs, processes, and outputs within an environment. When I looked at stems, I saw that music is also a system. A master recording consists of individual stems working together as a team to create a system. As music producers, you put this system together from scratch. It's a non-linear process that becomes linear. Stems reveal this system in plain sight. You can see how each instrument relates to another instrument and the purpose of each instrument in the system.

- You can see how one instrument works on its own.
- You can see how instruments work together as a subgroup.
- You can see how the subgroup of instruments work together with other subgroups of instruments.
- You can see how they are all grouped as one into the stereo output.

When analyzing stems, I looked at them through the "lenses" of the first frameworks – techniques and principles. The stems then lit up and revealed all the secrets in plain sight.

When I produced my music after analyzing stem files, I noticed that my layering decisions started to become that of the great producers of all time. I knew the right amount to layer to ensure I didn't underproduce or overproduce. I had seen so many examples of how to layer the right way that the patterns began to form in my mind. I began to think of each track I produced as a stem file. *How can I create the best stem file? How can I make the best stem file group that works well together? How can I create the best stem files that create the best track?*

It made me feel like I was a composer from the 1800s, layering an orchestra; each stave on the page a stem. I *became* the orchestra. But the most significant benefit of all felt almost esoteric. I felt like I connected to the composer's "energy", or "paradigm". Because I knew their secrets, I felt like I had the same "energy" when I went to compose myself. I began to feel like a master. Making masterful decisions while creating felt effortless.

In this section, I will explain how to analyze stem files. You can then get into even more detail with your music production analysis. You will then know how to layer like a world-class music producer.

Stems Thinking: Layering

Classical/Romantic era composers from the 1700s and 1800s were masters of layering. They used composition, arranging and orchestration to achieve this. They didn't have computers. They wrote their music as notation and then got the orchestra to play the different parts.

Not all classical composers did this, but a lot of the time, they'd use a piano to compose. The piano was like a mini-orchestra for their hands. They could compose the different layers they wanted on the piano. This gave them an idea of what the orchestra would be playing. Then, they just had to transfer the notes from the piano to other instruments in the orchestra to get the textures they wanted.

For example, if the composer needed a high instrument, they could use a flute or violin. They would use those instruments to replace the melody line they had composed on their piano. If they needed a low instrument for example, they might use a cello or a trombone depending on the effect they were after. They had all these different textures and colors they could use.

Their job was to think about how they could layer the arrangement. Did they want a solo flute or four flutes playing the same line? Did they want two flutes and two violins playing the same line? Did they want two flutes playing a foreground hook? Then two flutes playing a different secondary hook? The different combinations are endless. They composed on the piano, but they used different instruments to create a textured arrangement.

The same holds true today in modern music production and arranging. You do the same thing inside your computer. You play the keyboard/keypad and choose the instruments and samples inside the DAW. You are looking at the individual parts through the lenses of the core principles. You are then layering those parts using different textures.

You are the orchestra, and layering is your foundation.

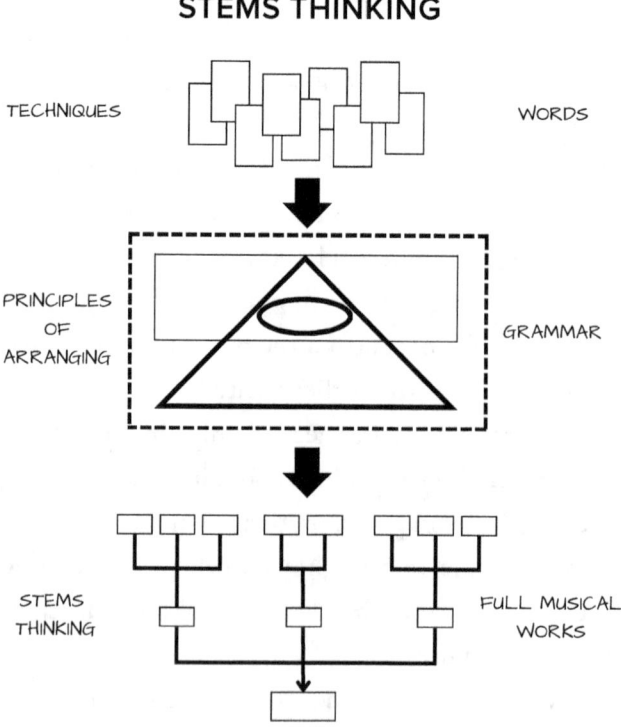

So far, you have learned Level One: Techniques. These are the building blocks of tracks. Then, you learned Level Two: the Ten Core Principles of Arranging. In this section, I will take you through Level Three: Stems Thinking.

Stems Thinking is layering tracks, a skill set that has been around for generations. How does this relate to music production analysis? We are going to learn and master *layering* by analyzing stem files.

Stems Thinking is knowing what the composer has done to create layers. Analyzing stem files helps you understand layering on a master level. We will bridge the gap between the classical era and the modern day. We do this by thinking about our arrangements as if we were the orchestra.

With Stems Thinking, you discover how each instrument works. Then, discover how groups of instruments work together. Then, discover how groups of instruments work with other groups of instruments. Then, discover the whole arrangement as one. Once you learn how the greatest producers use layering, you can do the same. Stems Thinking will take your arrangements to world-class layering.

Stems thinking is layering techniques (words) and principles (grammar) to create complete musical works (which consist of individual tracks and sub-groups, into one final mix/master).

WHAT ARE STEMS?

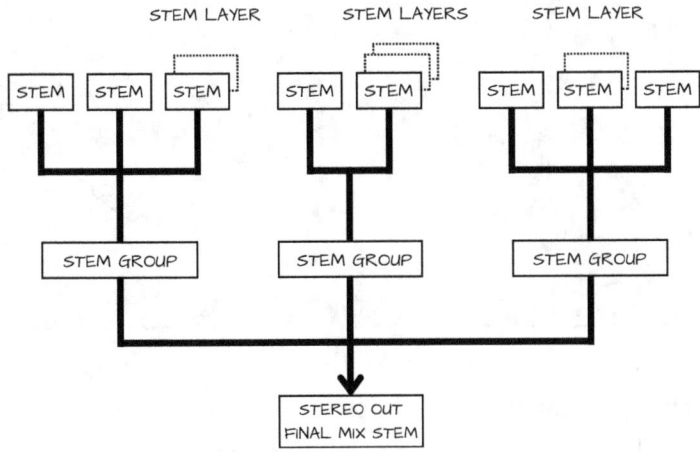

Stems are the final produced and mixed audio form of the instruments in an arrangement. There are many types of stems. Some stems are from production sessions (generally called *Multitracks*). Other stems are from mixing sessions (*Stems*). It depends on where you get the files. **For the purpose of this book we will use the term Stems to include multitracks and stems of any kind.** Stem files are usually in their final form when you collect them from a producer or mixing engineer. So they are ready for analysis. You can find stem files online or from other producers.

Example One: "Orange Tree" by Rachelle Rhienne, co-written and produced by me. Sometimes you'll get stems that look more like this:

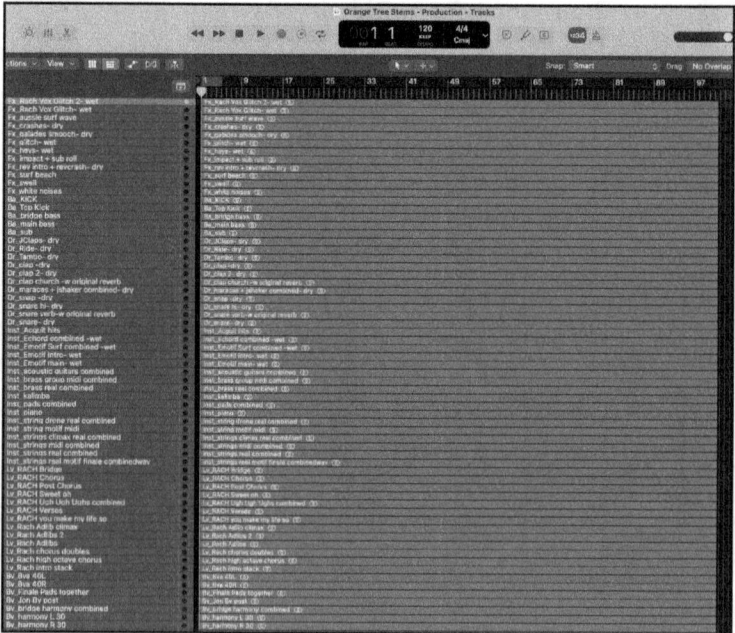

These are production stems (Multitracks) ready to be sent to a mixing engineer for mixing - but the full production is complete. Sometimes you'll even have all the production stems but they are mixed too. These mixed stems also look like this. **Note: The complete set of production stems that are also mixed are the ideal to analyze.** That is because they are in their final form yet give you the most information.

Example Two: The next set are the same stems from "Orange Tree" after being mixed into groups. These are the mixed stems from the full arrangement bounced from groups into single files. Sometimes you'll get stems that look more like this. In this example, all the bass instruments were bounced as one stem. All the brass instruments were bounced as one stem. All the background vocals were bounced as one stem. The drums, FX, guitars, lead vocals, strings, and synths were also bounced from their groups into one stem each.

Example Three: This last example is the final mix and master of the same track "Orange Tree". This is after the original production stems have been mixed and bounced into a single mix. Then, after mastering turned into a master file.

Here is what the flow chart would look like with real instruments and groups:

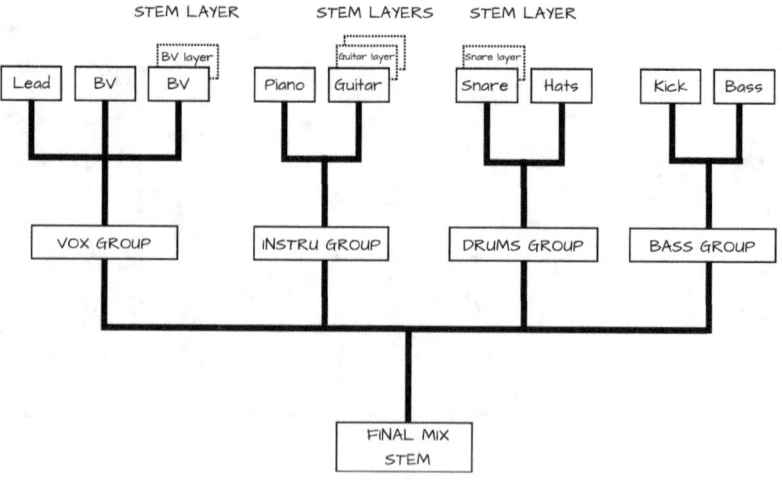

Part IV: Stems Thinking

HOW TO GROUP YOUR STEMS FOR ANALYSIS

Here is the secret to talent hacking using stem files: Analyze stem files through the lenses of the technique and principle levels.

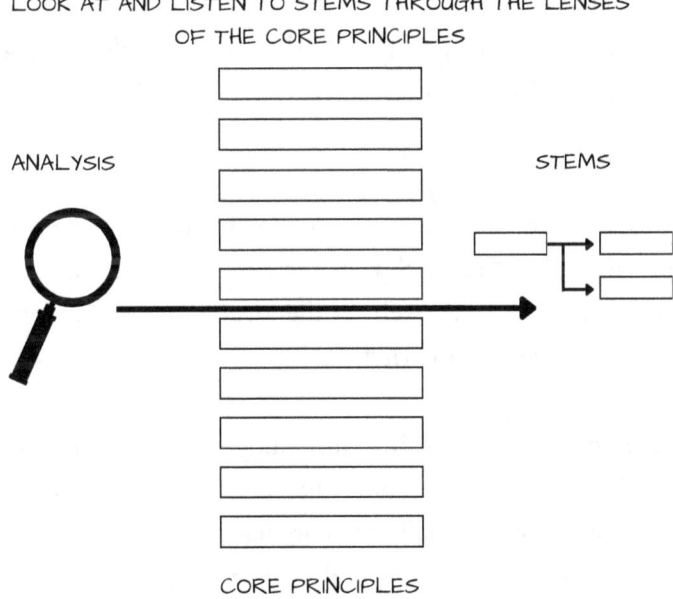

As you can see here, the stems are on the right-hand side. You're analyzing them through the lenses of the Ten Core Principles of Arranging.

STEMS GROUPINGS

IT IS EASIEST TO GROUP THE STEM FILES INTO THE FOLLOWING GROUP TYPES:

CORE RHYTHM ISOLATED DRUMS	CORE RHYTHM ISOLATED INSTRUMENTS	COUNTER RHYTHMS	SPATIAL PRINCIPLE TYPE GROUPS	FOREGROUND BACKGROUND HOOK GROUPS

Stems are easiest to view through the core principles when grouped. The easiest way I found to layer stems into principle groups is as follows:

- **Core rhythm isolated drum group:** Includes all the drums that flow with the core rhythm in their own group. Usually the kick, snare/clap pattern. As well as other drums/percussion instruments that flow with the core rhythm.

- **Core rhythm isolated instruments group:** Includes all the harmonic/melodic instruments that flow with the core rhythm in their own group. Usually the core harmonic rhythmic driver and instruments that flow with that. For example: bass line, piano chords, guitar chords, strings, brass, synths, etc.

- **Counter rhythm group:** Any counter rhythmic instrument that doesn't flow with the core rhythm can go into this group.

- **Similar instrument groupings within spatial principle:** For example, lead vocals are in a lead vocal group. Lead vocal group can include lead vocals, double tracks, whisper vocals, etc. Anything that flows with that grouping.

- **Foreground and background hook level groups:** Primary hooks as one group. Secondary hooks as one group. Hidden hooks as one group.

You can switch between solo stems, group stems, then two groups at a time, whole track, and back to solo to compare.

What if an instrument fits in multiple groups? When you group instruments, some may fit in multiple groups. Find the group that makes the most sense for the instrument and what you want to learn about the instrument.

For example, if it is a secondary hook, but is also a core rhythm instrument. Where you put it depends on what you want to know about it.

Don't be afraid to have it in more than one group. You can find the information you want from one group, then move it to another group to find more information. Sometimes the group you put it in can bring new information to light. You see this by how it relates to the other instruments in that group. You'll then see the other arranging principles in an obvious way including:

- Core Structure Principle
- Core Harmonic Structure Principle
- Energy Principle
- Call and Response Principle
- Repurposing Principle
- Synergy Principle

All the Ten Core Principles of Arranging will become evident when grouped.

STEMS GROUPINGS

IT IS EASIEST TO GROUP THE STEM FILES INTO THE FOLLOWING GROUP TYPES:

CORE RHYTHM ISOLATED DRUMS	CORE RHYTHM ISOLATED INSTRUMENTS	COUNTER RHYTHMS	SPATIAL PRINCIPLE TYPE GROUPS	FOREGROUND BACKGROUND HOOK GROUPS

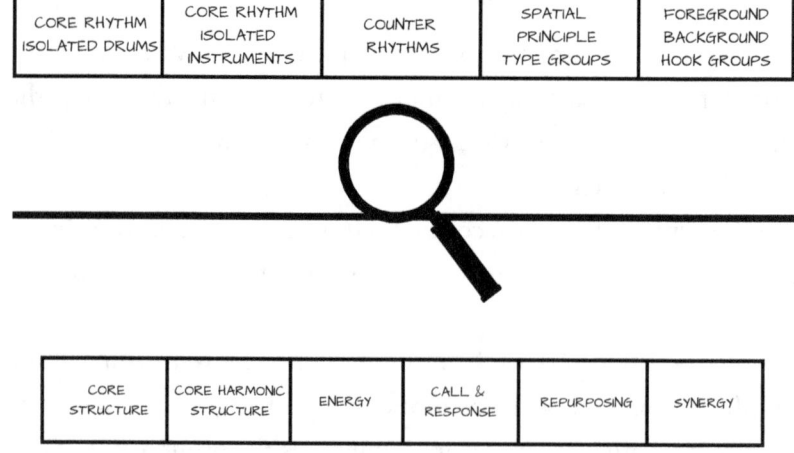

CORE STRUCTURE	CORE HARMONIC STRUCTURE	ENERGY	CALL & RESPONSE	REPURPOSING	SYNERGY

AFTER THE STEMS ARE GROUPED PROPERLY, YOU'LL BE ABLE TO SEE THE OTHER PRINCIPLES IN A CLEARER LIGHT

Note: These are the groups I recommend. But you can organize stems into any groups you'd like depending on the track and what you want to learn.

Example: "Orange Tree" by Rachelle Rhienne. Here are the same production stems I showed you before. But I moved the stems into the recommended group types for analysis. Here is how I would lay them out in my DAW.

All the production stems you saw earlier are grouped into "folders" within Logic Pro X.

Important: These groups are for analysis purposes only. These recommended groups are not for grouping your own music while producing or mixing. When producing and mixing your own music you can group them in ways that make sense for your arrangement and workflow. This practice is known as *routing*, which we'll cover later in this part.

LAYERING TYPES IN STEMS THINKING

There are three primary layering types you find in Stems Thinking.

- Layering Type One: Individual Stem Layering
- Layering Type Two: Groups of Stems Layering
- Layering Type Three: Groups and Groups of Stems Layering

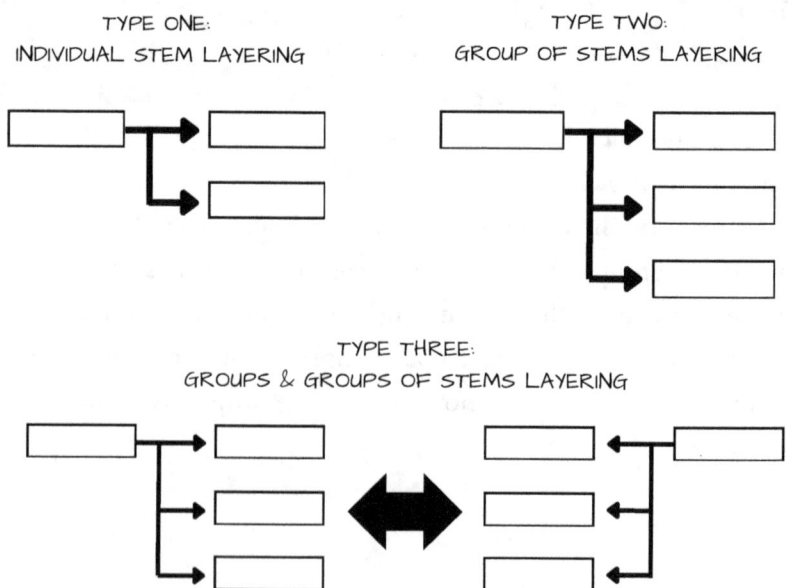

LAYERING TYPE ONE: INDIVIDUAL STEM

Layering Type One: Individual Stem. The individual stem is solo or layered with other instruments, doubles, or textures.

When you receive stem files from a producer, some of their stem files may be multiple tracks bounced as one stem file. These stem types can be deceptive as you may believe they are one sound. But sometimes, more than one sound is layered and bounced as one stem.

For example, say the stem is a guitar part. Have they used one recorded guitar? Or is this stem layered with other instruments, doubles, or textures playing the same part?

Sometimes, the single stem file is just one recorded instrument. It depends on the stem files you get and how the producer has chosen to layer and bounce those stems.

LAYERING TYPE ONE: INDIVIDUAL STEM

IS THE INDIVIDUAL STEM ITSELF SOLO OR LAYERED WITH MULTIPLE INSTRUMENTS?

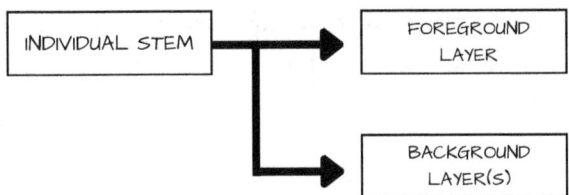

In the diagram, the left rectangle is the individual stem. That individual stem you're listening to includes the foreground instrument and background instrument layers. Sometimes, it is the only instrument in the stem file. Occasionally, the stem will have another instrument(s) layered with it.

Layering Type One: Individual Stem Examples

LAYERING TYPE ONE: INDIVIDUAL STEM EXAMPLE ONE

IS THE INDIVIDUAL STEM ITSELF SOLO OR LAYERED WITH MULTIPLE INSTRUMENTS?

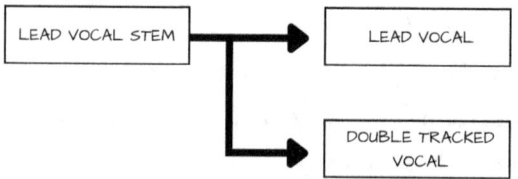

Example One: Say you have a lead vocal stem in your DAW that you've got from another producer. Inside that lead vocal stem, you notice a lead vocal, the foreground instrument. Then you notice a double-tracked vocal underneath is singing the same part. That's what you're going to listen out for. Does this individual stem have layers and other instruments inside that same stem file? In this case, there's a double-tracked vocal underneath the lead vocal.

LAYERING TYPE ONE: INDIVIDUAL STEM EXAMPLE TWO

IS THE INDIVIDUAL STEM ITSELF SOLO OR LAYERED WITH MULTIPLE INSTRUMENTS?

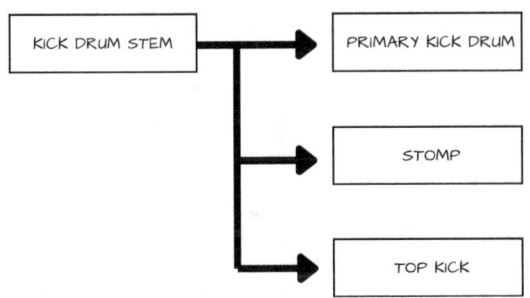

Example Two: This one is a kick drum stem. But inside that kick drum stem, there are three kicks layered. The primary kick is the one that's in the foreground. But I also notice that there's a stomp sound in the kick stem as well. Then, underneath that, there's a top kick. Within that one kick drum stem are three different kicks as one layer.

That's layering type number one. *What is this individual stem doing? Is it just one instrument, or is it layered?*

Example from the DAW: This is the track "Orange Tree" by Rachelle Rhienne. Here is an example of one stem file: a guitar. However, it is actually multiple guitars playing the same part. I played this same line four times, panned two guitars left, and two guitars right. Then bounced them all as one stem file.

LAYERING TYPE TWO: GROUPS OF STEMS

LAYERING TYPE TWO: GROUP OF STEMS

ARE THE STEMS WITHIN THEIR GROUP PLAYING SIMILAR IDEAS WHETHER THAT IS THE SAME THING OR A VARIATION FOR THAT GROUP?

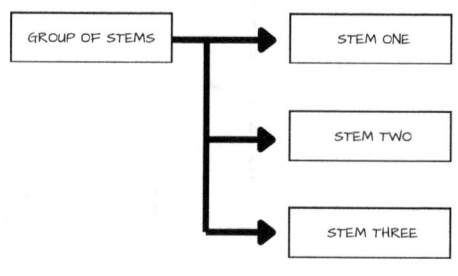

ETC.

Layering Type Two: Stems within a group playing similar, following, or variations of ideas to each other.

You have the groups you've made using the five group types I mentioned earlier in the book. Then, inside those groups, you have individual stems. When you analyze the groups, look at what the individual instruments are playing. Then, look at how those instruments are connecting with each other inside that same group.

Part IV: Stems Thinking

Layering Type Two: Groups of Stems Examples

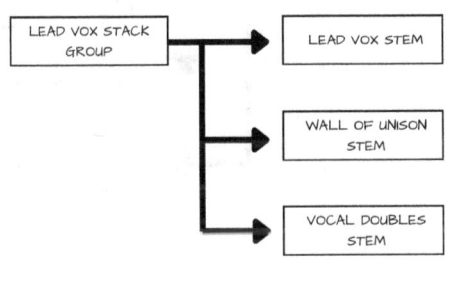

LAYERING TYPE TWO: GROUP OF STEMS
EXAMPLE ONE

ARE THE STEMS WITHIN THEIR GROUP PLAYING SIMILAR IDEAS
WHETHER THAT IS THE SAME THING OR A VARIATION FOR THAT GROUP?

ETC.

Example One: Lead vocal stack group. You have the lead vocal stem. Then it's layered with a vocal that's an octave higher and then one an octave lower. Then you have a stem that includes panned left and right vocal doubles. They only double certain words of the lead vocal. As you can see, they're one group. They're playing the same, similar, or accompanying parts. But there is variation in those ideas.

You will then be able to reveal how they all connect within that group. Soloing one stem, then analyzing how that stem relates to another stem by soloing that stem. You can continue this until you find all the combinations of layering.

LAYERING TYPE TWO: GROUP OF STEMS
EXAMPLE TWO

ARE THE STEMS WITHIN THEIR GROUP PLAYING SIMILAR IDEAS
WHETHER THAT IS THE SAME THING OR A VARIATION FOR THAT GROUP?

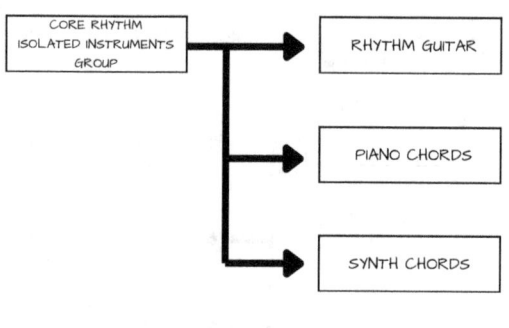

ETC.

Example Two: Core rhythm instruments that flow with drums group. Say the guitar plays the core harmonic rhythmic driver. But then, the piano and synth in the group only play accented parts on the core rhythm. In that case, they're playing a similar variation on the guitar line in that group.

Example from the DAW: As you can see in the following example from "Orange Tree", I've put the instruments playing pads into the same group. You can then hear how the piano, synth pad, and string pads are all connected. You can also see when they layer with each other.

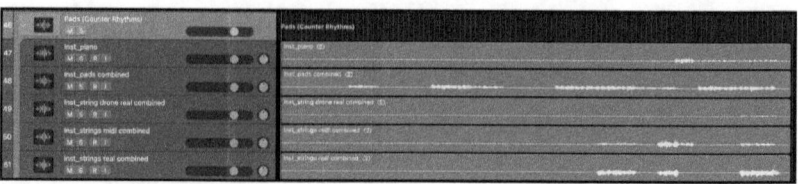

Part IV: Stems Thinking

STEMS ANALYSIS TYPE THREE: GROUPS AND GROUPS OF STEMS

LAYERING TYPE THREE:
GROUPS AND GROUPS OF STEMS

ARE THE GROUPS RELATING TO, FOLLOWING, OR PLAYING SOMETHING SIMILAR OR OPPOSING TO ANOTHER GROUP?

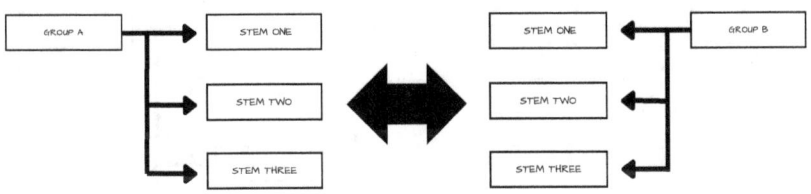

Layering Type Three: Groups relating to, following, or playing something similar or opposing to another group.

This type is when you analyze how one group of stems interacts with another group of stems. By groups, I mean the ones you have created using the five primary group types. You can compare any stems and groups you created to see how they connect.

- On the left-hand side is Group A, which has its own stems.
- On the right-hand side is Group B, which has its own stems.
- How does Group A connect to Group B within the arrangement?

Layering Type Three: Groups and Groups of Stems Examples

LAYERING TYPE THREE: GROUPS AND GROUPS OF STEMS EXAMPLE ONE

ARE THE GROUPS RELATING TO, FOLLOWING, OR PLAYING SOMETHING SIMILAR OR OPPOSING TO ANOTHER GROUP?

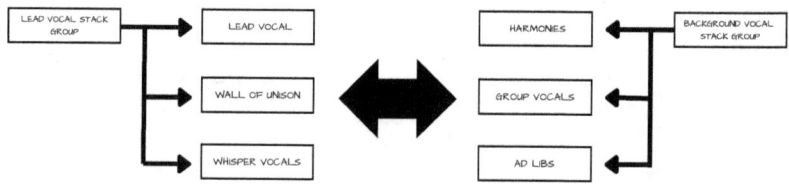

Example One: How are the lead vocal stack and the background vocal stack connected?

LAYERING TYPE THREE: GROUPS AND GROUPS OF STEMS EXAMPLE TWO

ARE THE GROUPS RELATING TO, FOLLOWING, OR PLAYING SOMETHING SIMILAR OR OPPOSING TO ANOTHER GROUP?

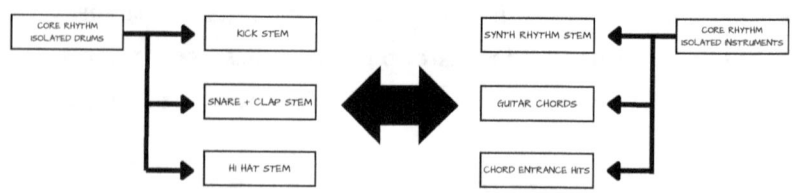

Example Two: How is the core isolated drum rhythm group working with the core isolated instruments group?

Example from the DAW: Here is the "Orange Tree" by Rachelle Rhienne example. As you can see, I can compare the core rhythm drums with the core rhythm instruments that flow with those drums.

Core rhythm drums and core rhythm instrument elements:

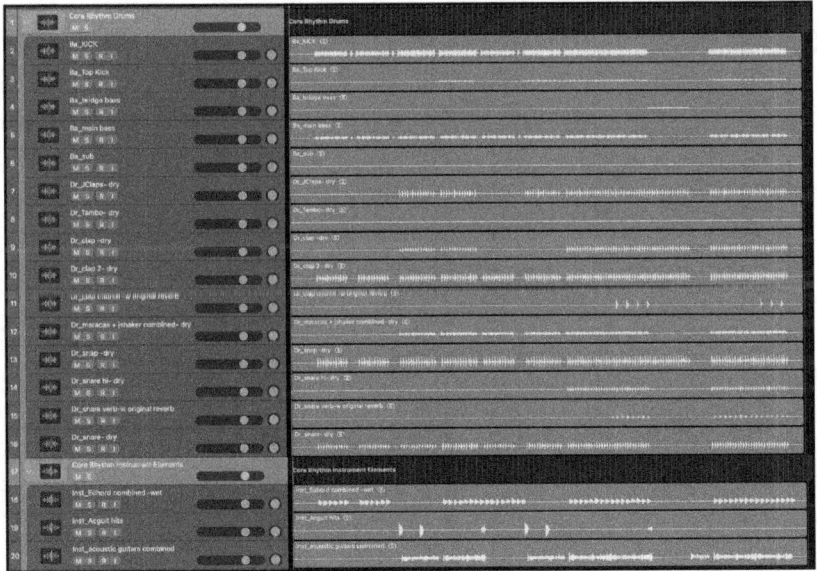

STEPS TO ANALYZE STEM FILES – SUMMARY

Here is a step-by-step guide on how to analyze stem files. As an example, I use the stem files of "Treasure" by Bruno Mars to illustrate this process.

Stems Analysis Pre-Frame

Look at the stems through the lenses of the core principles and find one technique at a time. Focus on the stems to see how they connect – eventually techniques are revealed.

Stems Analysis Step One

Choose which world-class stems to analyze. Where do you find stems? When I found stems from hit songs online, it was on a remix stem packs site that no longer exists. Sites that have them are popping up all the time. If you type in your search engine: "remix packs", "stem files", or "multitracks" and do some searching, you may find gold. Finding the original stems is best. Even finding just one stem files project from a world-class producer is enough to shift your paradigm.

    A second-tier option, which isn't as good but can still work, is using AI to break down a stereo track into stem files. The quality isn't as good because the stems aren't the originals. But do what you can for now.

    I have chosen the stem files of "Treasure" by Bruno Mars for this summary.

Stems Analysis Step Two

Lay the stems into your DAW on new tracks. Usually, the more individual and detailed the stems are, the better. Sometimes, you can find stem files that only have their pre-mixed group types. However, stems with more files are better for analysis. That is because you can group them yourself and find more information.

"Treasure" by Bruno Mars Example: Here is what the stems looked like when I first put them into the DAW.

The first thing I did was re-label the stems so they were clearer.

Stems Analysis Step Three

Once the stems are all on the DAW, analyze them through the lenses of the core principles. You do this by stacking them into groups where they flow together.

"Treasure" by Bruno Mars Example: I put the "Treasure" stems into core principle groups and color coded them. Here they are grouped.

Here are the same stem groups showing the tracks inside each group.

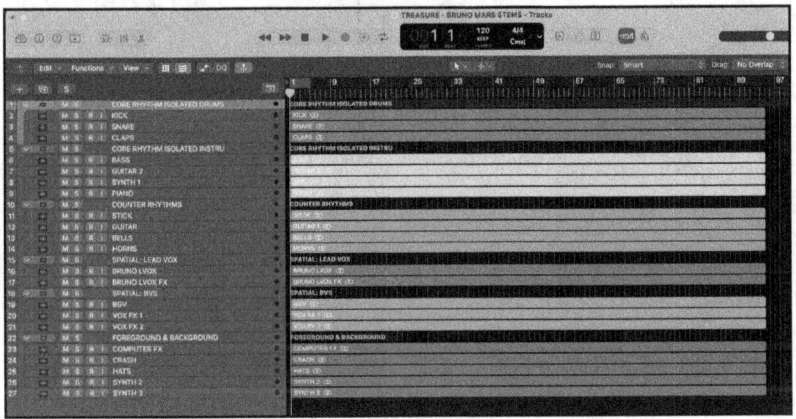

Stack them into the recommended group types:

Core rhythm principle groups:
1. Isolated core rhythm drums (kick and snare/clap and drums/percussion that flow with them).
2. Isolated instrument elements that flow with those drums (core harmonic rhythmic driver, etc.).

"Treasure" by Bruno Mars Example: As you can see I put the "kick", "snare", and "claps" into the core rhythm isolated drums group. I then found the core rhythm isolated instruments and put them into their own group. This included the core harmonic rhythmic driver in the "guitar 2" that flowed with the "bass". The "synth 1" and "piano" flowed with the core harmonic rhythmic driver.

Counter rhythm group: Once you have the core rhythm groups, counter rhythms will be easy to find. These instruments will be anything counter rhythmic that is not the core rhythm.

"Treasure" by Bruno Mars Example: Because I'd already found the core rhythms, the counter rhythms were easier to find. I placed the "stick", "guitar", "bells", and "horns" in this group. These instruments all played hooks that were counter rhythms to the core rhythm groups.

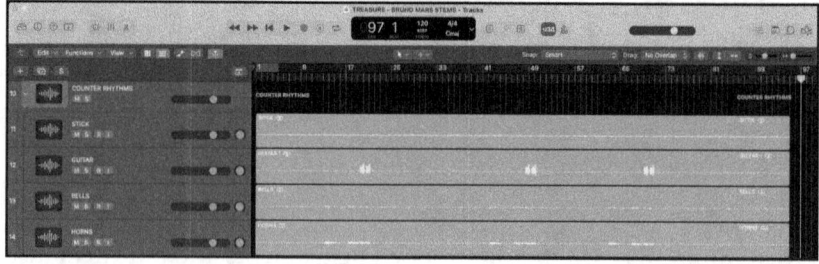

Spatial principle groups: Any instrument groups that are the same can go in these groups. Examples are lead vocal stack, background vocal stack, etc.

"Treasure" by Bruno Mars Example: The lead vocals and background vocals were all connected. I placed these into spatial principle groups. Most of these vocals flow with each other in a call and response way. I placed "Bruno LVOX" and "Bruno LVOX FX" in one group. I then placed the pack vocals "BGV", "VOX FX 1", and "VOX FX 2" in another group.

Foreground and background hook groups: If there's anything left over, place it in this group. For example, FX layers or random sounds that don't have a place in the other groups. Categorize them as primary, secondary, and hidden hooks.

"Treasure" by Bruno Mars Example: The last group I created was a foreground and background principle group. This group contained all the secondary and hidden hook instruments. This included a "computer FX sound", "crashes", "hat hits", "synth 2", and "synth 3".

Note: These groups are for analysis purposes. These recommended groups are not for grouping your music while producing or mixing. When you produce or mix you will group your instruments according to your routing.

Stems Analysis Step Four

Analyze the three types of layering in the stems.

Layering Type One: Analyze individual stems first. Look for whether the stem is a solo instrument or whether it is layered with another texture.

"Treasure" by Bruno Mars Example: I noticed that the "BGV" vocals had multiple layers in one stem. This included the lead vocal, and an octave lower vocal. It also included different vocalists stacked together. Whereas in the "piano stem", you can tell it is only the one piano playing. It is not layered by anything else within that individual stem file.

Layering Type Two: Analyze the stems within the groups you have made. Figure out how the individual stems within each group connect.

"Treasure" by Bruno Mars Example: I noticed that the core rhythm isolated instruments group was all connected. The "guitar 2" stem file is the core harmonic rhythmic driver. Playing "guitar 2" with the "bass" stem file, I could hear how these two flowed together rhythmically. I then noticed that the "synth 1" and "piano" stem files flowed with the "guitar 2" and "bass" stems, but only in the choruses. That tells me they only reserve the "synth 1" and "piano" for the choruses for energy development. I can also discover more information, such as where each stem sits in the frequency spectrum and where they are panned, etc.

Layering Type Three: Analyze how the groups of stems connect with the other groups of stems.

"Treasure" by Bruno Mars Example: I can now find the counter rhythms easier by comparing them to the core rhythm groups. The "stick" stem file plays a straight pulse on every beat. This runs counter to the syncopated funk of the core rhythm "guitar 2" stem file. The "bells" and "horns" stem files each play the same call and response hook that is a counter rhythm. The "bells" are an octave higher than the "horns". This exposes the layering methods they have used to develop the energy.

Stems Analysis Step Five

Analyze the stem files using Level One - Techniques. Analyze the stem files through the lenses of all core principles. You can do this using the core principles insights from Parts III and V. Also, look for all the layering decisions the producer has made. Then, find one technique at a time and place it in your technique library.

"Treasure" by Bruno Mars Example: I can go through each stem file using the three layering types. Once I find a technique, I can place it in my technique library. Say I discover that the "bells" layer the "horns" an octave higher during the call and response line they play. I may want to put multiple layering techniques into my technique library. Technique one is the "bells" layering the "horns" an octave higher. Technique two is the call and response hook with the lead vocal using the "bells" and "horns" that run counter to it. The list could go on.

HOW TO STEMS THINK WITH YOUR MUSIC

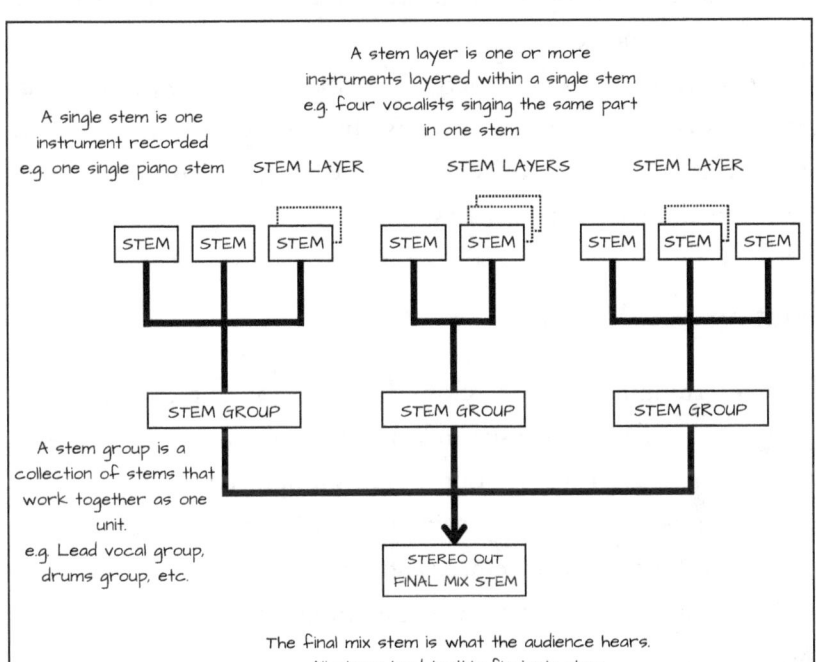

After you have analyzed the stems of the great music of all time, you will have educated decision-making. You will know how the great producers think about layering. You can then use the Stems Thinking framework to create your own music.

As learned in the foreground and background principle, you only need so many hooks in your arrangement to be effective. But the way you layer those hooks makes the arrangement sound world-class.

First, you decide what hook an instrument in your arrangement is: primary, secondary, or hidden. Then, you must determine what layers it needs. Some instruments can be strong by themselves - others will need layers. It's up to you to decide. This will come down to sound selection. The better your sound selection choices, the more original and world-class your track will sound.

Move through the three layering types for each instrument in your arrangement. Then, use your educated decisions from your analysis to make layering choices.

Stems Thinking is the synergy principle at play. You think of individual stems, then groups of stems, then groups of groups of stems and how it's all connected. With this layering knowledge, you can do advanced arrangement subtleties.

Routing

In Stems Thinking analysis I showed you core principles of arranging groups that will make it easier to learn techniques. In Stems Thinking your own music, usually routing will be grouped according to spatial principle types. Use routing inside your DAW to create groups that make sense for your arrangement and mix.

For example, here are a few common grouping options for your own music:

- Individual lead vocal stems routed to a lead vocal group.
- Individual background vocal stems routed to a background vocal group.
- Individual instrument stems routed to an instruments group.
- Individual drum stems routed to a drums group.
- Individual FX stems routed to an FX group.
- Individual bass stems routed to a bass group.
- Then route all of those groups into a premaster.
- Then route the premaster into the mix bus.

It is up to you how you set up your routing. You can use Stems Thinking while producing and mixing, regardless of how you choose to route your groups.

The Final Test

When you analyze stems, you see those stems in their final version. When making your own music, you have world-class, final-quality stems to compare to. You will then know whether your music is reaching the standard of world-class music. Your mind will form an invisible checklist. You will base it on the knowledge you gained from analyzing world-class stem files.

Here is the final test you can put your music through to level up your skills:

1. Solo each stem in your arrangement. Ask yourself, *Does this individual stem sound world-class?*
2. Solo each group of stems you have in your arrangement. Ask yourself, *Does this group of stems sound world-class together?*
3. Solo each group of stems with other groups of stems in your arrangement. Ask yourself, *Do these groups of stems sound world-class together?*
4. Listen to your whole piece of music as one. Ask yourself, *Does this whole track sound world class?*

You should be able to find any holes in your arrangement when you do this. Fix any holes and iterate until your arrangement sounds world-class.

ACTION STEPS

PART IV: STEMS THINKING - ACTION STEPS	
ACTION STEP ONE	APPLY THE STEMS THINKING ANALYSIS STEPS TO STEM FILES. DOWNLOAD STEM FILES AT WWW.POLYMATHPRODUCER.COM/RESOURCES
ACTION STEP TWO	APPLY STEMS THINKING TO YOUR OWN MUSIC CREATIONS BY THINKING IN THE THREE LAYERING TYPES
ACTION STEP THREE	APPLY THE FINAL TEST TO YOUR OWN MUSIC STEMS BY ASKING, "DO THESE STEMS SOUND WORLD-CLASS"?

Congratulations! You now know Stems Thinking. You now know how to layer techniques (words) and principles (grammar) to create full musical arrangements. You now know the entire system to master the art of arranging music. Now, we'll learn how to master the art of sonics.

Part IV: Stems Thinking

SUMMARY OF THE STEMS THINKING FRAMEWORK	
STEP ONE	CHOOSE WHICH WORLD-CLASS STEM FILES TO ANALYZE
STEP TWO	PUT THE STEM FILES INTO YOUR DAW ON NEW TRACKS
STEP THREE	ONCE THE STEMS ARE ALL ON THE DAW, LOOK AT THEM THROUGH THE LENSES OF THE CORE PRINCIPLES OF ARRANGING AND SONICS
STEP FOUR	STACK THEM INTO THE RECOMMENDED GROUP TYPES: • CORE RHYTHM DRUMS • CORE RHYTHM INSTRUMENTS THAT FLOW WITH CORE RHYTHM DRUMS • COUNTER RHYTHMS • SPATIAL PRINCIPLE • FOREGROUND AND BACKGROUND HOOKS
STEP FIVE	ANALYZE THE THREE TYPES OF LAYERING IN THE STEMS. • TYPE ONE: ANALYZE INDIVIDUAL STEMS FIRST • TYPE TWO: ANALYZE THE STEMS WITHIN THE GROUPS YOU HAVE MADE • TYPE THREE: ANALYZE HOW THE GROUPS OF STEMS CONNECT WITH THE OTHER GROUPS OF STEMS
STEP SIX	• ANALYZE THE STEM FILES THROUGH THE LENSES OF ALL CORE PRINCIPLES OF ARRANGING AND SONICS • ALSO, LOOK FOR ALL THE LAYERING DECISIONS THE PRODUCER HAS MADE • THEN, FIND ONE TECHNIQUE AT A TIME AND PLACE IT IN YOUR TECHNIQUE LIBRARY

PART V:

Sonics

[Analysis Level Four]

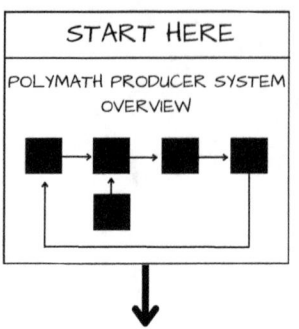

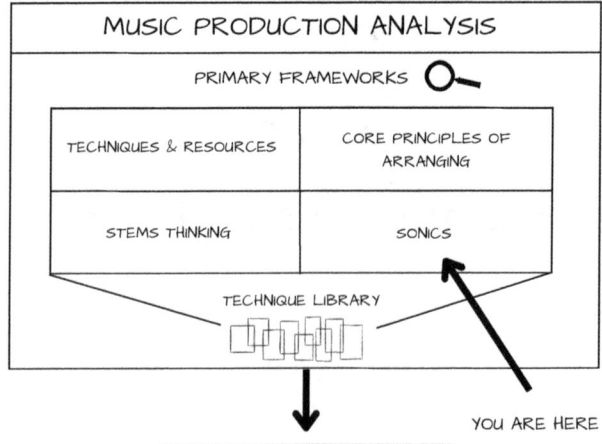

YOU ARE HERE

Sonics Confession

I HAVE A CONFESSION: I didn't know how to hear sonics until only a few years ago. When I learned about music production analysis, my entire life became about arranging. I convinced myself that arranging was the only thing that mattered. I thought, *Someone else can take care of the sonics who does that full time. Outsourcing to specialists is a great strategy. Most top-level producers will outsource the mixing and mastering of their tracks. So I should, too.*

In my conviction, I ignored sonics and took my arranging skills as far as possible. Soon enough though, I had to learn about sonics because the industry demanded it. My team and I needed to show our music to industry professionals, and I was the music producer on the team. If I couldn't mix and master, we would have to outsource it. That would cost thousands, which we didn't have at the time. I felt embarrassed. I had been producing for years; *how could I not know this yet?*

I hated the fact I had holes in my knowledge and skill set. If there were holes, it could be another situation where "I don't know what I don't know." I wanted to understand the end of the production chain – mixing and mastering – so I would know where I was going. I wanted to have the end in mind. Then, if the industry demanded that I mix and master, I could do it to an industry standard if I needed to. I refused to let this missing piece ruin opportunities that came my way.

I no longer wanted sonics to be a secret, either. The truth is it felt intimidating. I wanted to reveal the entire music production chain once and for all. I wanted to be able to complete the entire music production chain myself. Usually as a music producer – arranging, recording, and editing are the primary things you focus on. However, knowing mixing and mastering gives you an advantage because you'll have the end in mind. As the music producer, I was responsible for overseeing the entire production chain. So it was my responsibility to know mixing and mastering.

For some reason, even though most of the information I found online was about mixing and mastering, it took me years to finally "get it". I never had sonics explained to me in a way I could understand. I read every book I could get my hands on; I did every program I could buy. I watched the great mixing and mastering engineers of all time do their craft. I listened to their philosophies. I cross-analyzed everything. I tried to find the underlying fundamentals that made someone a master of sonics.

After years of searching, I found three learning fundamentals that changed everything. These fundamentals took me from struggling with sonics for years to learning sonics fast. I also found the *Core Principles of Sonics*, which helped me to know where to focus my attention.

Learning Fundamental Number One: Ear Training. I noticed that the professionals could hear frequencies. I couldn't yet. Becoming great at mixing and mastering required training my ears. I needed to be able to hear sonics. So, first, I trained my ears on sonics using a software called "SoundGym". I learned to hear volume, frequencies, compression, FX, and saturation. It took less than 26.5 hours of training time to hear and know frequencies.

Learning Fundamental Number Two: Hear the Truth. I realized that when I tried to mix in the past, my speakers and headphones gave me false information. That was because my room, speakers, and headphones weren't optimized. So, I discovered the best ways to "hear the truth". By "truth", I mean the frequencies became unaffected by the equipment and room I was hearing them from. Once I could hear the "truth", I could use my trained ears to mix and master accurately.

Learning Fundamental Number Three: Analyzing Sonics (reference matching). I knew that when I analyzed arrangements from the great producers of all time, I could now analyze the sonics too. I then wrote down the steps one would go through to record, edit, mix, and master a track. If the principles process worked for arranging it should also work for sonics. I found the principles in plain sight. There were certain principles that every top engineer would focus on. These principles gave me a guideline – *focus here*. You will learn the Principles of Sonics later in this Part.

Once I developed this framework, I tested it with my music production analysis. After doing this, I noticed a dramatic shift when I mixed my own tracks. I could use reference tracks as feedback. Because of ear training, I could hear the sonics. Because I optimized my room, speakers, and headphones, I could also hear the truth. To top it off, I knew the principles of recording, editing, mixing, and mastering to focus on. I could then hear a clear difference between what my track needed compared to the reference track.

This process finally bridged the gap for me. I would mix a vocal and place it next to an Ariana Grande vocal, and I could hear the difference. I could match the quality using the principles and my ear. To my shock, I had finally *matched* industry standards. I finally felt like I understood the "invisible" world of sonics.

With this missing piece of the puzzle, I became a 100%er. A complete Polymath Producer. If I want to, I can write a song, produce it, arrange it, record it, edit it, mix it, master it. I can do the entire production chain myself.

The industry demands a fully mixed and mastered track. This is true even if you just send a "demo" to a label on spec. It will help you in any area of the industry you work in.

I became a complete Polymath Producer through this. I often prefer to outsource mixing and mastering, but I now understand this part of the language. I now know what I want and how to get there. So I can set the track up to have even more success before I send it to a mixing or mastering engineer now. Or I can do the whole production chain myself when I want to. The choice is now mine. The truth is this has been the most liberating feeling creatively. Knowing that any idea I have I can make a reality to industry standard if I choose to. My confidence is at an all-time high, and it only grows stronger.

In this section, I will take you through this same transformation. You will learn the exact steps needed to learn and master mixing and mastering. Let's become a complete Polymath Producer.

LEARNING SONICS

LEARNING AND MASTERING sonics requires three steps:

1. Ear training.
2. Correctly set up room, speakers, and headphones to hear the truth.
3. Analyzing Sonics (reference matching) – matching your music to the sonic standard of references.

In this part we will go through each of these in more detail but first...

WHAT ARE SONICS?

You can view sonics as the "pronunciation" of the language of music production. Sonics are how the language sounds when played. Sonics can have different names compared to musical arrangement names. For example, a note on the keyboard can translate to a music note A4 or a frequency note 440Hz.

You will be using Techniques, Sonic Principles, and Stems Thinking with sonics too. Everything you have learned so far is the foundation for this part on sonics.

THE MUSICAL ARRANGEMENT VERSUS SONICS

Musical arrangements use notes like C, D, E, F, G, A, and B. You use melody, chords, and rhythms.

With sonics, you're using frequencies from 0Hz to 20kHz+. You're using volume, EQ, dynamics, saturation, and FX. You're using recording, editing, mixing, and mastering principles. We will go deeper into all these in this part on sonics. Sonics is all about acoustics and how acoustics work.

Sonics are like the code in the film *The Matrix*[14] – the information behind what you see. When the characters enter The Matrix, everything looks and feels natural. Think of that like the musical information that you're witnessing. It's going into your ears, and you're witnessing it in real time. The code is the computer-generated code behind the images in that movie. So think of the sonics like the code behind the music; it's the information behind the scenes. The audience will only really hear and see the musical arrangement. The sonics are the physics behind why it works.

To learn sonics, you must learn to recognize what a frequency sounds like from 0Hz to 20kHz+. When you can hear frequencies by ear, you can solve problems and get your tracks to an industry standard. You then want to learn to hear volume, dynamics, saturation, FX, etc. Then, you can solve all the sonic problems you face.

When you understand sonics, you can then record, edit, mix, and master your music. Then you can match your tracks to world-class references. Then, you can advance even beyond that. The fastest way to learn sonics is via *ear training*.

EAR TRAINING

We learned in Part I that the REPS method is one of the fastest ways to master a new skill. It involves Repetition, Engagement, Purposefulness, and Speedy Feedback in training. The more repetitions and variations you do in a short time, the faster your skill growth.

To get good at understanding sonics fast, I used a website called *SoundGym*. SoundGym covers the REPS method in their training. In the future, if this website doesn't exist, I recommend something similar that uses the REPS method. You can also do ear training by doing a lot of reference matching as explained soon in the *steps to industry standard*. But the SoundGym method uses the REPS training which means you can get a head start within a month. Here is why...

THE EXPERIMENT

I wrote this to myself in late July 2022:

> "Goal – Golden Ears in 30 to 90 days:
> Tim Ferriss has written many books about talent hacking and learning new skills.[15] He said you could get to the top five percent in the world in a skillset within three to six months with no prior experience. So, I will use talent hacking methods to see if that theory is correct. Will getting into the top five percent of hearing sonics take three to six months? Let's prove it.
>
> 1. I'll be using these mental models to learn faster:
>   - Deconstruct the skill.
>   - 80/20 the skill.
>   - Do it in the correct order of learning.
>   - Be consistent.
>
> 2. I'll also do deliberate practice, which is a practice that:
>   - Chunks the skill set.
>   - Has a lot of variation.
>   - Takes place in a short period of time.

3. I'll be soaking in sonics information until I know it all by heart.

4. I'll track progress and hours spent. What gets tracked gets measured.

5. I'll use SoundGym because it integrates the fast-paced REPS method in the training."

That was the plan and the experiment I wanted to try with sonics. I wanted to see whether I could go from not knowing sonics to being Golden Ears within three to six months.

THE JOURNEY

I started in late July 2022. I had no experience with frequency detection or technical ear training. As you can see, I went from zero score to a million score by December 2022. Which is top three percent in the world.

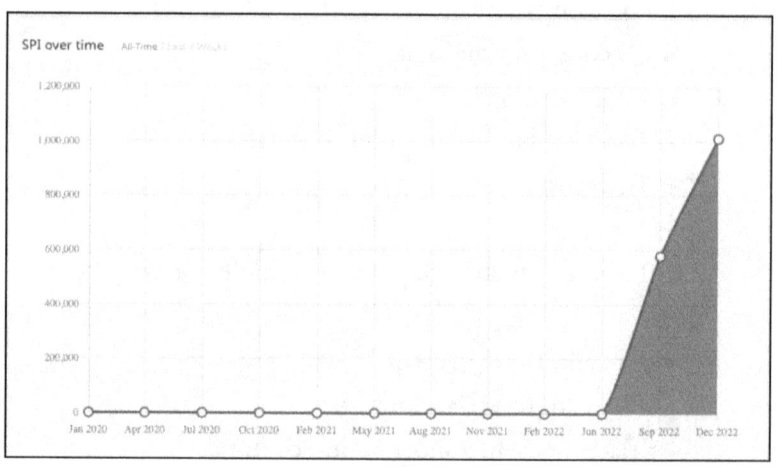

Part V: Sonics

Here's a post that I made in the Polymath Producer Community.

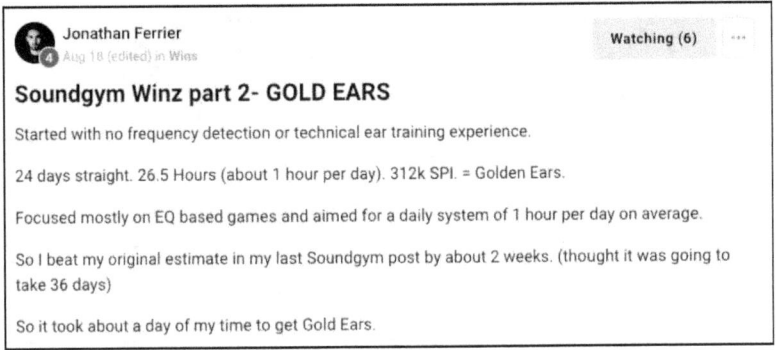

Here's my Golden Ears award, August 18th, 2022.

I started in late July 2022; it took me 26.5 hours to get to Golden Ears. The 26.5 hours of training took place over a 24-day period. Using this deliberate practice method, I got to the top ten percent of the skill within the first 26.5 hours of practice. As you can see, Tim Ferriss's theory is correct in this case. It took me within the first twenty to thirty hours of training to get to the top ten percent in the world. Then, by December 2022, within four months, I was in the top three percent in the world on SoundGym. Here are my stats from each game. They show you that I got into the top ten percent of every SoundGym game within those four months.

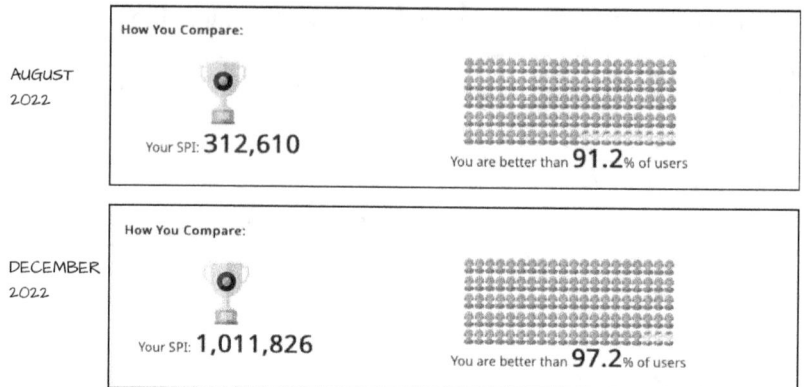

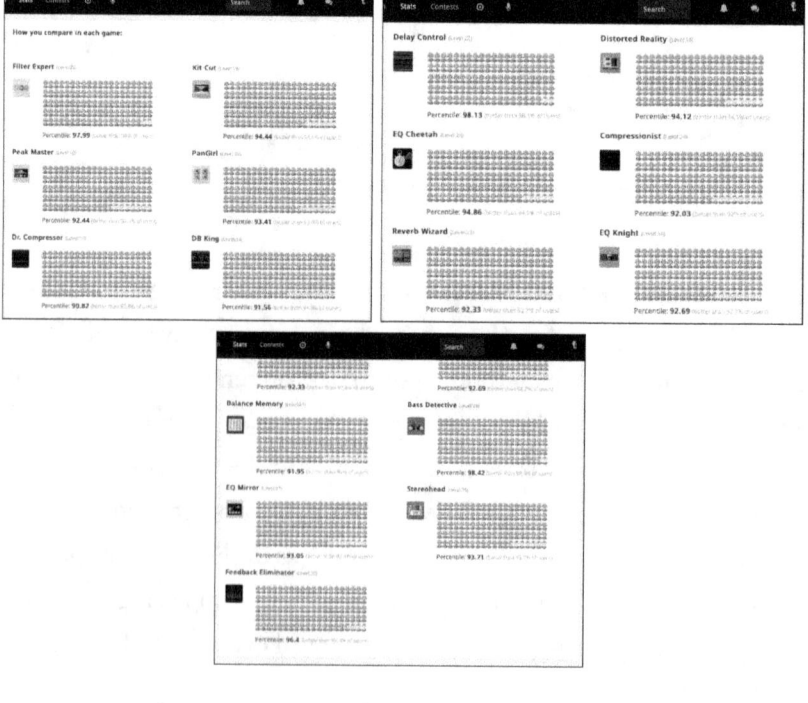

Top ten percent of all skills on the platform within seventy-five days.

Part V: Sonics

I tracked the data every day to keep track of my progress.

DAY	Ear Training/ rev eng	NOTES:	DAY	Ear Training/ rev eng	NOTES:
1		July 25 start	24	1.5hr	
2	1hr	started ear training tracking July 26	25	3hr	GOLD EARS- 24 days it took. 26.5hrs 300k
3	30m		26	1hr	
4	1hr		27	1hr	
5	1hr		28	1hr	
6	30m		29	1hr	
7	30m (4.5 for week)	sunday	30	30m	
8	1hr		31	1hr	
9	30m		32	1hr	
10	1hr		33	30m	
11	1hr		34	1hr	
12	1hr		35	1hr	
13	1hr		36	30m	
14	1hr (5.5 for week)		37	1.5hr	
15	1hr		38	1hr	500k SPI
16	1hr		39	30m	
17	1hr		40	30m	
18	1.5hr		41	30m	
19	1hr		42		
20	2hr		43		
21	30m		44	30m	
22	1hr		45	30m	
23	1hr		46	30m	
24	1.5hr		47	30m	

DAY	Ear Training/ rev eng	NOTES:	DAY	Ear Training/ rev eng	NOTES:
47	30m		69	30m	760k+ SPI halfway to diamond ears
48	30m		70		14 skills/17 90+% 3 at 80%
49	30m		71	30m	
50			72	30m	
51	1hr		73	30m	
52			74	30m	
53			75	30m	90%+ on all 17 skills on soundgym
54			76		
55			77		
56			78		
57			79	1.5hrs	
58	1hr		80	1hr	890k+ SPI
59	1.5hr	46hrs of training- Spi 650k-	81	30m	913k+ SPI
60	1hr	11 skills 90+ 6 skills 70+	82	30m	
61	1hr		83		
62	1hr	11 skills 90+ 6 skills 80+	84		
63	1hr	50 hours ear training			
64	30m				
65	1hr	700k+ SPI			
66	1hr				
67	1hr				
68	30m				
69	30m	760k+ SPI halfway to diamond ears			
70		14 skills/17 90+% 3 at 80%			

I started on July 25th, and I started tracking on July 26th. As you can see, I stayed very consistent for the first forty days. I was doing half an hour to an hour a day. Sometimes an hour and a half. Then, as you can see, I got to Golden Ears on day 24. As I continued, I started to get less consistent around day 50. I missed a whole week there. I began to get distracted by other things, but I started to pick up again on day 58. By day 75, I got to ninety percent plus on all seventeen skills on SoundGym. That's when I reached the top ten percent on all skills and the top three percent in the world overall. I did this by doing thirty minutes to one hour per day for the first few months.

This experiment proved that practicing a skill even for one hour a day has a compound effect. I gained the most growth within the first twenty to thirty hours. It took me twenty-four days to reach the top ten percent but four months to reach the top three percent.

Talent Stack

If you want to be in the top 1% or the top 0.01%, it's an exponential effect. It's going to take way more time to master that one skill. That's why sometimes you can stand out when you *talent stack*. Talent stack is a concept coined by author Scott Adams.[16] Talent stacking means being in the top ten percent at many skills. You then combine them to stand out. If you focus on one skill, it will take more time and more talent-hacking methods to get to that top 0.01%. To be in the top 0.01% of a single skill often requires a lifetime of dedication and mastery.

MY STRATEGY FOR GOLDEN EARS

Here's my strategy to get to Golden Ears within twenty-four days with SoundGym.

Golden Ears Step One

I started with *Feedback Eliminator*; that's a game on SoundGym. I used that to begin to recognize frequencies via tones.

While playing this game, I close my eyes, listen, and make a decision before I look with my eyes at what my options are. That's key because you want to train your ears, not your eyes. Then, after I see the options with my eyes, I make the final choice.

Golden Ears Step Two

I then moved on to EQ games in general, most notably *EQ Cheetah*. EQ Cheetah has rapid variation and instant feedback. I struggled with this one to start with. But I knew that it had the REPS principle within it. Although hard to begin with, this game teaches you EQ detection fast because of its fast feedback. You only have sixty seconds to answer twenty-five questions.

Golden Ears Step Three

I used a *frequency chart* to recognize frequencies through word labels. When I started, I had a frequency chart next to me as I played EQ games. I would then match frequencies I heard with words that described the sound closest.

When doing EQ Cheetah, you hear boosted frequencies. So if you hear something is muddy, for example, you know it will be around 200Hz. Looking at the frequency balance chart, you can see 200Hz sounds muddy if there is too much 200Hz. Then, if you hear something harsh, you know the answer will be around 1.5kHz to 5kHz, etc.

I would close my eyes and listen to it, and then I'd open my eyes, see the chart, and ask, what does this sound like? Is it piercing? Is it hissy? Is it rumbly? Is it boomy? Is it muddy? Is it boxy? Then, I'd answer based on the word I believed matched the sound. I did the same with boosts and cuts. There are games where they also cut frequencies, so you can use the chart to start with the language there, too. It helped me to identify words with the sounds to get me across a certain threshold in my ability.

Here are some words that reflect when a sound has too much of a frequency:

- 20Hz-50Hz: Rumbly.
- 50Hz-100Hz: Boomy.
- 100Hz-400Hz: Muddy.
- 400Hz-800Hz: Boxy.
- 800Hz-1.5kHz: Honky.
- 1.5kHz-5kHz: Harsh.
- 5kHz-10kHz: Piercing.
- 10kHz-20kHz+: Hissy.

Here are some words that reflect when a sound does not have enough of a frequency:

- 20Hz-100Hz: Weak.
- 100Hz-400Hz: Thin.
- 400Hz-800Hz: Hollow.
- 800Hz-1.5kHz: Scooped.
- 1.5kHz-5kHz: Distant.
- 5kHz-10kHz: Dull.
- 10kHz-20kHz+: Lifeless.

Here are some words that reflect when a sound is well-balanced in frequencies:

- 20Hz-50Hz: Deep.
- 50Hz-100Hz: Full.
- 100Hz-200Hz: Punchy.
- 200Hz-800Hz: Warm.
- 800Hz-1.5kHz: Natural.

- 1.5kHz-5kHz: Present.
- 5kHz-10kHz: Crisp.
- 10kHz-20kHz+: Airy.

Golden Ears Step Four

When I started on SoundGym, I used full-band instrumentals and songs. I didn't do individual instruments like a solo piano, a solo shaker, a drum kit, etc. I focused on full arrangements. You can choose one of the options to be "songs", which is a full track and song. Full songs allowed me to look at it more as a mastering engineer than a mixing engineer. Learning from this place creates rapid growth because it is easier to hear frequencies in a full arrangement.

I dropped the frequency word chart once I could detect frequencies without words and only by ear. Then, I moved on to solo instruments to make it more complicated.

Golden Ears Step Five

After getting all the EQ challenges to level twenty, I then moved on to other games like compression, volume, saturation, and FX. I then got all games to a ninety percent plus ranking. You can also do ear training on other platforms, but SoundGym was the one I used.

Once you do this, you should be able to understand sonics and read them like a book. Ear training is the first step to doing music production analysis of sonics.

Yes, 26.5 hours sounds like a long time. But if you committed to one month using this strategy. Only thirty to sixty minutes daily. Then, by the end you could hear frequencies and sonics. Isn't that worth it? That is how I went from being unable to detect sonics to knowing how to and gaining golden ears in 26.5 hours.

Mixing Headphones and Monitors

I recommend using your mixing headphones and monitors for ear training. This way, you can hear the subtle details. But it is important that even with mixing headphones and monitors you have an accurate listening experience. This brings me to the next part...

CAN YOU HEAR THE TRUTH?

Now that you can hear sonics, you must ensure that what you hear is the truth. You might not be hearing the truth because of these problems:

- If your room isn't the right room.
- If your room isn't treated correctly.
- If your desk and speakers inside the room aren't positioned correctly.
- If your room and speakers aren't calibrated from accurate data.
- If you haven't calibrated your headphones.

The above points explain why you could hear false information in your studio setup. You could impair your sonics' decision-making ability if you can't hear the truth. Impaired decision-making will mean your experiments will be flawed. If you know how to hear sonics but still aren't getting results, your environment and tools could be to blame.

Pro Studios Versus Home Studios

The best studios in the world have what is called a *flat frequency response*. That is because pro studios are designed with optimal acoustics in mind. In the best studios, every frequency band from 0Hz to 20hHz peaks within +/- 2 dB while listening to the music on speakers. So it's around 0 dB flat. With a flat frequency response, you are hearing a sound that is as close to "truth" as possible. It is not altered by the acoustics in the environment. This makes decision-making accurate in these environments.

By default, home studios aren't designed for studio purposes. They are standard rooms. So, having any frequencies in your room plus or minus in dB will skew your perception of reality. It will be a false representation of the truth.

For example: If you have +10 dB around 80Hz in your room, whenever you mix or master, you hear that 80Hz +10 dB too loud. So it's no wonder you must keep doing trial and error and waste thousands of hours because you aren't hearing the truth. A lot of the time, it isn't your fault.

Have you experienced this? You know how you create a mix, and then you finally believe you have achieved industry standards. Then, you do a car or iPhone test and find out that the low end has too much volume or too little. It is probably because, in your room/ headphones, the low end is +/- beyond the truth. You do not hear the truth. This practice means more trial and error, time-wasting, and frustration.

To Fix This Problem in Your Studio Will Require You to Manage Four Things:

1. Early reflections.
2. Decay times.
3. Room modes.
4. Inbuilt equipment frequency responses.

What Are Early Reflections?

Early reflections are the sounds that bounce off the closest walls to your speakers.

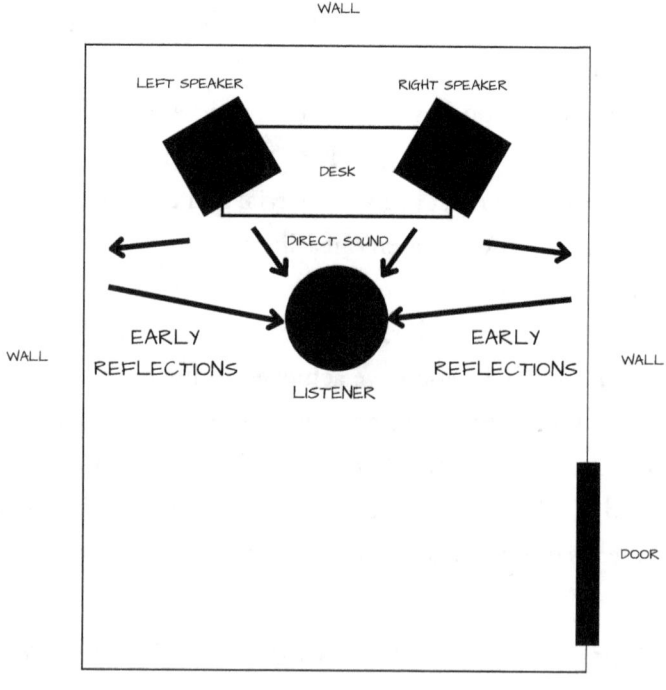

This diagram is an example of what early reflections look like inside a room. You've got a wall behind the studio, a wall on the left, a wall on the right, and a wall behind the listener. Then you've got the door at the back right-hand corner of the room. You've got the desk positioned in the center of the room. You've got the left speaker and the right speaker on the desk. The listener is in front of the desk.

The arrows represent the sound coming out of the speakers to the listener. That's the direct sound. The early reflections are the arrows (sound) that bounce off the walls back to the listener. It's coming out of the speakers, hitting the walls, and returning to the listener. Those are what early reflections are. These early reflections can sometimes impair the truth of the sound you're hearing.

What Are Decay Times?

Decay times are the duration for a sound source to decrease and stop existing. When someone speaks or claps in a church the sounds feel like they last long. That is because the decay times are long. When you clap in a church, it echoes through the room acoustics. The decay times are short in a small room, but can still bounce back and forth off the walls. These decay times can sometimes mess with the truth of the sound you are hearing.

What Are Room Modes?

When a speaker plays in a room, room modes are the collection of low-end frequency build-ups. They occur at different frequencies and places. Room modes can sometimes mess with the acoustics in the room. They can especially mess with the low-end frequencies in a bad way.

What Are Inbuilt Frequency Responses?

Many monitors and headphones, as well as gear in general like microphones, can have inbuilt frequency responses. Meaning certain frequency curves are built in. Some frequencies will naturally be boosted or cut depending on the gear.

When you have a lot of early reflections, decay times, and room modes building up, this mixture of sound can create a mess. Then, combine those with equipment that has unique inbuilt frequency responses. This mess of sound can cause you to inaccurately hear the truth.

To Fix These Problems You'll Need:

- Proper room choice.
- Correct position of the desk, speakers, and listening position within that room.
- Tools to analyze the room accurately, identify weak spots, and collect data. You can use programs like Room EQ Wizard and Sonarworks to gather data.
- Use of room treatment to treat the specific weak spots in your room. Treat the spots that need acoustic treatment based on the tested data.
- Speaker, room, and headphone calibration.

In-depth acoustics are beyond the scope of this book. Acoustics could be an entire book within itself. However, I wanted to inform you of the primary problems you may face when you work with sonics. I also wanted to explain why you may have inaccurate sonic information while producing and analyzing music. But here is an easy solution...

THE GOAL FOR POLYMATH PRODUCER WITH SONICS

Our goal is to master the language of music production with music production analysis. In this case, music production analysis of sonics. You can do this with headphones. Headphones won't have the problems your room/speakers may have: early reflections, decay times, and room modes. However, like rooms and speakers, headphone models vary in frequency response. To hear the truth, it is usually best to get a software to give your sonics headphones a flat frequency response. Using software to give your headphones a flat frequency response will let you hear sonics accurately. I used *Sonarworks Sound ID* for a flat frequency response. There are other programs too, so use the one that works best for you.

Hear the Truth

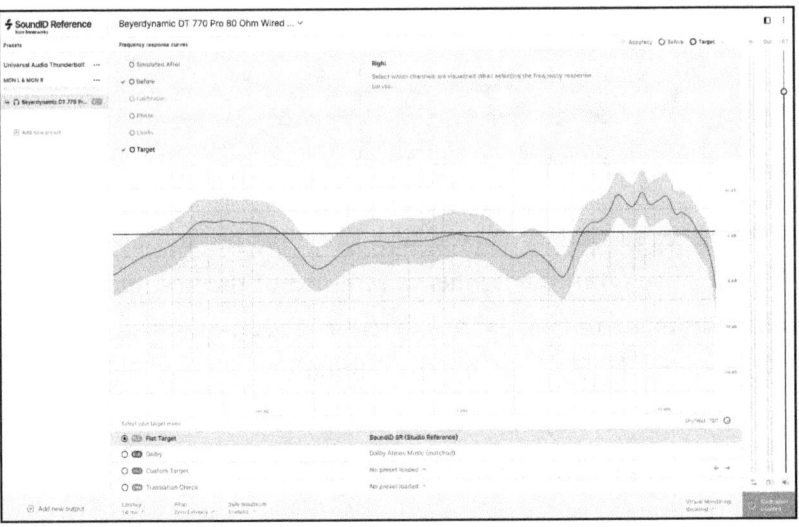

Here is the Sound ID reference program by Sonarworks. The above is a frequency response graph of my Beyerdynamic DT 770 Pro headphones. Look at the primary curved line: the headphone's frequency response curve. If you can see the frequency response curves, there are dB peaks; +5 dB at 6kHz to 10kHz. You can see there are dB dips to -6 dB at 3kHz. You can also see dB dips to -5 dB at 200Hz. You can see the flat black line is the target. The target frequency response is zero dB; that's a flat-frequency response.

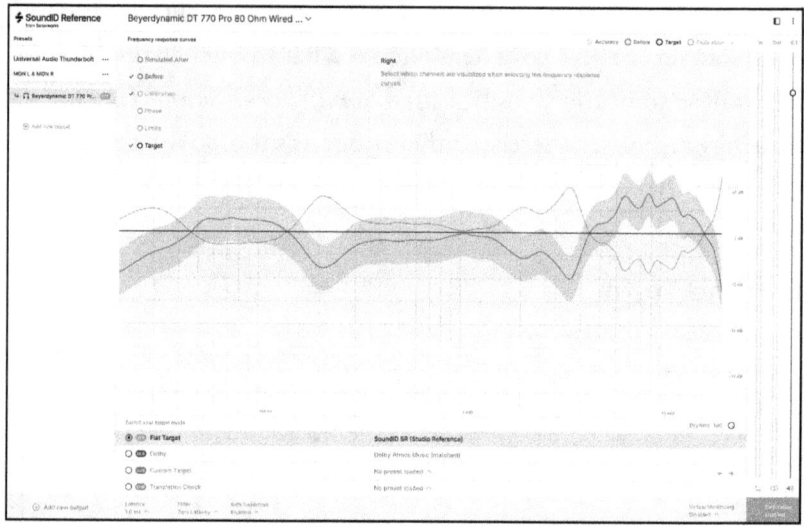

The other secondary curved line is the calibration applied. The calibration evens out the frequency response of the headphones. This calibration made my headphones' frequency response flat. Now, I'm hearing the truth after enabling the calibration.

Speaker Emulation Plugins

If you have to use headphones only, you can create and analyze music in your DAW using flat frequency response software. Then you can combine that with a speaker emulation plugin. I use the 112 dB plugin called *Red Line Monitor*. Red Line Monitor plugin is speaker emulation software. You put it in your stereo output while analyzing or mixing/mastering music in your DAW. It creates a sound like you have external speakers in your headphones. So you can mix on headphones anywhere, any time. This plugin is an optional addition to your sonics analysis and workflow.

Further Education

Solving the acoustic issues of your room requires more in-depth education, time, and money. I recommend getting a proper studio setup when you are ready. It will make the sound you're hearing even clearer when done well. Having a proper studio setup is integral, and I highly recommend it, but not everyone's ready to do that yet. If you have the money and the time, I suggest you get more education. If you want to go further, get your room and speakers properly set up, treated, and calibrated. I will leave suggestions of where to do this at: www.polymathproducer.com/resources.

Our Purposes for Calibrated Headphones

Our purposes when using calibrated headphones will be for the following:

- You will be able to hear the truth. This means the sounds you hear while ear training, analyzing, and producing sonics will be accurate.

- You will then be able to analyze more effectively. You will discover techniques from the top mixing and mastering engineers. You will learn what they do to achieve their sounds.

- With this accuracy, you can match your sonics with reference tracks much more easily. This will improve your standard. You can cross-compare your track with those of the greats to understand industry standards. The difference between yours and theirs will give clear information to bridge the gap. There will be clear data about what you must do to make your tracks sound industry standard.

This section covered specific software such as SoundGym, Sonarworks SoundID, and the 112dB Redline Monitor plugin. If these do not exist in the future, I recommend software that achieves the same thing.

You have ear training, and can hear the truth. Now, you are ready to analyze and produce sonics.

Analyzing Sonics

In this part you will learn how to master sonics with analysis.

We will cover:

- The Core Principles of Sonics
- Analyzing sonics (reference matching)
- Producing sonics
- Iteration and feedback to industry standard

As you know, sonics are the pronunciation of the language of music production.

Ear training shows you how to *hear* the pronunciation.

Analysis will show you how to *speak* the pronunciation.

When you learn a second language, the first step is learning how to speak the vowels and the consonants. Once you learn them, you can speak words. It simplifies everything because every word is made up of the same vowels and consonants arranged in different ways. In sonics, the vowels and consonants are the *Sonic Principles*.

I will not tell you how to record, edit, mix, or master in this book. Each professional has their own Technique Library. Therefore, each professional has their own way of doing sonics. However, just like there are core principles of arranging, there are also core principles of sonics in every track. All producers will work through these sonic principles in a production chain.

The music production chain has four primary sonic areas on which we will focus.

They are:

- Recording
- Editing
- Mixing
- Mastering

Each primary area of sonics contains four core principles. Learning these core principles, is like learning the vowels and consonants of pronunciation. These principles are in every track you'll ever record, edit, mix, and master. Once you learn them, you can then learn to speak them. These principles give you focus during your analysis and production of sonics.

PRINCIPLES OF SONICS

The following principles guide you on what to look for within your analysis and production of sonics. I made it as simple as possible. Each principle in recording usually occurs in successive order. Editing, mixing and mastering principles usually occur in successive order too; but, they can be flexible depending on the task and where you are in the process.

PRINCIPLES OF RECORDING, EDITING, MIXING & MASTERING

RECORDING	EDITING	MIXING	MASTERING
SOUND SELECTION	PHASE/ POLARITY/ BLEED ISSUES	BALANCE	VOLUME
PERFORMANCES	TIMING	FREQUENCIES	FREQUENCIES
ENVIRONMENTS/ ROOMS	COMPING/ TUNING	DYNAMICS/ SATURATION	DYNAMICS/ SATURATION
RECORDING SIGNALS	CUTS/ FADES/ UNWANTED NOISE	SPACE/ FX	LOUDNESS

Principles of Recording

Principles of recording are when you take a sound source and record it for your arrangement. Ideally, you get the recording principles correct from the source. That is because the choices you make here will feed into all further parts of the chain. If you make the right recording choices, you won't have to edit, mix, or master as much.

- **Principle One: Sound Selection.** The sound selection is what sounds you choose to play the parts in your arrangement. Sound selection is every sample, instrument, and performance you choose for your arrangement. This is one of the most important principles as all other principles follow this one. Your musical taste can influence these choices.

- **Principle Two: Performances.** This principle is who you get to perform the sound selection choice, and how it is performed. As producer you can guide the creative vision for the performers (instrumentalists and vocalists) and the parts they play. You can also perform the instrument(s) as well as choose and create samples yourself. It is your responsibility to guide and capture the best performances for your vision and standard.

- **Principle Three: Environments/ Rooms.** This principle is where you get the performance to take place in. If you are using pre-made samples these were already recorded in an environment. If you are recording people, you need to decide what rooms to record in. If you are recording virtual instruments this happens inside the computer.

- **Principle Four: Recording Signals.** This is how you record the performance in the environment with tools. This includes the mics, mic position, mic chain, virtual instruments, and direct inserts. As you record the performances, you must know what microphones you are using. You must know what microphone positions will work best for your goal. You will also need to know the microphone chain you are using, including microphone choice and audio interface choice, as well as any additional choices, like pre-amps or compressors. You may even be recording into your computer using direct input instruments, e.g., guitar into the interface. Or you could be recording in your computer using virtual instruments. Or you could be using sample creation/placements.

Principles of Editing

Principles of editing are when you fix any problems with the recordings. These problems are the focus of the editing principles. Ideally you avoid most problems in your recording by getting it right from the source; then editing won't be as necessary. Sometimes the editing process brings awareness to problems; you then re-record the parts you need to. But if further editing is necessary, you will then use tools to fix the problems.

Here are the editing principles to focus on:

- **Principle One: Phase, Polarity, and Bleed Issues.** If these issues are built into the recording, you can use DAW tools and plugins to tame them if necessary.

- **Principle Two: Timing.** Fix any parts of the performance that are out of time, or not "in the pocket". You can fix them here with manual timing in the DAW or with timing plugins. You can also use manual timing to "humanize" samples.

- **Principle Three: Comping/Tuning.** If there are lines of a recording that aren't ideal, you can comp them into a better line using multiple takes. You can also tune any lines that need it using plugins. You can also use manual tuning to "humanize" samples.

- **Principle Four: Cuts, Fades, Unwanted Noises.** You can clean up the audio with cuts and fades. You can also clean up excessive noises with plugins like de-click or de-noise.

Principles of Mixing

Principles of mixing are when you take each stem and balance them with the other stems. You do this by routing the arrangement from individual stems, into groups, then into a final stereo mix. Along the way, you use the principles of balance, frequencies, dynamics/saturation, and FX to give the track synergy. You also honor the core principles of arranging by optimizing them.

- **Principle One: Balance.** This principle is where you make your arrangement sound balanced. It is where each instrument is positioned in the stereo field. You do this using the following: gain staging, volume, panning, and automation. This part includes routing and gain structure within the digital audio workstation.

- **Principle Two: Frequencies.** This principle is where you control the arrangement's frequency balance. You use EQ cuts and EQ boosts to achieve that. Frequency balance is like volume balance but on specific frequency bands.

- **Principle Three: Dynamics/Saturation.** This principle is where you make sure each instrument is balanced further with dynamic processing (if needed). You can also shape tone and rhythm using dynamic tools. You can also use saturation to model the analog world. Saturation is used to add pleasing harmonics and perceived loudness. This also includes tape emulation.

- **Principle Four: FX/Space.** This principle is where you place room reflections and depth onto your music. You do this by using FX processing like reverbs, delays, etc. This creates the space your arrangement sits in.

Part V: Sonics

Principles of Mastering

Principles of mastering are where you take the final stereo mix through to a completed master. You do this by moving through the principles of mastering. This process is more broad and requires subtle moves to polish the mix to completion.

- **Principle One: Volume.** Do you need to change the gain/volume before processing? Do you need to automate some of the sections up or down? This principle is where you do that.

- **Principle Two: Frequencies.** This principle is where you control the master's frequency balance. You use EQ cuts and EQ boosts to achieve that. Frequency balance is like volume balance but on specific frequency bands.

- **Principle Three: Dynamics/Saturation.** Fix any dynamic problems here. Apply further saturation for perceived loudness if necessary.

- **Principle Four: Loudness.** This principle is when you get that final push for industry loudness with your master. Usually, a limiter is used for this process.

With the different techniques you learn and tools you use, all roads lead back to these principles. These principles will guide you in analyzing sonics and as you record, edit, mix, and master your own music. Most tools and techniques you learn will be under the umbrella of these sonic principles.

STEPS TO INDUSTRY STANDARD SONICS OVERVIEW

The *steps to industry standard sonics* is the feedback loop you go through to master sonics.

We will cover all these in this section.

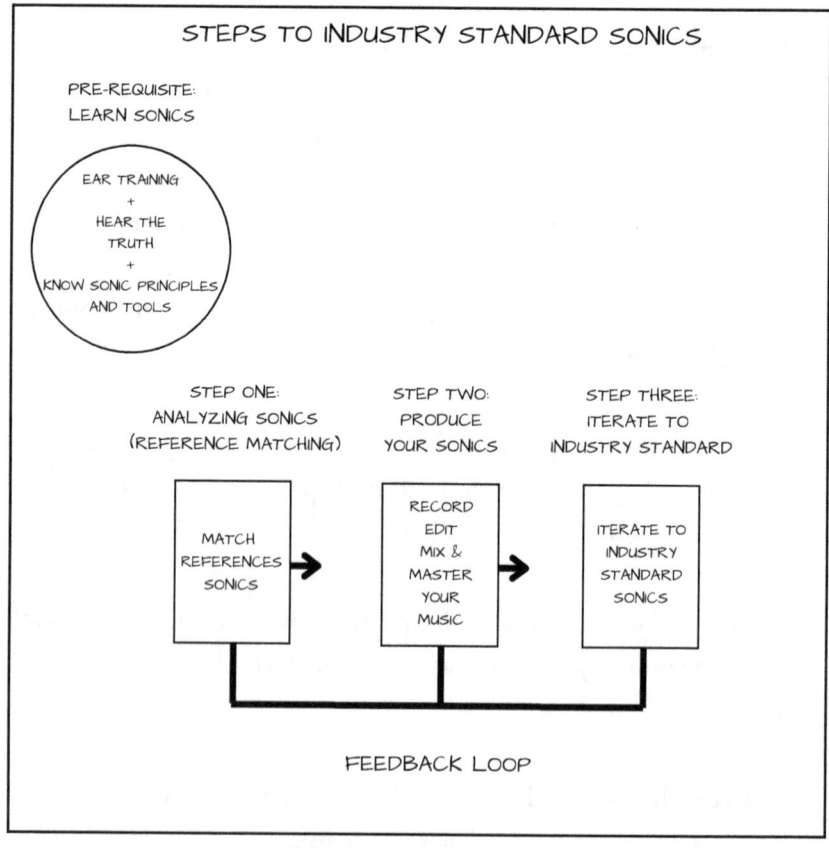

Part V: Sonics

Prerequisites: Ear Training, Hear the Truth, Know the Sonic Principles And Tools

PRE-REQUISITES

The prerequisites for this feedback loop to take place are:

- Ear training.
- Hear the truth – calibrate your headphones. Optional: Optimize and calibrate your room and speakers.
- It helps if you have a foundational understanding of the Sonic Principles.
- It also helps if you have a foundational understanding of your sonic tools. This includes tools like your digital audio workstation, as well as tools like gain, volume, panning, automation, EQ, compression, saturation, limiters, clippers, and FX.

Step One: Analyzing Sonics (Reference Matching)

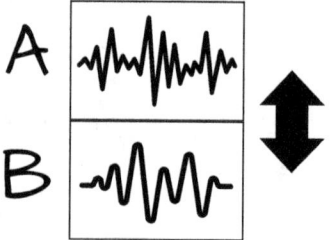

Reference matching is the sonics version of analysis. It is easiest to analyze sonics when you have contrast. So this is where you learn to "match" sonic principles through reference track analysis. With reference matching you are taking a track with industry standard sonics and comparing it with your own track. You will then use your ear training to find the sonic differences between your track and your reference track.

Using the core principles of sonics as a guide, you will go through each principle methodically to find the differences. With the data you find, you will then use tools to bridge the gap between your track's sonics and your reference track's sonics. Reference matching gives you the *why* you would use a tool to achieve something.

Step Two: Produce Your Sonics

Step Two is when you produce your sonics in your own track. This is where you bridge the gap between your own sonics and your reference's sonics. First you sonically matched your track to the reference track. You found the data. You will then discover the goals you need to reach, and the problems standing in your way to achieve those goals. This is where you use techniques and tools within the principles of sonics to fix the problems you face. Then you aim to achieve the goal of industry standard.

Step Three: Iterate to Industry Standard

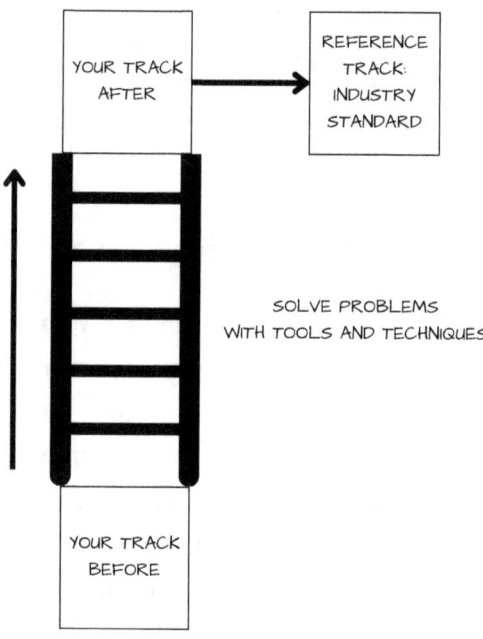

As you produce your sonics, you may sometimes hit a wall. This is common when you first start producing sonics. That is because you may still need to fill holes in your technique library. This is where resource mining and feedback will come in. You will fill the gaps in your knowledge through resource mining. You will also find mentors to listen to your track and tell you what they think is missing. You will then "learn what you don't know".

You will then iterate around this feedback loop of three steps until you reach industry standard. You will continue to go back to reference matching, producing, then feedback until you reach your goal. Solving every problem using tools and techniques along the way.

Note: The first time can take the longest. The first time I did this, it took me three months to get the track to industry standard. Each time around the cycle, I'd learn a new technique and way of fixing problems. These problems stood in the way of getting the track to industry standard. Soon, there were no more problems left. Soon there was nothing left to learn for that specific track. I reached industry standard. Now, I can take all that knowledge, and the next tracks become much faster to complete. Each time I go around this cycle with new music I become faster. Each time around the cycle I require less feedback from mentors, peers and clients.

Sometimes, it isn't a matter of being right; it is a matter of how little you can be not wrong.

REAL-LIFE EXAMPLE: "JUST LIKE ME" BY RACHELLE RHIENNE

I'll show you an example of the first track I mixed and mastered as a writer/producer. You'll see how I used this three-step process.

Prerequisites: Ear Training, Hear the Truth, Know the Sonic Principles And Tools – Example

I spent years resource-mining the best sonic techniques I could find. I used YouTube, books, programs, forums, and my own experience. I hadn't put these techniques into proper practice, and I had never aimed for industry standards with my own mix and master yet. I had achieved Golden Ears on SoundGym and could "hear the truth" on my DAW. This was my foundational knowledge.

Step One: Analyzing Sonics (Reference Matching) – Example

I found a reference at the sonic standard we wanted to match. It was

"Come Away with Me" by Norah Jones.

We A/B'd that master with our master. We had enough ear training to discover the differences in their track from ours.

Here is the data we found using the principles of sonics as a guide:

REFERENCE: NORAH JONES - COME AWAY WITH ME	
MIXING	Goal: Reference match lead vocal and overall quality and standard.
BALANCE	The lead vocal is quite up front and in your face. The use of panning allows for a lot of side information to take place out of the way of the vocal.
FREQUENCIES	The lead vocal has a prominence in the 2000kHz range that makes it feel forward. The production in general feels like it has a sparkle on the high end and a strong low end. Any other frequencies we can match that will work?
DYNAMICS/ SATURATION	The track is dynamic and not overly compressed. But remains very loud by industry standards. Can we match that loudness? How?
SPACE/ FX	Norah's lead vocal sounds like it has one prominent reverb on it, no delay. Or if it does have delay very little. Can we match a similar vibe?
MASTERING	Goal: Reference match frequencies and LOUDNESS
VOLUME	
FREQUENCIES	Can we match the frequencies here or is the arrangement too different?
DYNAMICS/ SATURATION	
LOUDNESS	Why is Norah Jones track so LOUD? What is making it do that? Is it the arrangement and the song, or is it the mixing and mastering?

Step Two: Produce Your Sonics – Example

I then mixed/ mastered my track to the best of my ability, using the skills I had at the time. With my co-mixing engineer, Marina Bennett, we took it to a certain level.

Step Three: Iterate to Industry Standard – Example

First, I used my technique library to solve the problems and match the reference standard. But when I found problems I couldn't solve, I turned to the Internet to ask questions. I then asked mentors as a last resort. I always thought critically and experimented. I didn't follow advice unless it worked for our vision.

I continued around this loop. Each time I cycled around this loop, I solved new problems with new solutions. My technique library grew while mixing and mastering.

It also revealed insights into the entire music production chain. I wouldn't have discovered these insights unless I had mixed and mastered the song. I found out there were flaws in the recording process of this track that required a large amount of editing and mixing time to fix. In hindsight, I would have gotten them re-recorded. However, I was already too far into the process to turn back. It is a blessing in disguise though. Because it was such a hard track to mix, I learned hundreds of techniques. I became a better Polymath Producer because of it. But what is good about this is that I won't make the same recording mistakes in the future. So by mixing and mastering my track, it gave me recording insights I wouldn't have learned otherwise.

Here are some of the results:

	MIX AND MASTER: RACHELLE RHIENNE - JUST LIKE ME	
MIXING	**Goal:** Reference match lead vocal and overall quality and standard	
BALANCE	We made the lead vocal louder simply by using the volume fader. We wanted to match how Norah Jones' vocal stood out. However we didn't want our lead vocal to feel separate from our track. So we found a healthy balance there. (Think for yourself)	
FREQUENCIES	Our lead vocal had a lot of high end from the microphones frequency response causing quite a lot of issues. But we found that the 2000kHz range was safe to boost 0.5dB in the mix. We frequency matched further frequencies at 800Hz, 3kHz, 5kHz, 8kHz, and 10kHz and above for the whole track. We aimed to get each instrument it's own space in the mix with cuts without over EQing.	
DYNAMICS/ SATURATION	We discovered that the use of saturation created more perceived loudness. We placed saturation on the instrument bus and the pre-master. We had to find the balance so we didn't risk over doing it.	
SPACE/ FX	We used the Capitol Chambers reverb to instil an 'old school' vibe onto the track. We matched a similar vibe to Norah Jones track, although made it more in line with ours once we found the balance.	
MASTERING	**Goal:** Reference match frequencies and LOUDNESS	
VOLUME	Rather than using a bunch of limiters on the track and running the risk of over processing, we moved the clip gain up from -8db peak to -0.5dB peak.	
FREQUENCIES	We used frequency boosts and cuts to match the overall vibe and quality of the Norah Jones track.	
DYNAMICS/ SATURATION	We used tape emulation and saturation to create perceived loudness without raising the gain. The balance was tough to find as we ran into distortion issues if pushed too hard. We eventually found a happy medium.	
LOUDNESS	Because we'd already made the track loud with clip gain, we then used a maximizer and a limiter to get it to industry standard loudness. I'd say hers is still 0.5dB louder. But that could be down to arrangement choices and song. We couldn't push it louder with a limiter or it would cause a squashed feel and distortion. So we went in favor of allowing the song to have dynamic flow.	

Standards Are Key

In that example, I would not stop until it was within range of industry-standard sonics. I refused to give up. Some say, "Do quantity, and the quality will come." But I knew that for every cause, there is an effect. If there was a problem in my mix and master, there was a cause for that problem. There must also be a solution to the problem. I refused to release something that was not at industry standard. I refused to give up until I could A/B my master with my reference master and hear little to no differences in sonic quality. Having that standard for yourself is key to reaching that standard.

I never lost sight of the standard. I pushed ahead, and although it was painful, I learned the lessons. Moving forward, I'll have these lessons for life. I decided these lessons needed to happen with this one track instead of many tracks. All you need is to get one track to industry standard sonics, and you'll know how to do it again. It only takes one.

Now you have a general overview of the steps to industry standard sonics. Let's discuss each step in more detail.

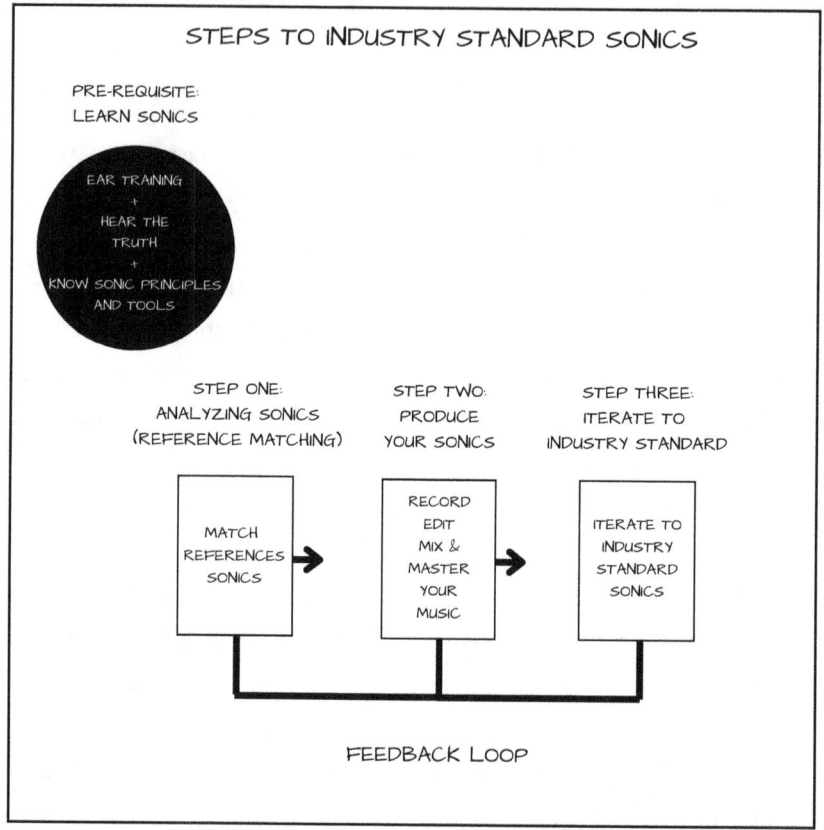

PREREQUISITES: EAR TRAINING, HEAR THE TRUTH, KNOW THE SONIC PRINCIPLES AND TOOLS

If you haven't done ear training and learned your DAW, sonic principles and tools at a basic level, do that before moving on. This section won't make sense to you unless you have covered the prerequisites. The good thing is that most YouTube videos, books, manuals, and programs focus primarily on these subjects. So it should be straight forward to learn them. Go through them using the same resource mining technique framework from Part II of this book. Most online information is about using tools to fix sonic problems.

If you would like my own recommendations of where to learn these foundational tools head to www.polymathproducer.com/resources.

Use the Core Principles of Sonics as a guide of the areas to focus on. Learn the fundamental techniques within them.

PRINCIPLES OF RECORDING, EDITING, MIXING & MASTERING

RECORDING	EDITING	MIXING	MASTERING
SOUND SELECTION	PHASE/ POLARITY/ BLEED ISSUES	BALANCE	VOLUME
PERFORMANCES	TIMING	FREQUENCIES	FREQUENCIES
ENVIRONMENTS/ ROOMS	COMPING/ TUNING	DYNAMICS/ SATURATION	DYNAMICS/ SATURATION
RECORDING SIGNALS	CUTS/ FADES/ UNWANTED NOISE	SPACE/ FX	LOUDNESS

Common Sonics Tools List

Use this sonics tools list to know where to focus your attention on.

DAW: Know your digital audio workstation of choice.

Recording Tools:
- Sound selection: Samples, instruments, voices, and loops.
- Performances: People or samples performing.
- Environments/rooms: Rooms, room emulations, computer.
- Recording Signals: Different mics. You can use different mic positions. You've got mic chains like interfaces, preamps, and compressors. Computer virtual instruments. Direct input instruments.

Editing Tools:
- Phase, polarity, and bleed issues: Phase plugins, noise gates.
- Timing: Manual timing in the DAW, timing software.
- Comping/Tuning: Comping, pitch correction software, auto-tune.
- Cuts, fades, and unwanted noise: DAW cut and fade tools, de-noise plugins.

Mixing Tools:
- Balance: Routing, gain staging, volume faders, pan knobs, automation.
- Frequencies: EQ and saturation.
- Dynamics/Saturation: Compression, limiting, clipping, saturation, tape.
- Space/FX: Reverbs, delays, modulation, stereo imagers.

Mastering Tools:
- Volume: Gain staging, volume, and automation.
- Frequencies: EQ and saturation.
- Dynamics/Saturation: Compression, limiting, clipping, saturation, tape.
- Loudness: Limiting, saturation, clipping.

Fastest Way to Learn These Tools

If you struggle to learn the tools, first learn what each knob and button, in general, does on the tool and why.

For example, every compressor has some version of: threshold, makeup gain, attack, release, and ratio. Some have fewer features, some more, but the fundamentals apply.

Then, read the manual for the tool you are using. It is the fastest way to learn new tools. Then, experiment with the tool to hear how each control affects the music. Soon you'll find that you can use most new tools easily. This is because their fundamentals overlap. The learning curve compounds. Keep it simple. Reading manuals sounds boring, but it is the fastest way to start using tools with clarity.

Note: Most advanced processing will be a variation on one of the tools mentioned. For example, dynamic EQ is a regular EQ with a slightly different function. Dynamic EQ and regular EQ both take place within the frequency principle.

As you use the tools during reference matching, your understanding of tools will become refined.

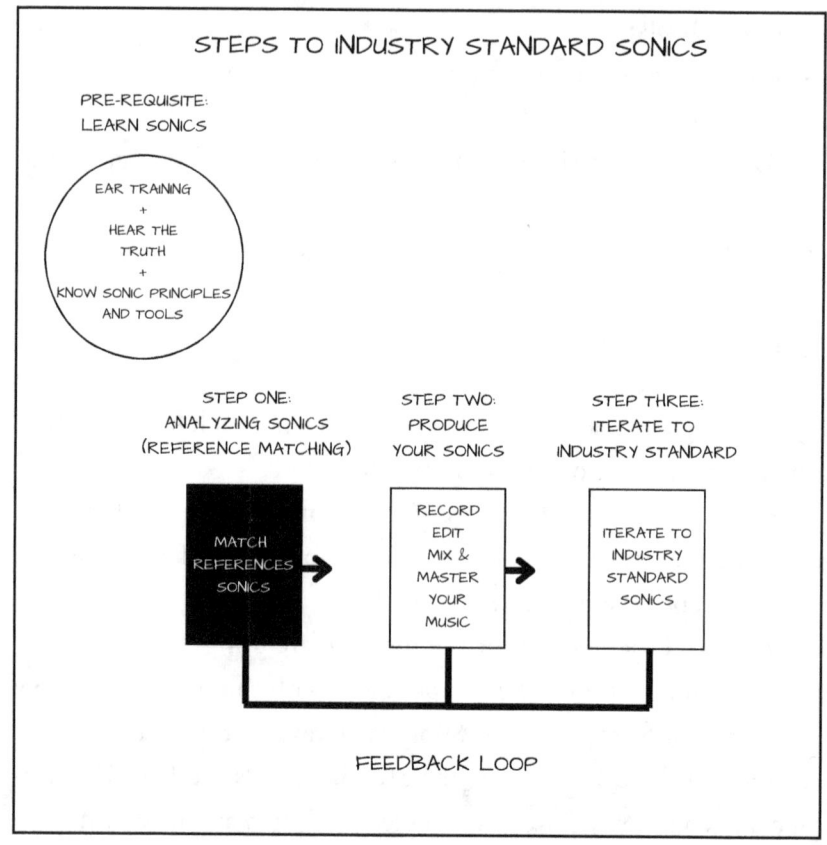

STEP ONE: ANALYZING SONICS (REFERENCE MATCHING)

Reference matching is when you choose an industry standard track with the sonics you want to match. You then place it on your DAW and find the differences in sonics between your track and theirs.

As mentioned earlier, when you learn a new language, the pronunciation of vowels and consonants are the first thing you learn. The vowels and consonants of sonics are the Core Principles of Sonics.

So when you match your reference track you are matching what you hear within the sonic principles. This becomes the analysis we use in the sonics section. Because sonic techniques are more "invisible" than arrangement techniques, sonics analysis is best learned through comparison and contrast. That is why we use reference matching to learn and master sonics.

Here is how it works:

SCIENTIFIC METHOD OF REFERENCE MATCHING

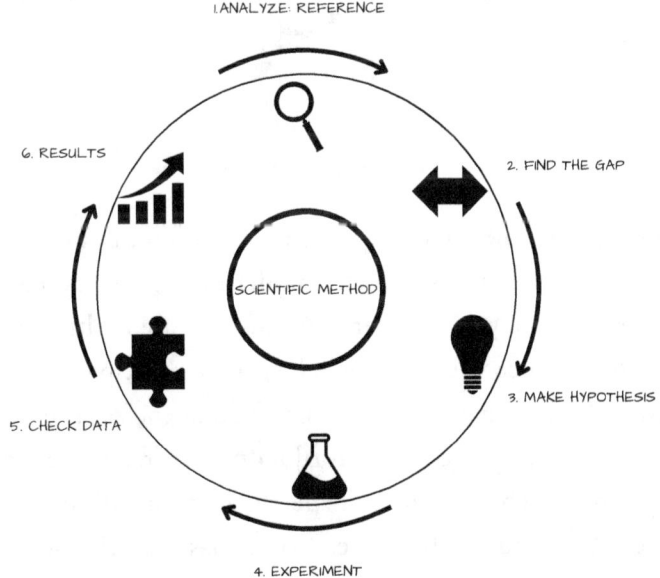

1. Analyze the reference
2. Find the sonic gaps between your track and the reference
3. Make a hypothesis – decide what techniques could bridge the gap
4. Experiment – produce your sonics
5. Check the data on your produced sonics
6. Results, feedback loop and iteration

Number One: Analyze the Reference

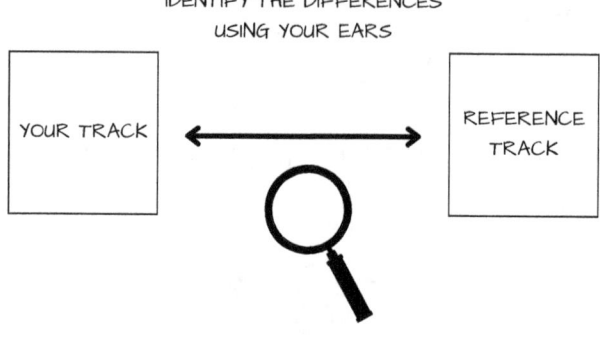

- First choose the reference track that you want to match sonically. The reference works best at a modern-day industry standard but suits the style you are after. You can also use multiple references. Each reference will be to match specific principles. For example, one reference may be best to match frequencies. The other reference may be best to match for loudness. A reference may also be used to match the sonics of specific instruments and techniques used. For example, how a lead vocal has used the principles and techniques of sonics.

- Place your own track onto the DAW. Then place the reference track onto your DAW.

- Analyze the tracks by A/Bing the tracks on solo and mute until you find the differences.

- As you do this, work through each principle to find the differences. The techniques they have used to make their track industry standard will become clear.

- You can use your DAW, but there are also plugins available that help with A/Bing like *Metric AB*.

Number Two: Find the Sonic Gaps Between Your Track and the Reference

ARE THERE ANY DIFFERENCES IN THE FOLLOWING PRINCIPLES BETWEEN YOUR TRACK AND YOUR REFERENCE TRACK?

RECORDING	EDITING	MIXING	MASTERING
SOUND SELECTION	PHASE/ POLARITY/ BLEED ISSUES	BALANCE	VOLUME
PERFORMANCES	TIMING	FREQUENCIES	FREQUENCIES
ENVIRONMENTS/ ROOMS	COMPING/ TUNING	DYNAMICS/ SATURATION	DYNAMICS/ SATURATION
RECORDING SIGNALS	CUTS/ FADES/ UNWANTED NOISE	SPACE/ FX	LOUDNESS

LOOK AT THE BIG PICTURE, THEN FOCUS ON ONE PRINCIPLE & ONE INSTRUMENT OR TRACK AT A TIME

- Find sonic gaps in standard. Do this by comparing the Core Principles of Sonics of your track compared to your reference track. Use A/Bing to achieve this.

- Focus on one principle at a time and find the difference. Are there any differences in the principles between your track and your reference? Look at the big picture, then focus on one principle and one instrument at a time. Use the principles of sonics to know where to focus your attention. For example, if you focus on the principle of frequencies in mastering, maybe your reference track has highs above 10kHz boosted by 1dB+ more than your track. You can now test on your track using an EQ on the mix bus or master and boost an EQ shelf by 1dB+. Then maybe your reference track has their 150Hz 2dB- less than your track. Maybe the 150Hz range for your track sounds muddy compared to theirs. You can test on your track with an EQ cut in that range.

- Use Stems Thinking to notice how all the sonics within the tracks and groups work together.

Number Three: Make a Hypothesis — Decide What Techniques Could Bridge the Gap

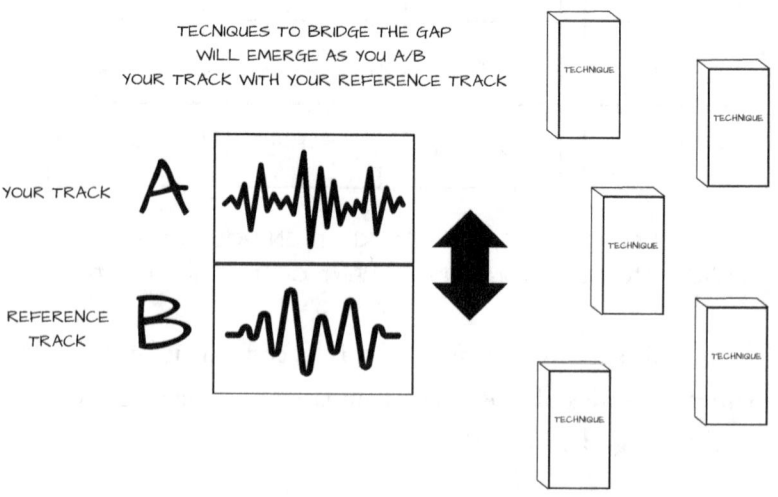

A hypothesis is an assumption of what you believe to be correct before testing. So in this part you are making assumptions of what techniques will bridge the gap in sonic standard based on the information you find.

What is the difference between your track and the reference track? What would the best techniques be to bridge that gap in standard? Make your educated decision in your mind.

As you are A/Bing your track to your reference track, techniques to bridge any gaps will flow into your mind. You will have a bunch of potential techniques that could work. There could be multiple different techniques to bridge the gap. Choose the techniques you believe will work best. Then experiment through the list until you find the correct answer.

Number Four: Experiment – Produce Your Sonics

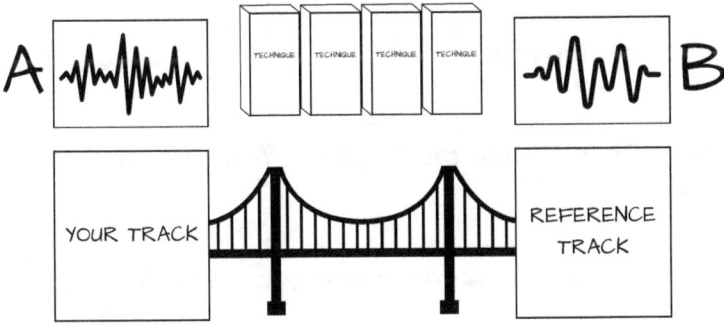

Now that you have a collection of techniques you can use, it is time to experiment. Use your technique library to bridge the gap and match your reference if necessary.

Say your reference had a superior EQ curve. You would match your track to their EQ curve if necessary. You'll then find the techniques needed to bridge the gap between your track and your reference track. You will then learn *why* there was a difference in standard.

To do this, you will do the following:

- Use the techniques in your technique library to bridge the gap. You may already know the answer to match it. For example, if there is a 2kHz boost in the lead vocal making it more present in your reference, that could be as simple as a 0.5 dB EQ boost in the lead vocal in your track to match it.

- Use the sonic principles to guide where to find gaps and techniques.

- If you can't figure out why there is a gap. Or you can't figure out the technique to bridge the gap. Find the answer from resource mining and ask the specific question. (Examples: books, programs, the Internet, etc.)

- Iterate until you find the answer.

Number Five: Check the Data on Your Produced Sonics

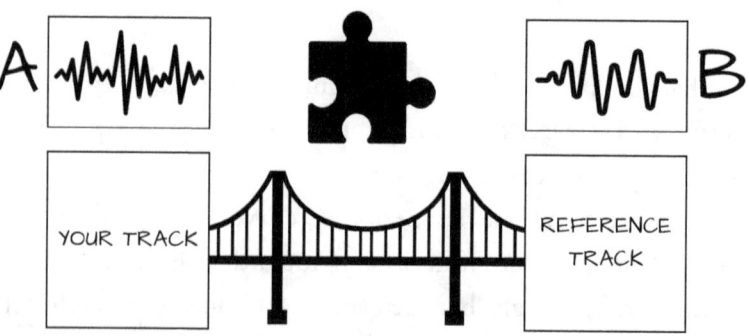

You have now used techniques you think will bridge the gap in sonic standard. A/B your track with your reference track again. Did you find the missing puzzle piece to the gap or not? You may have found the answer if your track matches the same sonic standard as your reference. If your track still doesn't match the sonic standard of your reference, you may still be missing something.

Number Six: Results, Feedback Loop and Iteration

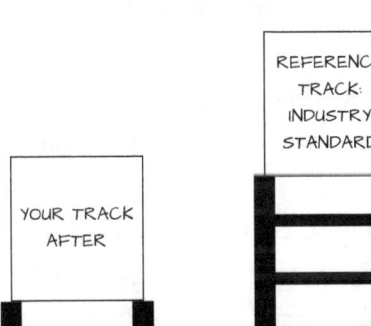

- If you found the answer, ask, *Why?* If your track sounds better because of it, leave it there. You will then understand the technique and be able to use it in future.

- If not, iterate. *Why did they have that difference compared to you? What were they doing that you weren't?* Then, return to the start and reference match again with new data. If you still can't find the answer, turn to resource mining to ask online, in programs and books, etc.

- If you can't find the answer after all that, getting a mentor can be a fast track. They can sometimes see things you can't. For example, I once struggled to get a track I mixed to be industry standard loudness. I could not figure out why I couldn't get there. I then got mentors to tell me their thoughts. I then cross-referenced all their feedback and discovered the answer. I recommend using three-to-five mentors for feedback, as sometimes mentors can be wrong. (See Part VI on Feedback.) Then repeat this process with the new technique(s) to see if you can match the reference.

You continue to repeat these steps until you reach industry standard. It is a feedback loop. Keep iterating until your track matches the same standard (or higher standard) as your reference track.

Sometimes you'll learn techniques from producers that don't work for your track. There are so many "rules" that float around. But sometimes these rules don't work for your track. That is where your own experience of life will come in. As you learn what works and what doesn't, the truth will be revealed. Sometimes you experiment and techniques work to bridge the gap because they just feel right. As long as you match industry standard and achieve your vision, it doesn't matter how you get there.

Document Techniques Into Your Technique Library

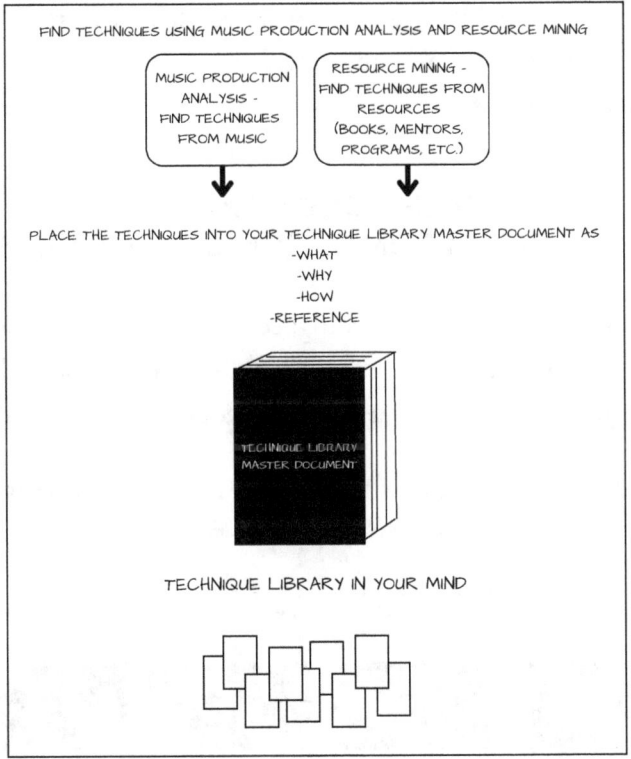

Once you have matched the difference and found techniques to match industry standards:

Write down the techniques – *what, why, how,* and *reference.*

You can match your track with the reference, but you need to discover *why* you are doing what you are doing. You will always have to reference match if you don't do this last action. This final action will solidify your sonic framework and move you toward mastery. The goal is to get to the point where you can learn *why* the top professionals do what they do. You can then transcend all this and make your sonics moves based primarily on feeling and intuition.

The principles will remain the same. The way those principles are used – the techniques – change depending on the track you analyze. After reference matching, you get a sense of where to start from – you then think for yourself. You innovate from there. You always only do things that make sense for your track.

TECHNIQUE LIBRARY: DOCUMENTATION OF SONIC TECHNIQUES

Focus on the principles of recording, editing, mixing, and mastering: then find techniques within them. Then, document the technique's *what*, *why*, *how*, and *reference* and build your sonic framework.

ANALYZE THE PRINCIPLES WITHIN MUSIC & RESOURCES TO FIND TECHNIQUES

CREATE THE WHAT, WHY, HOW & REFERENCE OF THE TECHNIQUE
BUILD YOUR SONIC FRAMEWORK

RECORDING	EDITING	MIXING	MASTERING
SOUND SELECTION	PHASE/ POLARITY/ BLEED ISSUES	BALANCE	VOLUME
PERFORMANCES	TIMING	FREQUENCIES	FREQUENCIES
ENVIRONMENTS/ ROOMS	COMPING/ TUNING	DYNAMICS/ SATURATION	DYNAMICS/ SATURATION
RECORDING SIGNALS	CUTS/ FADES/ UNWANTED NOISE	SPACE/ FX	LOUDNESS

Say you focus on mixing and want to learn how people use the Principle of Balance to create a proper mix. Look for volume, gain staging, automation, and panning tools and techniques.

Then, say you want to learn about frequencies in mastering. Look at frequencies in mastering; discover how engineers use EQs. You're looking at the reason why they use certain frequencies. *Why do they boost in specific frequencies? Why do they cut in certain frequencies?*

There will also be overlap. For example, songwriting, arranging, recording, mixing, and mastering can all impact frequencies. This focus will give you a holistic understanding of the entire production chain.

Document Sonic Techniques From Music Production Analysis

First, you will analyze sonic techniques during your reference matching.

- You will analyze the music through the lenses of Techniques, Sonic Principles, and Stems Thinking.

- You'll be analyzing one instrument/ track and one technique at a time.

- For each technique, write down the *what*, the *why*, the *how*, and the *reference*. Same as before.

- While listening, use the principles of recording, editing, mixing, and mastering. Finding techniques within these principles will make everything easier.

Find sonics analysis techniques and place them into your Technique Library as follows:

Music Production Analysis Sonic Technique Example

Principle Category: Mixing – Frequency Principle.

Name: Vocal Presence Technique.

What: When you boost the EQ of the lead vocal at around 2kHz, it helps the lead vocal push to the front of the mix.

Why: I noticed this technique used in "Come Away with Me" by Norah Jones. The 2kHz range is around the range where humans have the most sensitivity to volume. Making sure the lead vocal sits at 2kHz out in front will ensure the audience focuses on it the most.

How: If the vocal is already sitting right at 2kHz, all you need to do is move the volume fader up or down to make it sit right. If it isn't, you can try an EQ boost around 2kHz using the EQ of your choice. You can also try an EQ cut on the low end of the vocal. It may not work for every song. You can also EQ cut the instrumental around that position, but it may badly affect the instrumental. Use dynamic EQ on the instrumental instead. Or use intelligent EQ on the instrumental side-chained to the lead vocal for a more subtle effect. You can also use parallel saturation on the vocal around that frequency range too.

Reference: "Come Away with Me" by Norah Jones.

Document Sonic Techniques From Resource Mining

For every technique you find in reference matching (analysis), you can find the resource mining technique that gives you the "how to" achieve that using tools. Find resource mining sonics techniques and place them into your technique library as follows:

Resource Mining Sonic Technique Example

> **Principle Category:** Mixing – Dynamics/Saturation Principle.
>
> **Name:** Parallel saturation technique.
>
> **What:** Use parallel saturation to make your track louder without overdoing it.
>
> **Why:** To create perceived loudness. The secret sauce of a lot of mixing to make music louder. Models an analog workflow in digital.
>
> **How:** Create an aux track with a saturation plugin and dial it in. Or use the "mix" knob within the saturation plugin to make it less than one hundred per cent wet. You can use it on either one or more of the following: individual tracks, group buses, the mix bus, and/or the master. Using them in succession throughout routing can sometimes give you the best results.
>
> **Reference:** Josh Gudwin[17] & Jaycen Joshua[18] – "Mix with the Masters" videos.

REFERENCE MATCHING FOR EACH PART OF THE PRODUCTION CHAIN

For every technique you find through your reference matching; there are usually resource mining techniques that give you the "how to".

Reference Matching for Recording and Editing

While reference matching for recording and editing, you can sometimes find the best insights by using Stems Thinking. That is because you can isolate individual instruments and hear details on how they were recorded. You can listen through each individual stem and work through each principle of recording and editing. You can uncover extreme detail into each instrument's use of principles including:

- Sound selection
- Performances
- Environments/rooms
- Recording signals
- Editing

You can also find your best insights for recording and editing through resource mining. That is because there are techniques on mic positions, equipment setups, editing practices, DAW techniques – all of these can be found with resource mining. This will fill in any technical gaps from what you find in reference matching.

Reference Matching for Mixing and Mastering

When reference matching for mixing and mastering, you can find insights by using stems thinking for individual instruments. But, you can usually find the best insights by using the pro mixing and mastering workflow, which we will cover soon in Step Two of the steps to industry standard sonics. You then use resource mining to find the "how to" equivalent techniques.

SONICS VIA STEMS THINKING

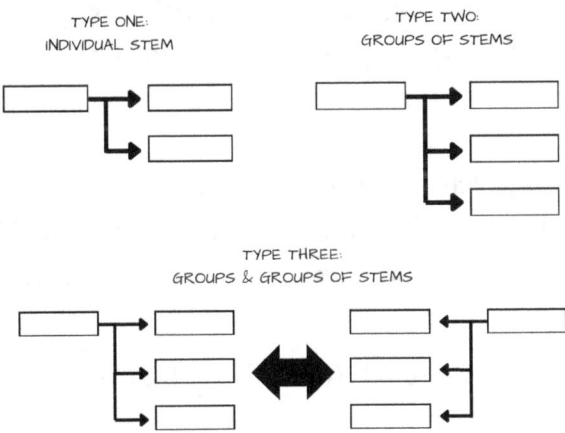

Mixed stems are a great place to analyze sonics for techniques and as references. You can hear the final processed tracks in their individual form. You can solo those tracks and listen to them. You can also compare stems on an individual layer, group layer, and groups of groups layer. For example, I used a Camila Cabello vocal stem, then A/Bed my vocal stem with hers. I could then discover the differences in EQ curves.

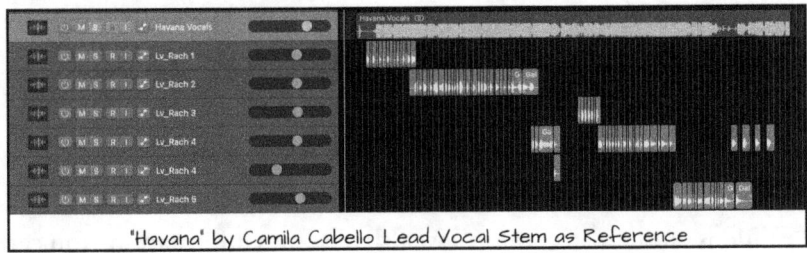

"Havana" by Camila Cabello Lead Vocal Stem as Reference

Stems thinking with sonics is the same process as we covered in Part IV of this book. This time, you're looking at it from a sonics lens. Use stems thinking as follows for sonics knowledge:

- **Type one:** Analyze sonics within individual stems.
- **Type two:** Analyze groups of stems. How do the sonics of each stem within the group interact with the sonics of the other stems in the group?
- **Type three:** Analyze groups of stems with other groups of stems. How do the sonics of a group of stems, interact with the sonics of another group of stems?

If you can't get the stems of a track, that is okay; a stereo master reference will have all the information you need. You should be able to get the same level of results from using just a stereo master reference.

VISUAL ANALYSIS OF SONICS

You can use tools in your DAW to show visuals of what you're hearing.

Look at the waveforms of tracks and stems. What do the peaks and transients look like? For example, what does a compressed versus uncompressed sound look like? What does comparing their processed track to your unprocessed track look like? What's the difference? When you process your track, does it look similar? Look at an EQ that shows visuals of the frequencies you are hearing. What are they doing? Where are they peaking? What do your loudness levels look like compared to your reference?

You shouldn't always follow these types of visual representations. You should always follow your ears. But it can sometimes give you clues of where to look for problems.

Videos online also contain a wealth of sonics information. You can see the stems of tracks from top producers that way. You can also look at visual representations when looking at "in the studio" videos. These videos can be gold mines for resource mining sonics techniques.

Important: Remember to always use your ears first.

SONIC PROBLEMS ALONG THE PRODUCTION CHAIN

Sometimes the problem in your sonics could be solved at any part of the production chain. It will be up to you to decide which part you want to focus on to fix the problem.

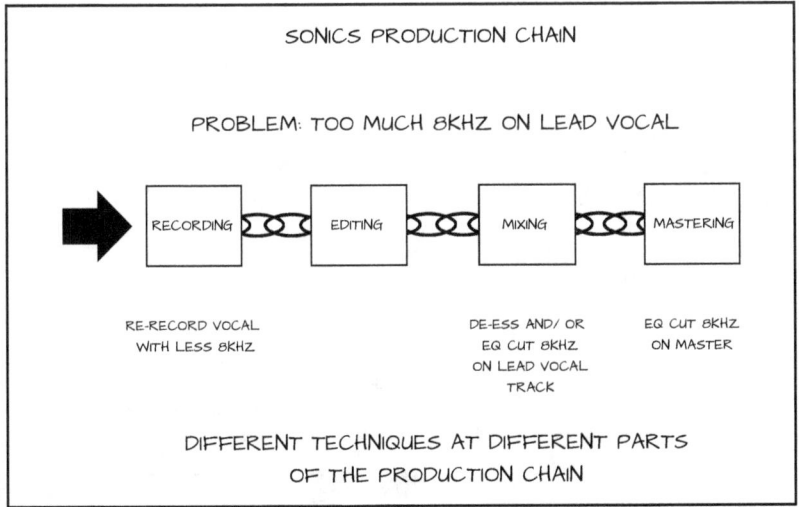

For example, if you find that your lead vocal has too much 8kHz you could solve that problem at any part of the chain:

- In recording, you could re-record it with a different mic or mic chain, making sure that the 8kHz frequency range isn't as harsh.
- In mixing, you could use a de-esser, or EQ dips on the 8kHz range.
- In mastering, you could use an EQ dip at the 8kHz range.

Keep in mind: As you move further to the end of the production chain you will have less control over the result. That is why I keep saying to get recording right from the source.

For example, if you EQ dip at 8kHz in the master, it will not only affect the vocal, but the entire arrangement. That is less control than if you EQ dip 8kHz on the lead vocal in the mix. But there are tradeoffs for every part of the chain. If you get the vocal re-recorded, you may lose the "magic" of the original performance. These decisions will be up to you, and you will learn these lessons over time.

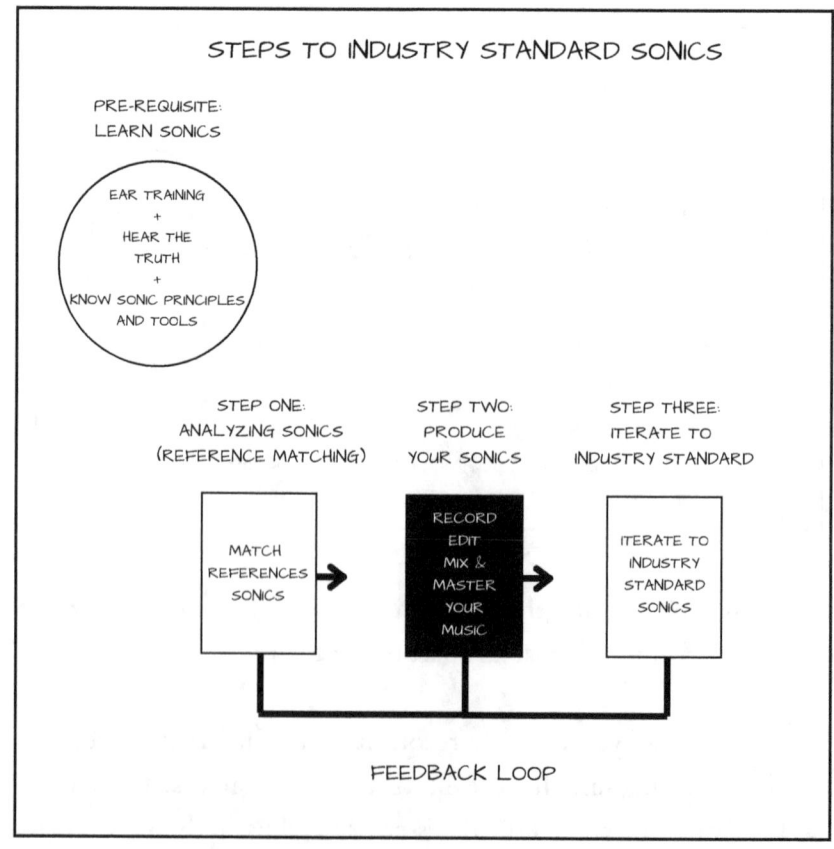

Part V: Sonics

STEP TWO: PRODUCE YOUR SONICS

Now that you have gone through the reference matching process, you will know the goals to match the reference. You will also be aware of the problems stopping you from reaching those goals. You will need tools to bridge the gap. In this part you will produce your sonics to industry standard.

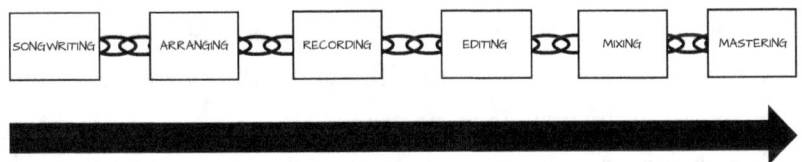

The top producers in the world complete each section of this production chain to the absolute best of their ability. This conscious approach lessens the workload of the section that comes after it.

- If you write the best song, the arrangement is easier to create.
- If you make the best arrangement, mixing and mastering is easier.
- If you record to the best of your ability, there will be less editing work.
- If you record and edit to the best of your ability, there will be less mixing work.
- If you mix to the best of your ability, there will be less mastering work.

A clear example is "Leave the Door Open" by Silk Sonic. When the mastering engineer Randy Merrill worked on it, he did the following:

- A little cut in the mid-range using mid-side EQ.
- A little boost at the very top using EQ.
- Used a limiter to catch the overs.

That was it. Randy said it is a well-recorded track and mix, so he didn't need to do much. This example proves the power of having each part of the chain to industry standard.[19]

HOW THE SONG AND ARRANGEMENT IMPACT THE SONICS

1. The song impacts the sonics of the arrangement because of the key of the song. The key impacts where the melody is sung and what harmony the arrangement uses. This influences where the arrangement sits in the frequency spectrum.
2. The arrangement choices are influenced then by how you use Techniques, the Core Principles of Arranging, and Stems Thinking.

Both the song and the arrangement then impact the sonics on a global macro level. These choices are the roots of everything.

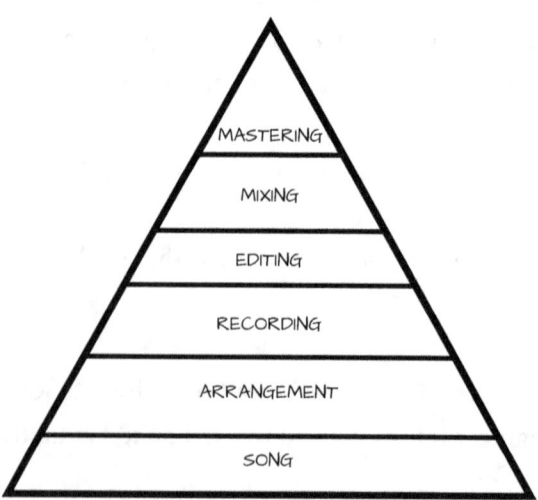

I recommend that when you create your song and arrangement, you stick to the Technique, Principles of Arranging, and Stems thinking frameworks from Parts II, III , IV, VI and VII. You create without necessarily worrying about sonics, but keep it in the back of your mind. You create based on how we mentioned in the other parts. This is because then you will have no creative limits.

Sometimes you may find a few flaws in your arrangements after you mix or master. Maybe you forget a piece of low-end material. Or maybe you don't put enough side information into the arrangement. That is okay, fix them, then remember those lessons and move on. Soon you will become so good at the entire production chain, that you will make fewer mistakes in each part of the chain.

LEARNING RECORDING AND EDITING

Learning recording and editing happens in four different ways:

1. You learn by resource mining; learning from programs, books, and mentors.
2. You then learn by experimenting with what you learn on your own recordings.
3. You can learn by reference matching your stem files to industry standard stem files using Stems Thinking.
4. You then learn by mixing and mastering, which then reveals any flaws in your approach to recording and editing.

As you loop around the production chain you will discover that all areas of the production chain will improve.

As I mentioned before, it is usually best to get the recording right at the source. This will help all stages in the production chain that evolve from it.

Sound selection is what makes the arrangement sound more unique. Sound selection is what makes the mix easier to do. The best recording engineers in the world, have the mix in mind as they record instruments. They also record well to minimize editing time.

For example legendary engineers like Al Schmidt can position a mic in the right way to accentuate the right EQ curves.

THE PRO MIXING AND MASTERING WORKFLOW

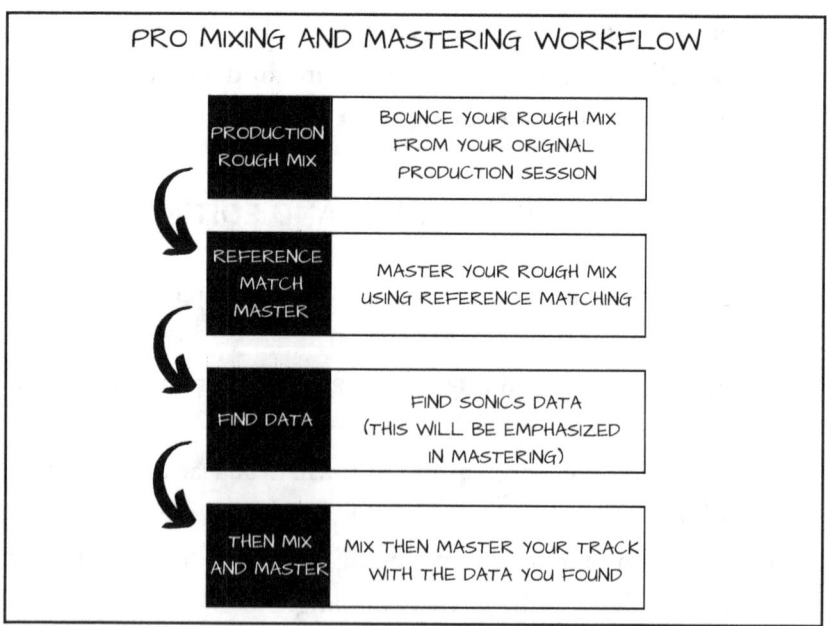

While analyzing the great mixing engineers of all time, I noticed a simple system they use. This system gets them superior results and speeds up their workflow. It utilizes the scientific method practically. It is reference matching in a way that reveals all the data you'd need to bridge the gap to industry standard. You do this by mastering your rough mix, which then reveals any flaws in the production chain. All flaws in the arrangement, recording, editing, and mixing will be revealed when you do this.

I call it the *Pro Mixing and Mastering Workflow.*

Clients in the Polymath Producer community whom I have shown this to tell me it was the missing link that allowed them to finally "get" to industry standard sonics.

Here are the steps to the Pro Mixing and Mastering Worfklow:

Step One: Bounce your rough mix from your original production session.

Step Two: Place your rough mix into the DAW of a mastering session.

Step Three: Select a reference master and place it into your DAW on a separate track underneath your rough mix on the same mastering session.

Step Four: Master your rough mix and aim to match the sonic principles with your reference master. Match volume, frequencies, dynamics/saturation, and loudness levels. Consistently A/B your master with the reference master as you do this. Do whatever is needed to match your reference master in sonic standard using the mastering principles.

Step Five: Note all the flaws with your rough mix compared to the reference by A/Bing. Because mastering uses subtle moves, all the flaws will be obvious. For example, if you have to boost 6dB+ at 150Hz, you'll know there is a mixing flaw.

Step Six: After you have exposed all the flaws in your rough master, you'll know exactly how to fix your mix. Go into your mix session and apply the changes. All the information you found in your rough master, will tell you what needs to be done in the mix. Use the techniques you've found through the principles of sonics to bridge the gap. Move through each principle in succession. Can you bridge the gap with balance? Can you bridge the gap with frequencies? Can you bridge the gap with dynamics/saturation? Can you bridge the gap with FX?

- Mix Bus – use the data you found from the rough master you did. "Master" your mix using the mix bus. Take off the limiters you use before you bounce the mix for mastering if necessary. Use the principles of mixing and mastering as a guide.

- Group Buses – This is where you can do more of the medium shifts that were needed from your rough master data. Use the core principles of mixing as a guide.

- Individual tracks – This is where you can make more of the big changes that were needed from your rough master data. Use the core principles of mixing as a guide.

Step Seven: Match your reference in the mix session until it essentially sounds "mastered" in your mix. The top mixing engineers' mixes barely need mastering because they apply this process.

Bonus: The alternative version is doing this in your mix session on the mix bus to start, using a reference in the session. Match the reference in the mix bus to expose what needs to be shifted in your mix. You will then know what to do on a mix bus, group bus, and individual track level. Then either leave the plugins on, or mute them and make your changes on an individual and group bus level.

I saw pro mixing engineer Shawn Everitt use this exact approach on the track "Slow Burn" by Kacey Musgraves.[20]

By doing this process you are analyzing, producing, and matching all at the same time.

Step Eight: Master your final mix in the mastering session. Repeat steps 1-8 until you reach industry standard.

REAL-LIFE EXAMPLE: MIXING AND MASTERING "LATE TO THE PARTY" BY RACHELLE RHIENNE

Here is a real life example of this process. As mentioned earlier, the first mix and master I did was "Just Like Me" by Rachelle Rhienne. The next track that I mixed and mastered was "Late to the Party" by Rachelle Rhienne. I wanted to test to see if I could match the reference we had without getting external mentor feedback. I wanted to do this one all on my own using the steps to industry standard sonics. I also utilized the pro mixing and mastering workflow.

Prerequisites: Ear Training, Hear the Truth, Know the Sonic Principles and Tools – Example
I had all the knowledge and techniques I'd learned from mixing and mastering "Just Like Me". Coming out of that mix I was feeling confident. I also had my backlog of techniques from analysis and resource mining.

Industry Standard: Step One – Analyzing Sonics (Reference Matching) – Example
I co-wrote and co-produced this song with Marina Bennett and Rachelle Rhienne. I already created a rough mix from the original "Late to the Party" production sessions. It was only balanced in volume and panning at this point. I found a reference at the sonic standard I wanted to match. It was "Havana" by Camila Cabello.

I then took our track through the scientific method.

1. Reference: "Havana" by Camila Cabello. I placed my rough mix and the reference master onto a DAW mastering session.

2. Find the gap: I used the pro mixing and mastering workflow to find the gaps. I A/B'ed the "Havana" master with the "Late to the Party" rough mix.

3. Make a hypothesis: Techniques started to form in my brain automatically. I had many techniques I could trial to match my rough mix with the reference masters sonics.

Industry Standard: Step Two – Produce Your Sonics – Example

4. Experiment: I then mastered my rough mix to match my reference. As I did this, I found all the data I needed. I had to use pretty drastic

EQ moves to match the reference. This told me where to make changes in the mix.

5. Check Data: I then moved the data I'd found into my mix session. I used the data to make my mix match the sonic standard of my reference. To do this I moved through the mixing principles. I used balance first (most important). Then frequencies. Then dynamics/saturation. Then space/FX. I started with the simplest solution first (balance), then moved to other solutions if needed.

6. Results: I then got closer to matching the reference master with my mix and master.

Industry Standard: Step Three – Iterate to Industry Standard – Example
I continued around the loop until I reached industry standard. I used my technique library to solve the problems and match the reference standard. I did this repeatedly. I would mix the song. Master it. See where the gaps were. Then mix it again. Then master it again. Eventually I got to the finish line.

When I reached the finish line, I had a few of my mastering mentors/peers check the master to let me know their opinions. (See Part VI on Feedback to know why I had multiple people check my master.)

Marina Bennett assisted me in the final mixing and mastering decisions. After a few more finishing touches it was ready to go.

Vision
"Havana" is such a different song and arrangement that I wasn't trying to match it completely in sonics. Remember, the song and arrangement also impact sonics. I was trying to get into a similar sonic identity, and then do my own thing. That is because our song has its own unique message and vibe. I mainly wanted to match this reference's EQ curves

and loudness. So each move I made added perceived loudness to the track. But I wanted to keep our laid-back vibe and vision. So, remember that although you can use reference matching to get to industry standard, know when you can move past the reference to achieve your vision.

EXPOSING THE PROBLEMS IN YOUR PRODUCTION CHAIN

Using the pro mixing and mastering workflow will reveal any "flaws" in your arrangement, recording, editing, and mixing. This is the benefit of knowing the entire production chain.

Example: While you mix and master your music to industry standard, you may realize that the lead vocal you recorded has too much 3kHz or 8kHz. Then these 3kHz and 8kHz frequencies cause a lot of issues in mixing and mastering. You will then know that when you record that vocalist in the future, focusing on the principles of recording will help to lessen that effect. This will then lessen your editing, mixing, and mastering time. That is what happened in the vocal recording for "Late to the Party". During the demo recording process, it was recorded on a bad mic in a bad room. But the performance was "the one". So, we opted to keep the performance, but the frequencies weren't recorded that well. We knew that it would require additional mix processing to fix those problems.

During this workflow, you may also realize that you are missing an instrument in your arrangement. Maybe there is a key frequency pocket that needed to be filled. It wasn't until you did reference matching that you revealed that flaw in your arrangement. For "Late to the Party", I noticed my reference had more sub 100Hz frequencies than my rough mix. So, I added in an extra 808 bass to play on certain notes. This was an additional arrangement choice added after we already created the initial arrangement.

By using the pro mixing and mastering workflow, you will reveal everything that needs fixing along the production chain. Then in future you will learn not to make those mistakes again.

Learning mastering is important for this to work. By understanding mastering, you will be able to do what one of my mastering mentors Blake La Grange calls *pushing back on the mix*.[21] Mastering is a subtle art form. By mastering your rough mix, any flaws in your production chain will be obvious. The flaws can then be fixed before doing your final master. That is what makes this process so effective.

By understanding the whole production chain, you will develop second-order thinking. Second-order thinking means there is not just one consequence to your initial actions: but a ripple effect of many consequences. Each decision becomes a chain reaction of cause and effect. Therefore, initial conditions are everything along the production chain. Second-order thinking will ensure you have the end in mind and that each decision is optimal.

During the pro mixing and mastering workflow, it helps to play your master on multiple speakers and headphones. This process can reveal even more potential problems. Do this after you bounce each master draft.

By using the pro mixing and mastering workflow you will know:

- Do you need to add or remove anything in the arrangement?
- Do you need to record anything better?
- Do you need to edit anything more or less?
- Do you need to mix it better?

Remember: I can't tell you how important it is to understand this: **record things properly.** It will save you weeks, even months of your life fixing the mistakes in editing and mixing.

Although, as with all creativity, sometimes mistakes become magic. Maybe you want to keep a bad recording of an instrument for the "vibe". But because you'll know what could cause problems, you can make that choice with a clear mind. For example, the acoustic guitar in "Late to the Party" had a frequency at above 3kHz that sounded like white noise. We chose to keep it because it gave a vibe to the track we missed when we took it out. Even though it sounded "bad", we chose to keep it.

As Brian Eno has said from his own technique library *Oblique Strategies*: "Honor your mistake as a hidden intention."[22]

Part V: Sonics

GOALS, PROBLEMS, AND TOOLS

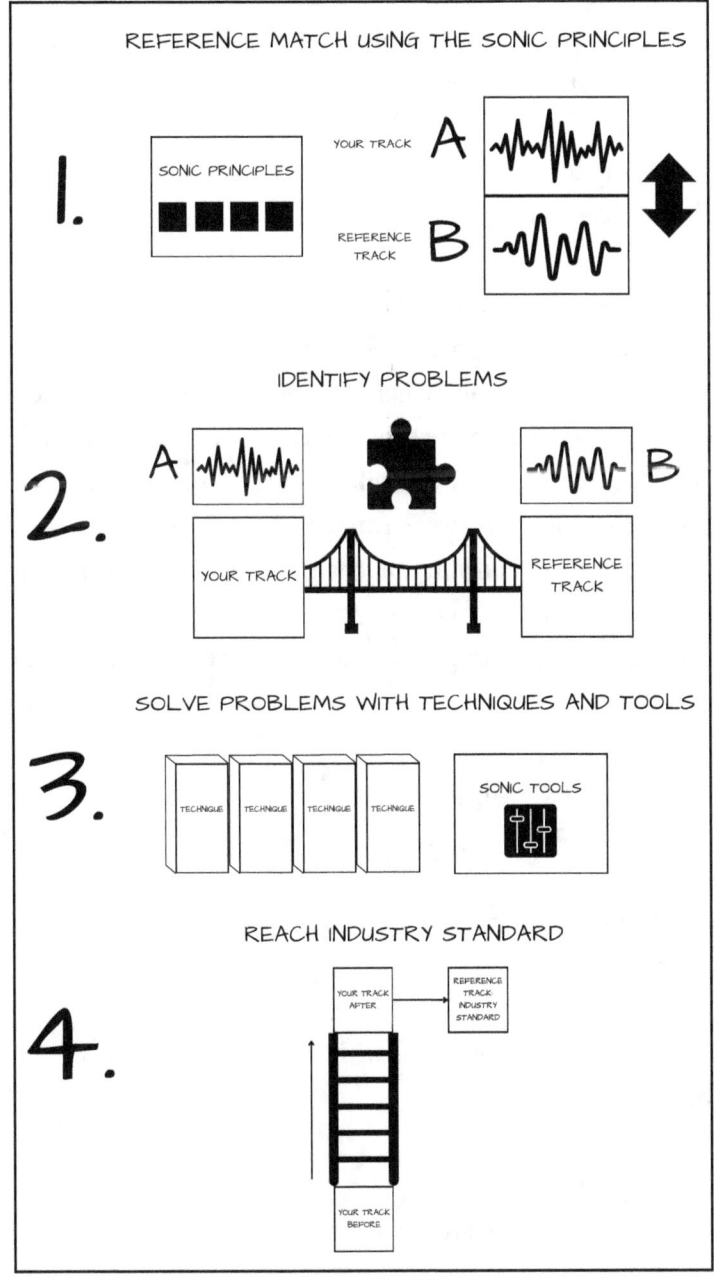

As you reference match, sonic problems will be revealed. These problems are the blocks between your track reaching industry standard sonics. You then solve those problems using techniques and tools. The goal being industry standard.

A great way to look at sonics:
Solve problems using tools.

How do you identify problems?
Ear training will heighten your awareness of sonic problems in your music. Use the Sonic Principles as a guide of where to look for problems. When you find the gaps between your track and a reference track, any problems you missed will become clear. This feedback loop will train your sonic framework further.

At each part of the production chain – recording, editing, mixing, and mastering, ask: *Are there any problems?* You're doing this for all the different Principles of Sonics. You can do this in successive order if you want to.

Recording. Are there any problems with the:
- Sound selections.
- Performances.
- Environments/rooms.
- Recording signals.

Editing. Are there any problems with:
- Phase/Polarity and Bleed.
- Timing.
- Comping/Tuning.
- Cuts/fades/unwanted noises.

Mixing. Are there any problems with the:
- Balance.
- Frequencies.
- Dynamics/saturation.
- Space/FX.

Mastering. Are there any problems with the:
- Volume.
- Frequencies.
- Dynamics/saturation.
- Loudness.

Go through each principle using the Technique and Stems Thinking frameworks. Then:

- Focus on one instrument at a time, one group at a time, and groups compared to groups.
- Then focus on the whole track as one.
- Then find the gaps between each sonic principle compared to the reference track.
- Then find the techniques needed to bridge the gap in standard.
- You then fix the sonic problems in your track using sonics tools. As shown earlier in the prerequisites.

ENTIRE FRAMEWORK WORKFLOW

1. As you record, edit, mix, and master, you move through each principle:
   - **Recording**: sound selection, performances, environments/rooms, recording signals.
   - **Editing**: phase, polarity and bleed issues, timing, comping/tuning, fades, cuts and unwanted noise.
   - **Mixing**: balance, frequencies, dynamics/saturation, and space/FX.
   - **Mastering**: volume, frequencies, dynamics/saturation and loudness.

2. As you do this, you will draw techniques from your technique library, i.e., techniques you found from reference matching (analysis) and resource mining.

3. You then face problems toward your goal of industry standard. So you use tools to fix the problems within the principles.

Sonics Stems Thinking Workflow

You can do this with stems thinking as well. You're mixing your stems, and then thinking of the groups of stems. You're mixing the group of stems, and then you're mixing the groups with the groups of stems and so on. As you are completing the sonics chain, you must maintain stems thinking to ensure that the synergy principle is maintained. Each individual stem relates to every other stem. Each group relates to every other group. The whole track becomes one unit. Therefore, it helps to view each individual group, group bus, and final mix bus, as if you are mastering each one.

Part V: Sonics

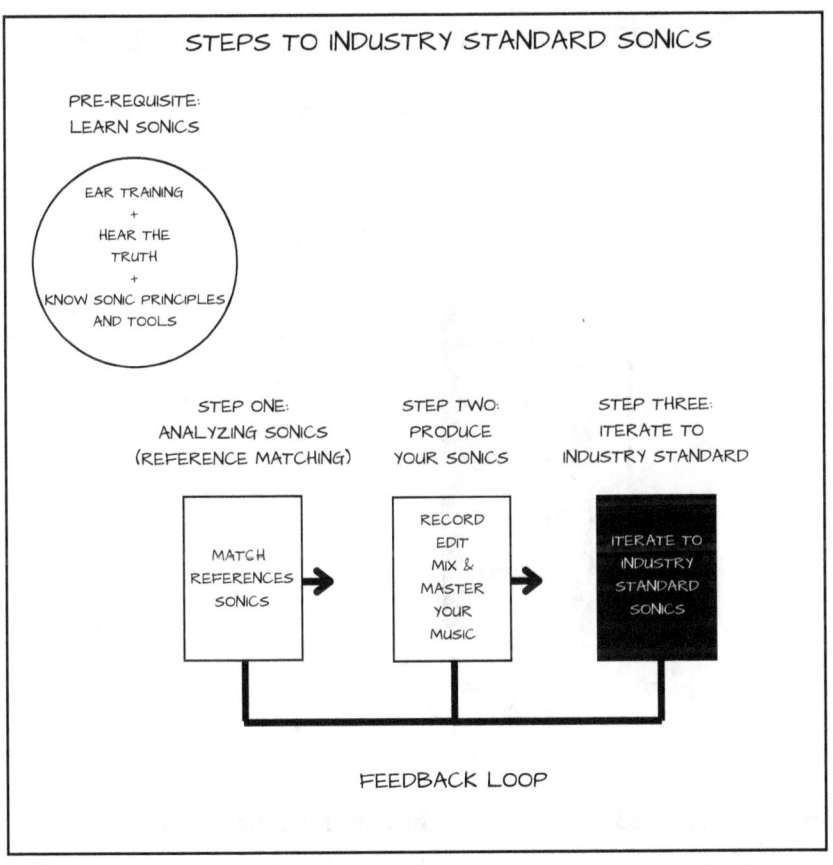

STEP THREE: ITERATE TO INDUSTRY STANDARD

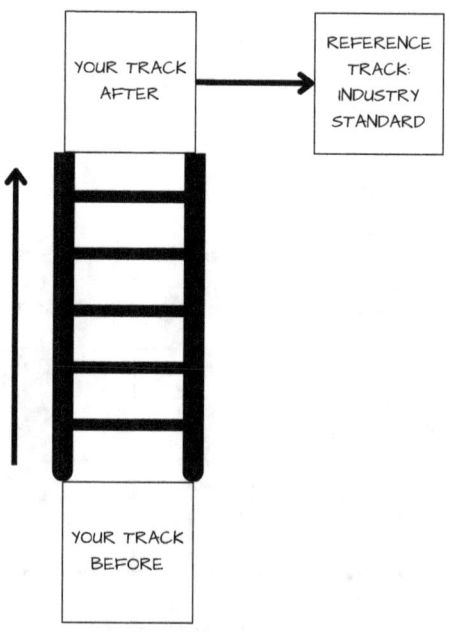

After you have taken your track through reference matching, you've found the data and then bridged the gap. You've mixed and mastered your own track. Maybe even changed your arrangement, recording, or editing to optimize them. You may find that you hit a wall and need external feedback. This is where if your technique library has holes, you'll need to fill those holes. Resource mining helps here as others may see things you can't yet.

FILL IN THE HOLES IN YOUR TECHNIQUE LIBRARY

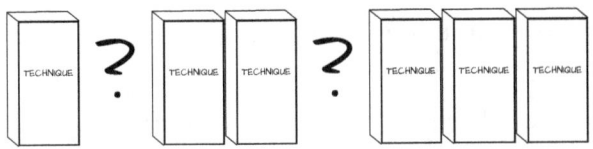

Your current skill level will determine if you need more resource mining.

For someone who has achieved industry standard sonics many times before, you may not need extra help. You may only need feedback from your client to move to completion.

But if you get stuck, get trusted mentors to give feedback on your track. There are:

1. Things you know.
2. Things you don't know you know.
3. Things you know that you don't know. (Get a mentor here.)
4. Things that you don't know that you don't know. (Get a mentor here.)

You then trial the new data you find and iterate back around to Step One and start over again.

- Repeat the steps to industry standard until you reach industry standard. Reference matching, producing sonics, and feedback/iteration.

- You may need to cycle through this process one time to hit industry standard. You may need to cycle through this process many times until you hit industry standard. Keep going, it will work.

- Document all the techniques you find from reference matching, resource mining, and your own experience. Then store the techniques into your technique library.

- The goal for Polymath Producers is to reach industry-standard sonics and beyond. Repeat the steps to industry standard until you achieve it. The key in this step is to hold that standard no matter what.

- Eventually you'll learn to recognize what you love in sonics based on musical taste.

- You'll develop an invisible checklist in your mind of what great sonics sound like. It will become your default. You can then innovate from that base line with your own music. (We'll cover more on *innovation* in Parts VI and VII.)

BENEFITS OF KNOWING THE WHOLE PRODUCTION CHAIN

The benefit of knowing the whole production chain is that you can always have "the end in mind". You will know whether you are falling off the mark at any given time during the production chain.

As a Polymath Producer, you are responsible for overseeing the entire production chain. You will always ensure each step is complete to standard before moving to the next step. You do so whether *you* are recording, editing, mixing, and mastering, or *outsourcing*.

Part V: Sonics

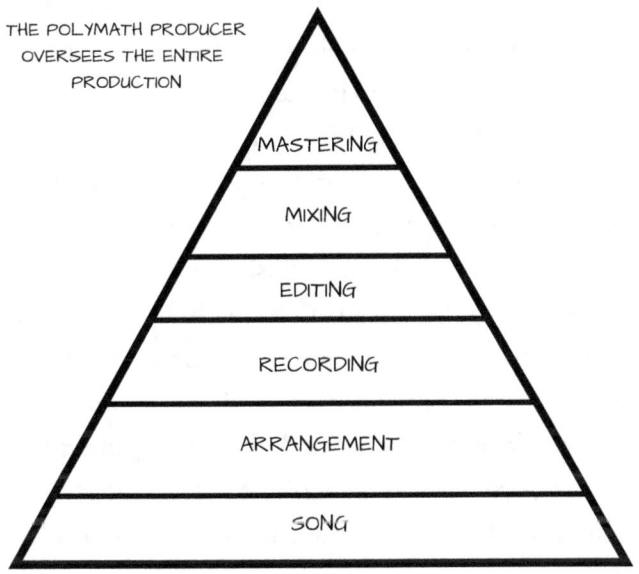

THINK FOR YOURSELF AND WORLD CLASS STANDARDS

While learning pronunciation, you learn by matching the sounds. I suggest when you're developing your sonic wisdom, aim to use *critical thinking*. Critical thinking is the objective analysis of something to form a judgment. Avoid assuming that if a producer has used a sonic technique in their track, it will work the same for your track.

For example, if a producer says they EQ boosted their lead vocal at 10kHz, it may not work for your track. What if the microphone you used to record with was already boosted at 10kHz? You could be adding too much 10kHz to your vocals when mixing.

Only use sonic techniques within your productions when necessary. You must be the judge of whether you need a technique or not.

The top producers in the world use critical thinking. They then trust their instincts about what they believe is best for the track. Then, they use techniques to help them achieve their goals. They also take care of the micro details that others miss. Top producers can spend hours micro-chunking tiny details to perfection during editing. It comes down to standards. Does it reach the standard or not?

Before we move on to Part VI, I want to say it again. You always need to think for yourself in this process. It doesn't matter if an industry standard track does something or a mentor tells you to do something. If you experiment with their insight and it doesn't work, do not use it. You have the final say as a Polymath Producer. You have the vision. You have the standard. Always keep the world-class standard, and you can't go wrong. The answers to all your problems will reveal themselves if you keep that standard. It did for me, and it can for you. Your own style of sonics will form over time the longer you do this. The ultimate aim will be to transcend and develop your own style.

*

Congratulations, you have now learned how to master sonics using the Polymath Producer System. You now know the pronunciation of the language. Use the action steps to get results.

You have the entire framework. Now, go and master sonics.

Part V: Sonics

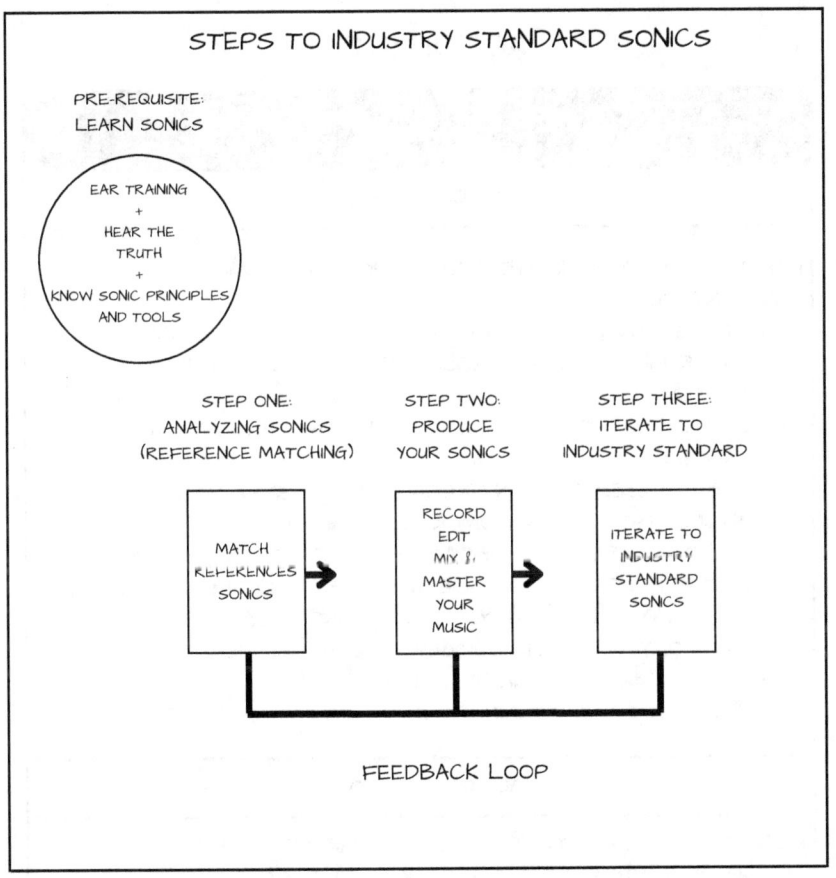

ACTION STEPS

PART V: SONICS - ACTION STEPS

ACTION STEP ONE

EAR TRAINING, HEARING THE TRUTH, KNOW THE SONIC PRINCIPLES AND SONIC TOOLS
- GET A SOUNDGYM MEMBERSHIP (IF NOT SOUNDGYM, USE A SIMILAR EAR TRAINING WEBSITE THAT INCLUDES THE REPS METHOD.)
- DO ONE HOUR PER DAY. FOLLOW THE MASTERS AND EQ FIRST STRATEGY.
- REACH GOLDEN EARS IN FREQUENCIES. MASTER VOLUME, PANNING, SATURATION, COMPRESSION AND FX GAMES.
- USE SOFTWARE TO CALIBRATE YOUR HEADPHONES TO HEAR A FLAT FREQUENCY RESPONSE WHILE TRAINING AND PRODUCING.
- IF YOU WANT TO TREAT YOUR ROOM AND SPEAKERS: HEAD TO WWW.POLYMATHPRODUCER.COM/RESOURCES FOR RECOMMENDED RESOURCES ON THIS TOPIC.
- KNOW THE SONIC PRINCIPLES, SONIC TOOLS AND YOUR DAW

ACTION STEP TWO

REPEAT THE STEPS TO INDUSTRY STANDARD SONICS
- ANALYSIS (REFERENCE MATCHING). USE SCIENTIFIC METHOD TO REFERENCE MATCH YOUR TRACK WITH YOUR REFERENCE'S SONICS IN RECORDING, EDITING, MIXING, AND MASTERING. DOCUMENT THE TECHNIQUES INTO YOUR TECHNIQUE LIBRARY.
- PRODUCE YOUR SONICS. MAKE EVERY PART OF THE PRODUCTION CHAIN THE BEST IT CAN BE. USE THE PRO MIXING AND MASTERING WORKFLOW. EXPOSE ALL PROBLEMS IN YOUR PRODUCTION CHAIN. USE TOOLS TO FIX PROBLEMS YOU FACE AND ACHIEVE GOALS TO REACH INDUSTRY STANDARD SONICS.
- ITERATE TO INDUSTRY STANDARD. USE ADDITIONAL RESOURCE MINING AND FEEDBACK FROM MENTORS IF NECESSARY TO FILL IN HOLES IN YOUR TECHNIQUE LIBRARY. KEEP GOING AROUND THE STEPS TO INDUSTRY STANDARD UNTIL YOU REACH IT.

Part V: Sonics

SUMMARY OF THE SONICS FRAMEWORK
PRE-REQUISITES
EAR TRAINING
CALIBRATED HEADPHONES. (OPTIONAL: OPTIMIZE AND CALIBRATE YOUR ROOM AND SPEAKERS)
KNOW THE SONIC PRINCIPLES
KNOW THE SONIC TOOLS AND YOUR DAW
STEP ONE: ANALYZING SONICS (REFERENCE MATCHING)
USE SCIENTIFIC METHOD TO REFERENCE MATCH YOUR TRACK WITH YOUR REFERENCES SONICS IN RECORDING, EDITING, MIXING AND MASTERING
DOCUMENT THE TECHNIQUES INTO YOUR TECHNIQUE LIBRARY
STEP TWO: PRODUCE YOUR SONICS
MAKE EVERY PART OF THE PRODUCTION CHAIN THE BEST IT CAN BE
USE THE PRO MIXING AND MASTERING WORKFLOW - EXPOSE ALL PROBLEMS IN YOUR PRODUCTION CHAIN
USE TOOLS TO FIX PROBLEMS YOU FACE AND ACHIEVE GOALS TO REACH INDUSTRY STANDARD
STEP THREE: ITERATE TO INDUSTRY STANDARD
USE ADDITIONAL RESOURCE MINING AND FEEDBACK FROM MENTORS IF NECESSARY TO FILL IN HOLES IN YOUR TECHNIQUE LIBRARY
KEEP GOING AROUND THE STEPS TO INDUSTRY STANDARD SONICS UNTIL YOU REACH IT

YOU'VE LEARNED THE FOUR PRIMARY FRAMEWORKS

You have now learned the entire set of analysis frameworks. You now know the language of music production. By following the action steps I've given you from Parts I-V, you will see phenomenal results.

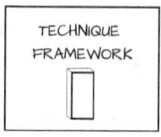 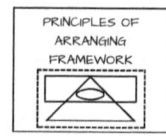 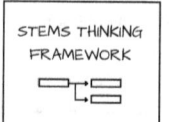 

Remember: Emotion, Emotion, Emotion

Emotion is the key. What emotion are you aiming to achieve in your listener? Analyzing music using the four primary frameworks will calm your technical, thinking brain. We do this on purpose so that your feeling and soul can come through when you create. You will automatically learn to trust yourself: your taste and instinct. That is the ultimate goal of this process. While using the Polymath Producer System, you are finding:

- The emotion behind techniques.
- The emotion behind the Core Principles of Arranging.
- The emotion behind Stems Thinking.
- The emotion behind sonics.

Once you internalize these, it is up to you while creating your own music, to create using your own inner compass. Create with your emotion. Create from your soul. This inner compass will form as you quiet your thinking brain and learn to trust your inner voice. That is what we'll focus on next in the parts on *Original Sound*, and *Transcendence*.

Part V: Sonics

MUSIC PRODUCTION IS....

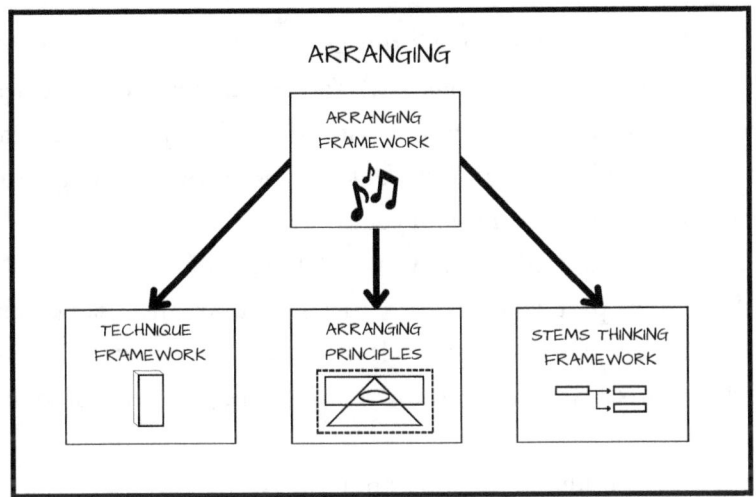

AND

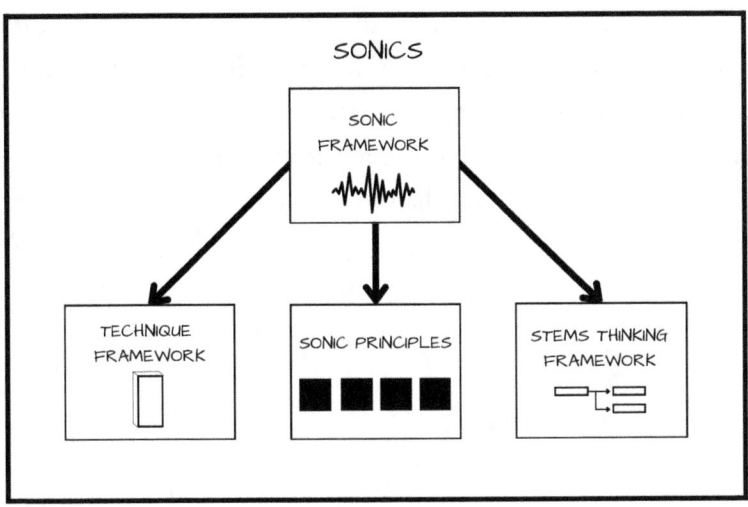

Pause and Reflect on How Far You've Come Now.

The fact that you've made it this far into the book shows me that you are different to everyone else. You're humble enough to learn more and motivated enough to master the skill. You also have faith that your time invested in this book will bring you amazing results. Thank you for trusting me with your time.

Now, trust yourself and move ahead. I believe in you.

In the next part, you will learn how to focus on these same frameworks to create your own music. This is where all your work from the previous parts pays off. This is where you create your original sounds.

But before we move on, I ask a quick favor…

I ask that you take sixty seconds of your time to review this book on Amazon. The more reviews this book gets on Amazon, the more it will be shown to producers who need it. By doing this good deed today you could help thousands of producers in the future. Producers just like you. But what's even more important is you'll be changing someone else's life for the better. So, thank you for helping others. You're an absolute legend.

Jonathan William Ferrier

Now back to the book.

PART VI:
Original Sound

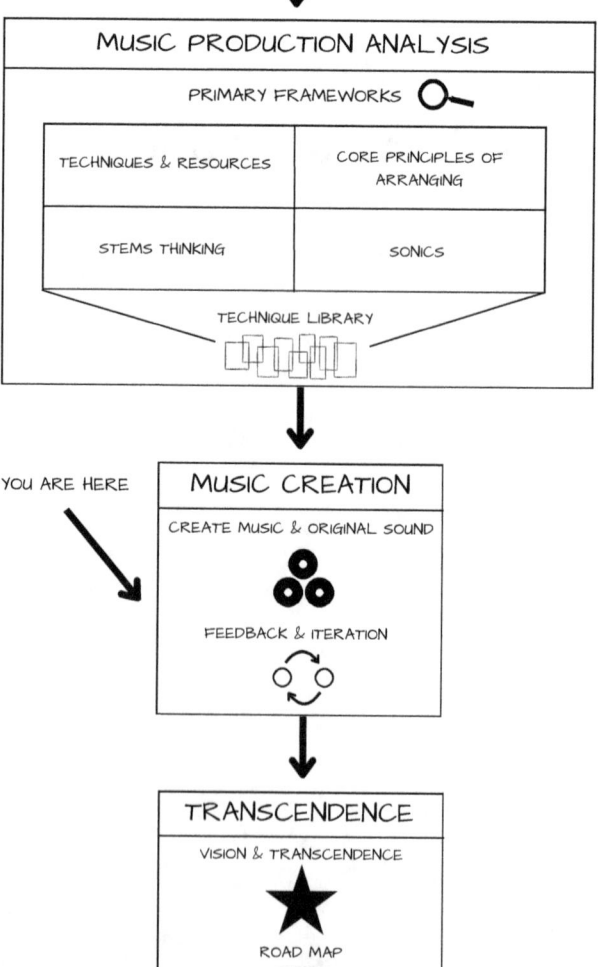

Building Blocks

I HAD A TUB full of Lego building blocks as a kid. If you don't know, when you buy a new pack of Legos from the store, the designs of the Legos are all part of a theme. The pieces of Lego are specific to the theme, and you follow the instructions to create the theme.

For example, one of the themes I had was a Wild West theme. If you follow the instructions, you create a Wild West town with all the characters involved. In a stereotypical scenario that includes: the sheriff, the outlaw, the saloons, the horses, etc.

Another one of the themes I had was an outer space theme. This one had future technology, spaceships, and aliens. The list of themes was endless.

What I did was I would finish the original theme that the instructions stated to create. But as the years passed, I didn't want to repeat the same thing. That became boring. I wanted to cure my boredom. So, to occupy my mind, I would do other things like climbing trees, riding my bike, or playing video games.

But one day, everything changed. My mother didn't want a bunch of Lego sets lying around in separate boxes, taking up valuable storage space in the home. So, she placed all the Lego theme packs together into a single tub of Legos. This decision shocked me to my core. Now, I'd never be able to create the original themes again. After mixing them up, there was no going back. They were all individual pieces in a pool of options that made zero sense together. *What was I supposed to create if I couldn't create the original themes? Was the Lego tub doomed to sit in the cupboard collecting dust? Or would I manage to make something from it?*

The initial shock from my mixed Lego sets became a blessing in disguise – like many of life's lessons. Being a child as children are, beaming with imagination, this mix of Lego empowered me. It also cured my boredom. I could now create whatever combination I wanted. I could create new combinations with these building blocks. The only limit was my imagination. I no longer saw the Lego building blocks as "themes". I saw the Legos as individual pieces I could use to create whatever I wanted.

So I did; I created massive spaceships out of the most random materials. I would add pieces from any of the themes I had. As individual pieces mixed, they worked. It didn't matter if it was a Western theme piece mixed with a spaceship theme piece. I used my imagination to combine the building blocks to create new, original creations. My creations were my own, so I was even more proud.

This game was one of my favorite things to do as a child. I would make the most over-the-top creations to see how big I could make them.

*

The same process is used in music production when I create original sound. The themes of Lego are like music genres. Pre-built, you can follow specific instructions (techniques) to make that genre. But when you combine building blocks from each Lego theme, in this case, technique building blocks, you create something original to you. I realized I was doing that again when I started to produce after using the Polymath Producer System. I started to take technique building blocks from any genre or track I wanted and combine them all. The combinations became limitless. This process became the cross-pollination of sounds – the method for creating new genres. I could now transcend genre and view production as a universal language. A language built of principles and technique building blocks.

With Lego, I could combine building blocks from a Wild West

theme with a spaceship theme to create something new. I could make gigantic spaceships. I could create huge towns that looked like a mixture of a Wild West town, a space town, a tropical island, and a castle. The mixtures were endless.

This was the exact process applied to music once I used the Polymath Producer System. When I didn't have to rely on copying genres, music finally felt like a universal language. I could mix building blocks from any genre I wanted to create new sounds – I could *transcend genre*. The amazing thing is that everyone's influences are unique to them. So everyone has the potential to create their own original sounds.

In this part on *original sound*, we will look at how you can reconnect with this child-like self again. Then view music production as building blocks to cross-pollinate and create your own original sounds.

Your Catalog Of Music

So far, you have analyzed music through the lenses of the four primary frameworks:

- Technique building blocks.
- The Ten Core Principles of Arranging.
- The layering of Stems Thinking.
- The Sonics framework.

The building blocks you're finding from analysis are becoming a technique library worthy of a master. You're mastering the language of music production. The part of the process we're about to cover now activates your genius. You will now see *your* music through the lenses of the four primary frameworks. Now, everything comes full circle by aiming your technique library at your own music.

THE FRAMEWORK

The possibilities are infinite when you aim the Polymath Producer frameworks and your technique library at your own music. You can draw upon any building block you have ever found from your analysis. Doing this is where you will discover that you have transcended genre. Music is now a universal language. Cross-pollination becomes effortless, and your original sound develops. Now, you can create your own music catalog and use this system to achieve whatever sound you desire.

You should find now that building blocks (in the form of educated decisions) will arise as you create. Your intuition will "know" what to do. Trial and error will decrease. You will start to create music faster. Decision-making will become world-class; so your music becomes world-class.

This diagram shows how you can now compose with the four primary frameworks and your technique library.

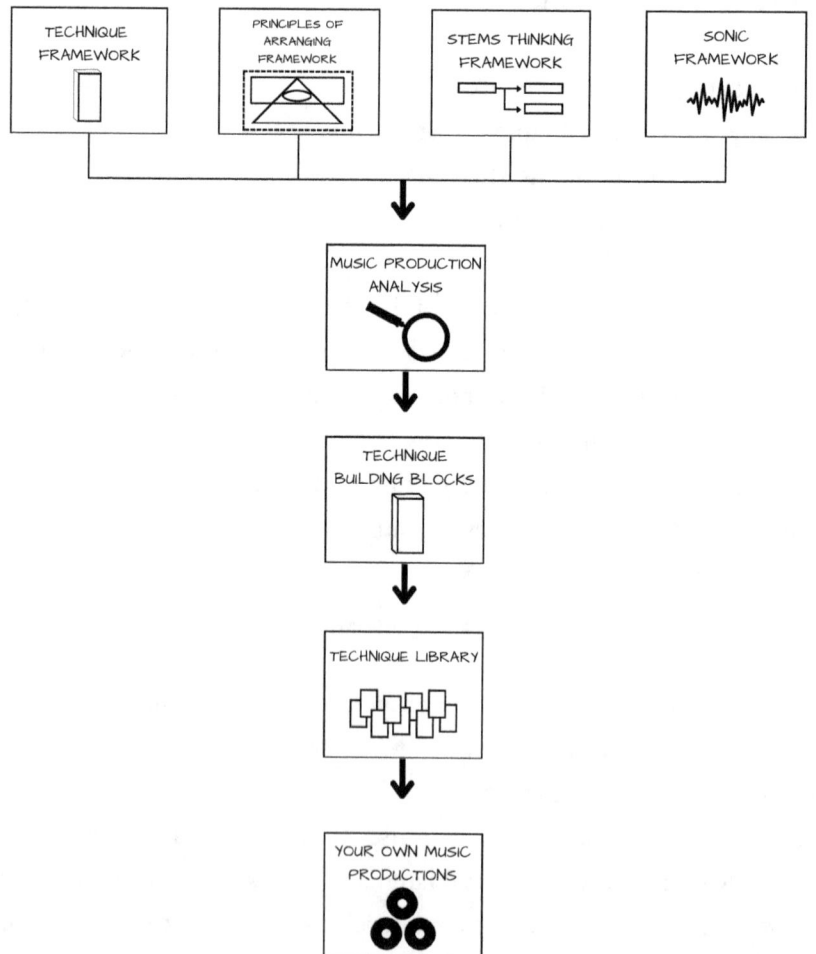

IMPORTANT: BEFORE YOU MOVE ON

Keep in mind that if you have done music production analysis using the four primary frameworks, as shown earlier in the book, you won't have to "think" about creating music with them. It will happen naturally in your own music creation.

- Techniques will pop up in your mind intuitively when you need them.
- You'll naturally think about the core principles as you create your arrangements.
- You'll intuitively know what kind of stem layering decisions you must make.
- You'll know when your sonics are reaching industry standards.

This will all happen if you follow the music production analysis action steps from Parts I, II, III, IV, and V. Your subconscious brain will do the work after all the experience you gain over time. When the language of music production is within you, it will happen naturally. Sometimes you may need more or less iteration to get the results you want. But you'll be confident you can always get results.

When you do music production analysis with the four primary frameworks they become a part of you. You'll then automatically know how to produce your own music with the four primary frameworks.

You must do the work for this process to take place in your mind. So, if you haven't done the work from Parts I-V yet, go back and do the action steps. Mastery could take more or less time depending on where you are at in your current skill level. In fact, you'll continue to use these frameworks for life.

For example, I studied techniques and principles for a year and a half before I got to Stems Thinking. I also did four years of them all before I got to sonics. That is because I had to develop this and figure it out alone; you don't have to. Use this gift and save yourself years of trial and error.

In the movie *The Karate Kid*,[23] the lead character, Daniel, wants to learn and master Karate. His mentor, Mr. Miyagi, a master of Karate, instead, tells him to do tasks that feel unrelated to Karate. Daniel reluctantly does these tasks. These tasks include waxing a car, sanding a floor, painting a house, etc.

Daniel doesn't realize this; by doing the tasks as Mr. Miyagi tells him, he has been learning Karate without knowing. Daniel then realizes when he begins to fight that he knows how to do Karate. He goes from a skeptical student to a believer in Mr. Miyagi's teachings.

Remember, in this book, I'm teaching you how to think for yourself. I'm not going to tell you "how" to produce. But when you use the action steps in this book from Parts I-V, you *will* know *how* to produce. If that sounds like a paradox, do the action steps for a month. Produce your music. Then read this section again. You will find that I have used a teaching style like Mr. Miyagi.

Appendix I of this book provides a complete list of these action steps in one place for quick reference.

THE GOAL WHEN CREATING YOUR MUSIC

You will create a catalog of music over your entire career. Your goal is to create, finish, and consistently release your best music. The catalog always remains the number one priority. At the same time, always move to the edge of your abilities. Doing this will move you toward what author Mihaly Csikszentmihalyi calls a *flow state*.[24] A flow state is when you are at the edges of your abilities – the perfect state to create and advance your skills. Your experience becomes heightened. Through this heightened experience, you learn and master skills much faster.

FEEDBACK AND ITERATION

You are applying the new techniques and growing your technique library. You're creating new music. The next step is *feedback*. Feedback will allow you to recognize where you are going right and where you are going wrong in your music. It will expose the holes in your skillset that you need to improve and iterate on. You then use music production analysis to fill those specific holes. Once you reach a certain level where you have filled the holes, you'll get less feedback and more praise.

This process is the scientific method, where you iterate over time until each track is at its best. Your standard rises to a world-class level because you analyze the greatest tracks of all time. You begin to develop an "invisible checklist" within your mind. This checklist creates an internal feedback system. You get a sense of how close you are to matching the standard of the great tracks of all time.

But there are other ways to get feedback. Another way is to get a mentor who can increase your speed of growth. Mentors can be another producer. Often, they can be industry professionals – someone who requires you to meet a standard. Mentors are most beneficial during the sonics process specifically. For arrangements, music production analysis is usually enough. But mentors and peers can help you there, too.

Mentors, Authority, Triangulation and 33/33/33

When asking mentors for advice, always take what they say with a grain of salt. Always use your own ears and critical thinking. You must be responsible for the standard of where your track goes. Always make sure you have the final say and think for yourself.

In Robert Cialdini's book *Influence*,[25] authority is a primary persuasion tool. If a human believes someone has authority, they're more likely to believe what they say. You can become free of this human bias by looking at feedback objectively – regardless of who it is from.

To counteract this authority bias, it is best to get at least three-to-five (or more) sources of feedback on a question. In his book *Principles*,[26] investor Ray Dalio calls this feedback process *Triangulation*. It means getting opinions from believable people on a question. Then you cross-reference the answers to find the truth.

Ultimately, you must hold onto your vision for the track. If what your mentors tell you doesn't align with your vision, then do your own thing. You must be confident and hold your vision for what you feel is true.

The last way to get feedback is through direct market feedback from music releases. We will discuss that later in the *transcending generations* section.

To become well-rounded: You can also use the 33/33/33 method. This method says for the highest skill development to spend:

- 33% of your time being mentored.
- 33% of your time working with your peers.
- 33% of your time coaching others.

The reason why this works is because, when mentored, you learn what's working. Working with your peers, you are creating and learning together. Coaching others has proven to be one of the best learning methods for memory retention. As theoretical physicist Richard Feynman stated, and I paraphrase, *"If you can't explain something in simple terms, you don't understand it."*[27] I mentor other producers in the Polymath Producer community. It helps me keep my mind sharp.

Keep iterating around the Polymath Producer System until you reach your desired goals.

EXAMPLE OF ORIGINAL SOUND

In 2006, Justin Timberlake, Nate Hills, and Timbaland finished their track "SexyBack". They created it using a mixture of their own technique libraries. The track was sounding like nothing else on the radio at the time. It had Justin Timberlake (traditionally an R&B singer) singing more in a rock style. The production behind it had a lot of electronic influences, but the song was like an R&B song. It was a mixture of pop, R&B, electronic influences, and rock. It had all these different influences in one track, and it didn't sound like anything else on the radio then.

When the record label A&R heard it, they believed it would be a disaster. They thought it was too weird compared to everything else doing well on the radio. They weren't keen on it being the first single. They didn't believe in it. But Timberlake had people in the studio who were his *audience* at the time. He saw how his audience was responding positively to the new sound. With the direct market feedback, he decided to push ahead and put the track out as the first single. What happened? "SexyBack" went Number One on the Billboard Hot 100, becoming Justin Timberlake's first solo number one.[28]

Here is the lesson: They got a sample of how the market would react on a micro-level, which scaled to a macro-level. They saw a sample of their target audience reacting in a certain way. The creators believed in the track. They created it from their original influences. They weren't trying to copy what the current trends were. They did what they wanted to do; they stood out and succeeded. It is important to remember this story as you keep reading Part VI.

MUSICAL TASTE

Musical taste is the invisible force that directs your decision-making process. It influences what you listen to and what you create. Some people are born with a musical taste that connects with many people. It is almost universally liked. Other musical tastes are more niched down, and only a select few enjoy them. Staying true to yourself is key here.

Keep in mind musical taste can impact how universally accepted your music becomes. That is because your taste can determine the decisions you make. Those decisions then either connect with an audience or not.

Reflect on the Justin Timberlake story on the previous page. Their taste in music created a new sound for them. The sound connected with a large audience to become a number one hit.

To conform means to go against what your musical taste and soul want to create. It will feel painful if you do that. This decision is up to you and what you want to create. *Can you stay true to yourself?*

THE MYTH OF GENRE

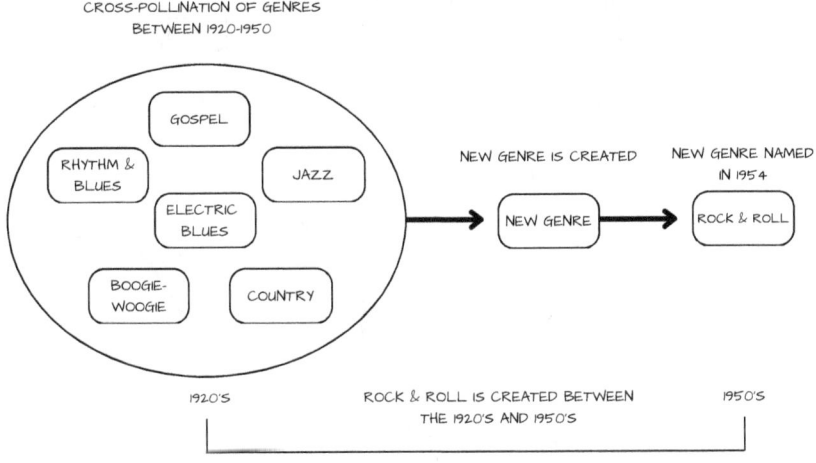

Genre is created before it is defined. If you look at the diagram: Rock was created, and then someone named it Rock. From the 1920s to the 1950s, various artists cross-pollinated techniques from genres like Gospel, Jazz, Rhythm and Blues, Country, Boogie-Woogie, and Electric Blues to create what became Rock and Roll. Then it was named Rock and Roll in the 1950s.

Genre is a cross-pollination of the building blocks from past genres. This evolution has taken place since music began. The key to cross-pollination is learning and combining techniques from various genres.

TRANSCENDING GENERATIONS

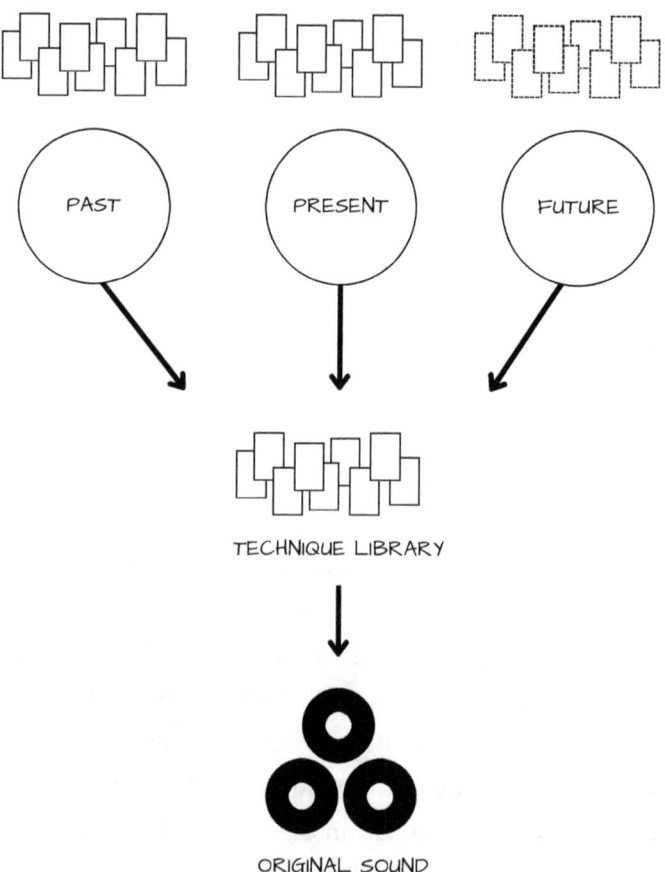

Genres are constantly changing. New generations want to be different from the generations that came before them. They like to rebel. It's a consistent cycle that's been happening for centuries. To stay relevant, you can cross-pollinate techniques from the past, the present, and the future. The current hot trends right now will change in a few years. Production is volatile and always changing. Because of the technological revolution, the generation gap has become closer. Society and art are progressing at a faster rate. To counteract this, avoid chasing trends.

Instead, think of the three time periods when creating:

1. Which generations from the past can I discover building blocks from?
2. Which modern generations can I discover building blocks from?
3. Where can I go in the future? The only way to find the truth for the future will be to test honest market feedback.

Doing this can help you transcend generations. Robert Greene discusses this concept in the *Laws of Human Nature* in the chapter on *Generational Myopia*.[29] If the current trends are not what you want to create, don't create them. Create for yourself and then test it on the market. If you create something fresh sounding, you won't know if it works until the market responds. Then, the reality of the situation will be true. It is about finding the link between what you want to create and what the audience wants. That is *product-market-fit*.

Apple co-founder Steve Jobs once said:

> *"Some people say, 'Give the customers what they want.' But that's not my approach. Our job is to figure out what they're going to want before they do. I think Henry Ford once said, 'If I'd asked customers what they wanted, they would have told me, "A faster horse!"' People don't know what they want until you show it to them. That's why I never rely on market research. Our task is to read things that are not yet on the page."*[30]

Trends come and go. The market doesn't know what it wants until you test it with them. This approach requires real market feedback with what you create.

The solution then, is to create music then release it to the market.

You will then know whether your music has product market fit. This is when your music and the market's interests link up. That is when the "truth" will be revealed.

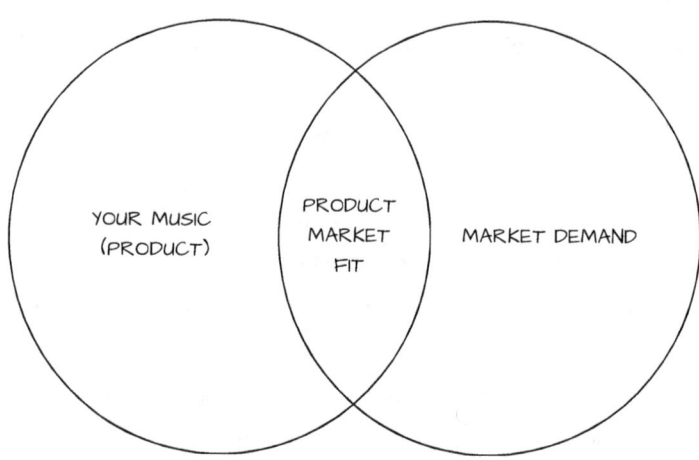

TRENDS VERSUS PERENNIAL SELLERS

What you can do to counteract trends is to aim to create what the author Ryan Holiday calls *perennial sellers*.[31] Perennial sellers are art that can stand the test of time. A perennial seller is a piece of work or art that compounds the length of its shelf life the longer it stays in mass consciousness.

For example, The Beatles have been listened to fifty years after they ended in 1970. According to this theory, the Beatles will continue to be listened to another fifty years from now. When they hit the one-hundred-year mark, they will likely be listened to for another one hundred years.

Ask yourself: *If this song is played fifty years from now, will people still enjoy it?*

WORLD CLASS SONIC STANDARDS

It helps to keep your standard at a world-class level to achieve perennial sellers. It also helps to apply modern-day sonic standards. Suppose your track sounds different from everyone else creatively. In that case, it can help to match the industry's modern sonic standard. But you can also innovate in sonic standard also. It is up to you.

You can also listen to the mainstream and soak in the "essence" of it. This essence is the times; it is a feeling. But if you embody it, you'll take it into your own tracks and match that standard, regardless of how unique your sound is.

EVOLUTION OF SOUND

What if you create the sound you're known for and don't want to be pigeonholed? When Prince created the *Purple Rain* album and was known for that sound, his next album, *Around the World in a Day*, sounded nothing like it. That's why his music catalog crosses many sounds and genres. He chose to use different building blocks in his follow-up album. He applied what's called *Musical Pressure.* This is stated in *Prince and the Purple Rain Era Sessions* by Duane Tudahl.[32] Apply musical pressure on yourself to create your genius. This musical pressure comes from music production analysis.

The Beatles also sounded like they ranged across all different genres. They evolved their sound by using different building blocks as their careers evolved. You can do the same if you choose to.

The constant between these great artists as they evolved their sound is that they continued to have great songs. We cover *songwriting* in this Part soon.

EVERY DECISION COUNTS

Every single decision you make along the way becomes your sound. Believe in an abundance of ideas. The more you complete, the more you make room for your genius to come. It's evolution. Some of the ideas will not work, but some will. You keep creating, and then the strongest ideas will survive. Everyone's technique library is unique. So, everyone creates uniquely.

COLLABORATION AND ORIGINAL SOUND

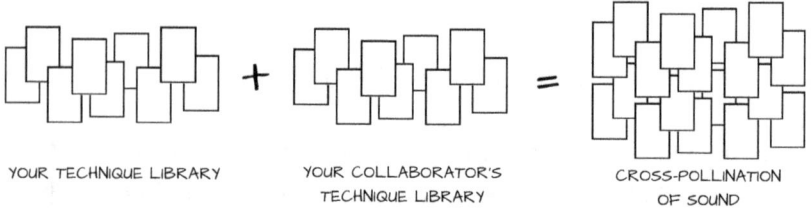

YOUR TECHNIQUE LIBRARY + YOUR COLLABORATOR'S TECHNIQUE LIBRARY = CROSS-POLLINATION OF SOUND

You can achieve original sound independently, but collaboration is another way. Each member of your team will have their own musical taste and set of influences. So, the technique building blocks will vary. Cross-pollinating these technique building blocks so that all musical tastes can work in harmony can be a recipe for an original sound. Multiple technique libraries merge.

There is a fine line, though. If you find someone with a very different musical taste from yours, it could be a recipe for genius. But, it could also be a recipe for a constant battle. Most of the best writing and production partnerships involve people with similar musical tastes. But, their tastes vary enough to create a unique combination. If their tastes vary too much, it will unlikely last long term as there will be too much battling.

The key to successful collaboration is finding people who match your musical taste but who bring a unique combination of building blocks. You will then have a shared mission. But you will each have unique technique building blocks to offer. Of course, creative battling is okay as long as the end goal is shared. If the musical tastes are so different that both people want the end goal completely different, it isn't the right match. Find your people first, and then the rest will follow. It is okay if you don't creatively match with certain people; you will find your matches if you keep looking for them.

The artists you work with will also impact the direction of the sounds you create. Before I start working with any artist, I'll ask them what influences they have, past and present. This will give me an idea of their technique library, which I can then cross-pollinate with my technique library to achieve what they want.

THE GOLDEN THREAD

(Diagram: three overlapping circles labeled PRODUCER(S), ARTIST(S), and SONGWRITER(S), with the center labeled HIT SONGS + ORIGINAL SOUND.)

The fundamental thread that links all success in original sound is the following:

- A producer links up with an artist with a ton of potential. The artist is often at the start of their career, but not always. Sometimes, it is an established artist who wants a new sound. The artist can also be the producer if they're a producer/artist.

- If needed, they also link up with other collaborators (songwriters, producers, artists), and they all write songs together. This approach works best when a "hit song" is written.

- The producer crafts an original sound with the artist. They do this by cross-pollinating past, present, and future influences. They achieve this by combining technique libraries. The music also meets modern-day sonic standards. The market then receives it well because it aligns with their musical taste but stands out.

I call this the *Golden Thread*.

A few examples of the golden thread in action include:

- Bruno Mars, Ari Levine, Phillip Lawrence.
- Mark Ronson, Amy Winehouse.
- Max Martin, Shellback, Taylor Swift.
- Quincy Jones, Michael Jackson.
- The Beatles, George Martin.
- Ludwig Goransson, Childish Gambino.
- Ian Kirkpatrick, Dua Lipa, Emily Warren, Caroline Ailin.

The list goes on.

However, the absolute meta of success in this industry has been and always will be *hit songs*. Especially hit songs that achieve product-market-fit using the golden thread as explained above.

Part VI: Original Sound

SONGWRITING

Many of the world's top producers recommend that you master songwriting as well. Producers like Ryan Tedder have said that songwriting is key to his success as a producer.[33]

Chris Gehringer is one of the world's top mastering engineers. He masters for artists like Dua Lipa. Often, Chris gets clients asking him to master a track to sound as good as a Dua Lipa track. He stated, "...a lot of the time it's just (because it's) a hit song."[34]

Songwriting is everything. Everything starts with the song. From my own experience, songwriting completely shifts the way that I produce. Songwriting is always first for me. I wrote songs for five years before I even touched my first DAW. It was and is my first love in the entire production chain.

Some of you may not want to do songwriting, which is also okay. Some of you may be doing instrumental music, like film music. This requires a different form of composition than composition around a song. But many of the same principles apply.

If you are making music with songs, finding the right songwriting team is crucial. This is especially so for a producer. Songwriters are key to achieving the golden thread. You can also write songs on your own, too, or not write songs at all. It is up to you what you want to do.

I'd already spent a decade songwriting before I created the Polymath Producer System. When I first learned songwriting, I learned by doing. I remember recording hundreds of song ideas on a digital recorder. I would do that day after day for years. As I reflect, musical taste plays a crucial role in how a songwriter's melodies, lyrics, and chord choices form. Even when I wrote my first song, I had the seeds of my musical taste come through. The same taste that I developed over time using the Polymath Producer System.

Can you use the Polymath Producer System on songwriting, too?

Yes, you can. In fact, I used the system on songwriting without realizing it. However, your musical taste will often govern your songwriting choices. Going against that will grate against your will. But yes, the Polymath Producer System in songwriting can help hone your craft.

For example, a technique in songwriting could be: Use a catchy melody in phrase one. Repeat that melody in phrase two. Then, do a variation melody in phrase three. Finally, return for a punchline in phrase four.

That is one approach to a chorus melody you could use. But if your musical taste doesn't like that, you won't do it.

Music production analysis of a diverse range of hit songs still applies. This will hone your standard and invisible checklist.

To complete this section on songwriting, I'll say the following:

- You can apply the technique and resource mining levels to songwriting.

- The principles of songwriting are *title, melody, lyrics, harmony,* and *structure*. Melody and lyrics being the primary focus. Most songwriting techniques fall under one of those principle categories. You can apply principles thinking, to songwriting as well. You do this by analyzing one technique at a time within the principles of songwriting.

- Songs are universal. You build a genre of music production around the song. A song can be turned into any genre by how it is played or produced.

- Stems thinking and sonics analysis don't apply to this category. Although the song impacts how stems thinking and sonics in a production can unfold. This was covered in Part V on Sonics.

Part VI: Original Sound

SONGWRITING PRINCIPLES

```
┌─────────────────┐
│   SONGWRITING   │
├─────────────────┤
│     TITLE       │
├─────────────────┤
│     MELODY      │
├─────────────────┤
│     LYRICS      │
├─────────────────┤
│     HARMONY     │
├─────────────────┤
│    STRUCTURE    │
└─────────────────┘
```

Songs are universal, but the genre of music production around the song can shift. This moves us to the key of original sound:

Cross-pollination.

CROSS-POLLINATION

Cross-pollination of techniques from multiple genres (including individual songs, tracks and influences) can become an original sound. Genres have characteristics that make them what they are.
These can include:

- The choice of Techniques used.
- The way the Core Principles of Arranging are used, especially core rhythm.
- The way Stems Thinking layering is used.
- The way Sonics Principles are used.
- Instrument/sound selection choices; because some genres have instruments typical to them, i.e., rock music = guitars, classical music = strings.
- Genre specific styles.

Cross-pollination is maximized by the decisions you make while creating your productions. As you move through techniques, principles, stems thinking, and sonics, you will make thousands of decisions. As you move through the production chain you will make thousands of decisions. There are countless moments along the path to cross-pollinate. This process is usually intuitive; meaning you let it flow through you. But it can also be intentional. You can *choose* to draw techniques from certain influences.

For example, songwriter/producer Burt Bacharach was known in the 1960s to draw core rhythms from many different genres. If you listen to "The Look of Love" by Dusty Springfield, that song has a Bossa Nova rhythm. This rhythm was developed in Brazil in the late 1950s/early 1960s. So Bacharach and producer Phil Ramone created a unique mix by adding that rhythm to a modern US pop song.

Part VI: Original Sound

CROSS-POLLINATION

HOW HAS THIS GENRE USED:
- TECHNIQUES
- PRINCIPLES OF ARRANGING
- STEMS THINKING
- SONICS
- GENRE SPECIFIC INSTRUMENTS
- GENRE SPECIFIC STYLES

HOW HAS THIS GENRE USED:
- TECHNIQUES
- PRINCIPLES OF ARRANGING
- STEMS THINKING
- SONICS
- GENRE SPECIFIC INSTRUMENTS
- GENRE SPECIFIC STYLES

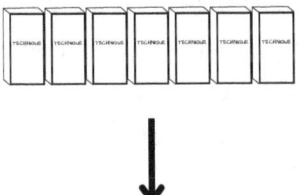
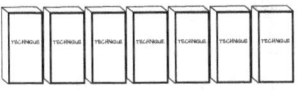

CROSS-POLLINATE GENRES TOGETHER
USING TECHNIQUES YOU FIND

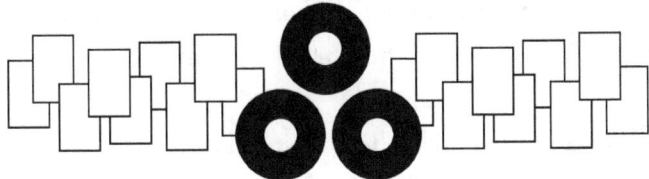

ORIGINAL SOUND

Cross-Pollination Case Study: "Walk This Way"

In 1986, "Walk This Way" by Run-DMC and Aerosmith became the first hip-hop song to reach the Top Five of the Billboard Hot 100.[35]

While producing the next Run-DMC album, Rick Rubin played the original version of "Walk This Way" by Aerosmith. At live shows Run-DMC would sometimes rap over the top of the first few seconds of the song on loop. So during the production of their album, Rick Rubin suggested that Run-DMC do their own version of the song.

This is where it gets interesting. The new version combined hip hop and rock *together*. The same drum beat pattern was used from the original "Walk This Way" by Aerosmith. But the *samples* used to make the drum beat pattern were from hip-hop. This meant the song *sounded* like a hip-hop beat because of the samples; but the core rhythm drum pattern technique was from a rock song. The lead guitar riff was the same from the original "Walk This Way". But the verses were rapped instead of sung now. So the techniques typical to the genres were mixed together.

From rock music, they used the guitars, the drum beat pattern, and the rock vocal chorus. From hip hop, they used the drum beat hip-hop samples and layering techniques. They also used rapping over the beat. Sonically the drums were hip-hop but the guitars were rock.

This combination used all of these to stand out:

- Techniques.
- Core Principles of Arranging.
- Stems Thinking layering.
- Sonics choices.
- Instruments/sound selection choices.
- Genre specific styles

This song is a clear example of how cross-pollination can create original sound. By 1986, rock music had been the dominant form of music for around thirty years. This track helped hip hop become more mainstream by bridging the gap between rock and hip-hop. They achieved the *golden thread*.

AIMING THE SYSTEM AT A GOAL

Luckily there are ways you can increase your chances of the golden thread happening for yourself and your team. You do this by aiming the Polymath Producer System at a goal.

Remember this formula?

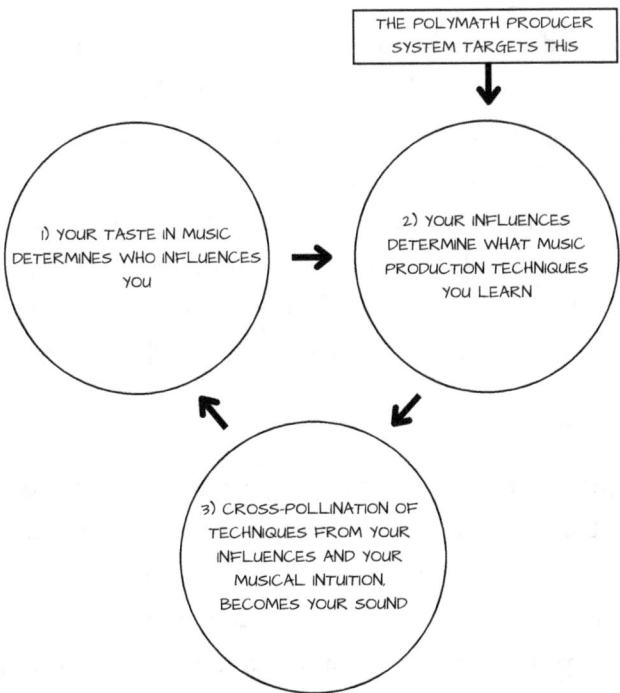

Goal: You want to create your own original sound, whether that is for you or the artists you work with. *What mix of influences best align with the sound that you're trying to achieve?*

Task: Aim the Polymath Producer System frameworks at that goal.

- The first approach is to target specific genres. For example, if you want to write great house music, analyze the great house music of all time. Learn the primary techniques. Whatever techniques you need to make world-class tracks. Target the system onto those influences that inspire you the most. Find the technique building blocks. Also discover how they use the core principles, stems thinking, and sonics.

- The second approach is to move to where your intuition and love for the craft take you. If you feel like using the system for pop music one day and classical music on another day, do it. Go where your curiosity takes you. If you're listening to Jazz, but it makes no sense to the music that you're currently creating, why not analyze it anyway? The influences you learn from could cross-pollinate with the music you're creating. Be open to analyzing where your curiosity takes you. You never know what depth of insights an analysis can give you. Everything connects.

- The third approach is to analyze music you don't love or listen to often, but you want to understand why people love it. This approach expands your musical palette. For example, you don't like rock music and only like to create trap music. If you analyze classic rock, you may find something you can use in your trap music. Maybe you find cool guitar riffs, and you combine that with your trap music to create a fresh sound.

- The fourth approach is to ask the artists and/or collaborators you work with questions about their influences (technique library). Once you find their influences, use music production analysis on them. Then cross-pollinate their influences with your technique library to create an original sound.

- The fifth approach is a mixture of two or more of the above.

The more techniques you gather, the more your "color palette" will broaden. The more colors you'll have to paint with to achieve your soul's sound.

So what do you want? What goal do you want to achieve? What does your intuition tell you to do? Rather than thinking about what other people are doing, think about what you want. The key is to fuse the rational with the intuitive. Internalize all the technique building blocks you're learning so you can let it flow out of you. Analyze the right influences aimed at the goal you want to achieve. Then get out of your own way and let your subconscious mind link the building blocks together. We will talk about this further in Part VII on *transcendence*.

"Talent hits a target no one else can hit;
Genius hits a target no one else can see." -
Arthur Schopenhauer[36]

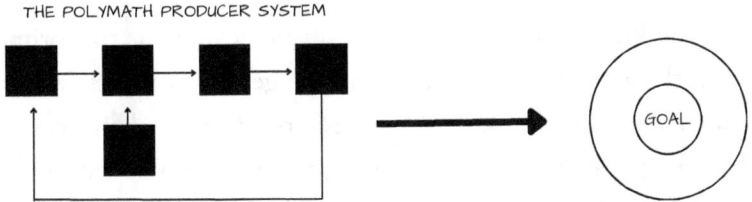

THE POLYMATH PRODUCER SYSTEM

ACTION STEPS

Congratulations, you've now learned how to aim the system at a goal to create your own original sound. The following are the action steps to do it.

	PART VI: ORIGINAL SOUND - ACTION STEPS
ACTION STEP ONE	BUILD YOUR CATALOG OF MUSIC - THIS IS THE NUMBER ONE PRIORITY. USE THE FOUR PRIMARY FRAMEWORKS AND YOUR TECHNIQUE LIBRARY TO CREATE YOUR MUSIC. USE FEEDBACK AND ITERATION UNTIL YOU ACHIEVE YOUR GOAL.
ACTION STEP TWO	THINK ABOUT THE THREE TIMES. THEY ARE PAST, PRESENT, AND FUTURE - DRAW TECHNIQUES FROM THEM ALL. AIM TO CREATE PERENNIAL SELLERS.
ACTION STEP THREE	FIND YOUR GOLDEN THREAD TEAMS BECOME A SONGWRITER COLLABORATE AND FUSE TECHNIQUE LIBRARIES WITH YOUR DREAM TEAM JOIN THE POLYMATH PRODUCER COMMUNITY AT WWW.POLYMATHPRODUCER.COM/RESOURCES
ACTION STEP FOUR	AIM THE SYSTEM AT THE GOAL YOU WANT TO ACHIEVE. ANALYZE INFLUENCES YOU WANT TO. CROSS-POLLINATE THE TECHNIQUE LIBRARY YOU BUILD TO CREATE YOUR ORIGINAL SOUND.

Bonus Tip: Music Business

Ensure you know that *publishing* and *masters* are your two primary assets in this business. Make sure that you get any contracts checked by lawyers. When you master the music production chain, you will likely start getting business deals sent your way. So, you will need to understand the business to ensure you are safe, this is a reminder.

Note on A.I.

In the future, A.I. may be able to use music production analysis to create original sounds. It may be able to analyze and collect the building blocks of a successful track. Then, it might cross-pollinate genres together to create new genres. What it will lack, though, is the soul behind the creation. Only time will tell what will happen, but until then, we will move toward transcendence. Use plugins and tools to assist your creation process, but aim to create from the soul.

Coming up Next

You have now learned how music production analysis can help you discover your own original sounds. This will help you think for yourself and make innovation more effortless.

If techniques are the words, principles are the grammar. Stems thinking is layering words and grammar together to create full works. Sonics are the pronunciation. Then original sound is creating your own works of art. You've learned how to master all of the fundamentals. You are now on your way to becoming what the industry calls a "100%er" – someone who can complete the entire production chain from start to finish... a Polymath Producer.

Now the final step is transcendence. This is where you embody this system and transcend your mind.

PART VII:

Transcendence

START HERE

POLYMATH PRODUCER SYSTEM OVERVIEW

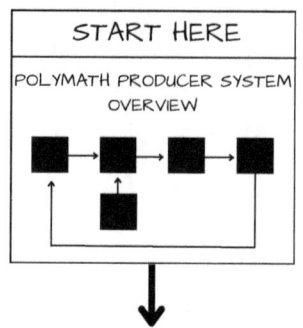

MUSIC PRODUCTION ANALYSIS

PRIMARY FRAMEWORKS

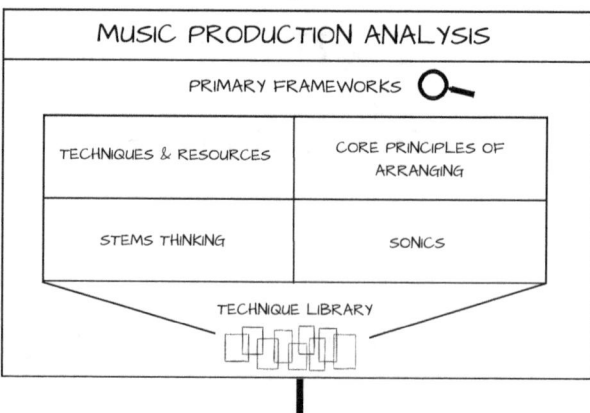

TECHNIQUES & RESOURCES	CORE PRINCIPLES OF ARRANGING
STEMS THINKING	SONICS

TECHNIQUE LIBRARY

MUSIC CREATION

CREATE MUSIC & ORIGINAL SOUND

FEEDBACK & ITERATION

YOU ARE HERE

TRANSCENDENCE

VISION & TRANSCENDENCE

ROAD MAP

Transcending The System

IN 2021, I started working with the artist Rachelle Rhienne. At first, I asked her questions to find the sound she wanted. It was a sound she had sought her whole life, but no one could help her create yet. During a short interview, she listed different sounds she loved. She told me about the artists who inspired her and where she saw herself going in her career. By the end of the interview, I had the logical information written down. The styles listed varied, but this information became my target.

What I wanted was to create a sound with her that was unique and blended with her voice. I wanted to make a sound that was a mix of all the influences she had told me about. I knew deep down that creating a unique sound with an artist means helping them carve their own category into the market. The unique sound is what helps an artist stand out. Besides a hit song, a unique sound is one of the top things you can offer an artist as a producer. My aim was to create hit songs and a sound unique to Rachelle. A sound she loved and that had the potential to stand the test of time.

I knew the project's long-term potential. When I discovered her, she wrote behind the scenes for other pop artists with another team. One of the first things I said to her was, "I don't understand… why is your team writing for someone else when they already have a star in the mix?" I believed she was a star, not only in voice but also in character, stage presence, and songwriting. I would not let an opportunity to be part of her career pass me by.

Although, the pressure was on. At the time, Rachelle had over a hundred thousand followers on social media. She had also already been on television. She was by far the most influential artist I'd worked with at the time.

In the past, I would have created the music using trial and error and hoped for the best. But after years of analyzing the great producers, I was confident I could achieve the sound she wanted.

My motivation ran high; I dove into the opportunity with no foot on the brake. Just like I was as a child, I saw the information she had given me as Lego building blocks to cross-pollinate. I had the building blocks within my subconscious; I knew what she wanted, but it was time to create it. I then did what is this system's last and most powerful piece; *I transcended my mind.*

When I came to the studio to create the tracks I let my intuition flow. I allowed the *inner source* to work through me. The building blocks from years of analyzing music came flowing through me. It was magic; every move I made was like my hands were moving by themselves. Sometimes, I used technique building blocks that weren't in Rachelle's original information. But they were building blocks that made sense for the track. That's where my intuition took me. I followed my intuition with complete trust.

I programmed my mind to head in a direction. Then, I let my intuition drive me there. I let my imagination run wild. I would grab a technique building block I learned from a 1950s track. I would combine that technique with techniques from a 2020s track. I would combine that with orchestration moves I learned from film score composers. So on it went until cross-pollination was there. Like I was when I was a child playing with Lego building blocks, I let it flow through me.

The Polymath Producer System gave me the confidence to trust that I would know the answers. My job then was to get out of the way and let that happen.

Once I had an entire arrangement, I knew when the flow was complete. I was then to return to my head for technical work. It was like a tap turned on; the creation came through me, and I knew once it was complete.

As Rick Rubin stated in that same Tim Ferriss interview mentioned earlier in the book:

> *"Try not to think too much, the job is more emotion and heart work than it is head work. The head comes in after to look at what the heart has presented and to organize it. But the initial inspiration comes from a different place and it's not the head. Creating art is not an intellectual activity, it is more inspiration."* – Rick Rubin[37]

What happened felt like a miracle. Every time it happens, it feels like a miracle.

I came to her with the music production I'd created around our song, "Sometimes I Think About You". It was the first song Rachelle Rhienne, Marina Bennett, and I co-wrote as the *3 Sparks* team. It was the exact sound Rachelle had known she wanted and now finally had. She loved the production; it was the perfect blend for her voice, which was a massive success for me. Now I knew I had found the sound; I only needed to create that with her in unique ways for her other tracks.

This process proved to me the power of the Polymath Producer System. I had analyzed the great producers and tracks of all time. In doing that, I had thousands of techniques in my mind from different genres and influences. When Rachelle told me what sound she was looking for, I could connect the dots. I knew what mix of sounds to use. The final step in the process, which happened naturally, was getting out of my own way. I allowed my intuition to flow. I trusted that I would have the answers. I trusted the answers would flow through me. I embodied the energy of someone who was a master. With this confidence, trust, and a clear goal, I let the *inner source* guide me where I needed to go. The techniques flowed effortlessly.

I had finally achieved what I set out to do at the start. Internally, I had become what I'd always wanted to become. I was also given gifts in other ways. The team I had found in *3 Sparks* was what I was looking for all along:

- The companionship of artists on a shared mission.
- Navigating the music industry.
- Working from the ground up toward success.

The Polymath Producer System was a tool that helped me help us. I knew my external world was about to change and that this was only the beginning.

In this next part of the book, I will explain how to get out of your own way to allow *transcendence* to take place.

Vision and Transcendence

WE ARE music producers who learn to analyze the great music of all time to become great ourselves. We become masters of the *language of music production*. If you have come this far and taken action on what I have shown you, you have become a Polymath Producer.

TRANSCENDENCE

When you have been using this system long enough, it becomes a part of you. You no longer have to do it. You will be it. You *become* a Polymath Producer. Eventually, you can stop writing down every technique you find onto paper, if you choose. You'll instead be able to hear, see, and feel techniques, and they'll become a part of you. You'll soak them in, and then you'll know how to use them while producing. This practice will become habitual – a part of who you are. You trust that it's happening in your subconscious at all times.

THE PARADOX OF HEART AND MIND

Technique building blocks work with the rational mind. This rationale is necessary to get the "program" into your mind in the first place. Transcendence is when you move out of your head, get out of your own way, and let the heart come through. Only then will you create authentically; authenticity is the key to transcendence. Learn as much as you choose to with your mind, but then transcend. It is a paradox. Most of the time, being free and playful is the key. There's a time and place for learning with your mind. But when it's time, you transcend the mind. Then it's all about balancing the rational mind and the intuitive feeling. This flow state is what we as music producers are searching for.

When you sit at the DAW, you have the skill set of a developed master. You know everything about the craft you need to create and push yourself to the edge of your abilities. But you have the risk-taking and imagination of an intuitive child. The decisions you make are playful and outside the box. You know the skill sets so well that you can break the rules. You follow your curiosity and run your own experiments to find new levels of growth. You embrace your soul's authentic musical taste using a color palette of unlimited techniques. This is mastery. Or what Robert Greene, author of *Mastery,* calls "when the rational meets the intuitive mind."[38]

MOVING INTO THE UNKNOWN

When you first started producing, the skill was unknown to you. Having used this system, you know what the greats of all time have done. Once you've learned what has worked for others, the next step is the unknown. You've come full circle. The unknown requires a life of experimentation, trial and error, and innovation. You begin to create your own experiments and techniques; this is transcendence at its fullest potential. Mastery is always becoming and evolving. You maintain a humble beginner's mind; mastery never ends.

FIND YOUR OWN TRUTH

The spiritual guru Osho claimed he had read thousands of books of immense value in his lifetime. He then decided to stop reading because, he said, "But then I got my own truth."[39] He read thousands of books by other people of immense value, and it was all rational information going into his mind. Then he stopped reading. He found his own truth inside himself, which was more powerful. It was the feeling and his own experience of life that became his truth. I'm calling you now to find your own truth, your own authenticity, to be your authentic self, and to play and have fun.

HUMANS ARE BORN TO SPEAK THE LANGUAGE

As a human, you are born to interpret language. First in the form of energy, body language, tonality, and an extension of those three – music – and then spoken language. You were born to create this language. In fact, newborn babies can feel beat and rhythm before speaking.

Before being immersed in the music of the cultures we were born into, we only knew the music of our mother's heartbeat. Or perhaps we knew the beats and melodies imprinted on our DNA from the echo of a thousand generations. Or perhaps we know music from our souls. We can now listen to any music we want through the Internet. We are being brought back to ourselves with access to any music we want to listen to. I hope that this system brings you back to yourself. I hope this system shows you it has been inside you all along.

HOW SIMPLE CAN YOU MAKE IT?

Another thing to consider is: *"How simple can you make this in the rational mind?"* A lot of the time, things can get overly complicated. In this book I've aimed to simplify music production into a language and its simplest truths. As you create, you can use this simplification to make things much easier. *"How simple can you make it?"* That is the question. That's something for you to experience yourself. Transcendence of the mind is when creativity will be at its most simple. It will flow through you effortlessly. You can use these systems and frameworks whenever you need to. Transcendence is a spiritual process of surrender. Surrender is allowing creativity to flow without judgment of what comes through. That is simplicity.

STANDARDS AND IDENTITY

I've mentioned standards in this book, and I'll say it one last time. Your identity and beliefs will shift as you become a world-class music producer. Your identity will be in constant flux. One day, you might think you're the best producer in the world; the next day, you may feel you aren't even professional yet. I recommend you claim the identity of a world-class producer. I recommend you believe that you are a world-class producer. But one of the best ways to remove this flux in identity on your way to this goal, is to focus on a standard.

Have the standard of: *"I create world class music."* Then it becomes less about you and your identity. It becomes more about: *Has this track I'm working on reached my standard yet*? If the track hasn't met the standard, continue to work at it until it has.

It doesn't have to be anything to do with you or your identity. It is either at a world-class standard or not. For every cause, there is an effect. If your track isn't at a world-class standard yet, some cause (or causes) is stopping it from being there. You can figure it out as long as you keep your standard.

BE > DO > HAVE

Have a vision for what you want to achieve in life and music. When you have that vision, get into the energy and essence of the master and the tracks you listen to. *Be, do,* then *have.* Sometimes when using the Polymath Producer System I'm not looking for techniques. I'm looking for something deeper. Another level I attained was to move into the energy and the essence of what the person had done. It was more of a *feeling* of what they had done. You'll have to experience it for yourself as it is indescribable. When you can sense the essence of what the person has done in the track, you can soak in the essence of the master. Then, when you go to create yourself, you be that essence. Then you create from that place. You become the master in energy. You Be, you Do, and then you Have a masterful track you have made that's original. It's more of an energy.

Creativity is a higher state of consciousness than the rational mind. *To transcend the rational mind, the way is spiritual surrender.* This surrender process is explained in the book *Letting Go* by David R. Hawkins.[40] You connect to this essence through the heart, and the feeling. You connect to this through intention. That is when genius flows; when you create through the heart. When you have fun and play in your own authenticity.

THINK FOR YOURSELF, FEEL FOR YOURSELF

In this book I've been showing you how to think for yourself using mental models and frameworks. The top producers in the world think for themselves. The most common thread of top producers is that they also *feel* their way toward genius. When you transcend the system, it becomes less about the mind and more about the feeling. Music is a feeling game. When you know how to feel, you become an intuitive master of the craft. You know what to do and when to do it, based on your inner source, your inner feeling. You have access to the inner source through your heart and your feelings. **Don't believe what you are told but what you experience to be true.**

INNER SOURCE

There is a higher power working through us. We need to get out of the way to let it flow through. This power is the genius within us all. It feels childlike. The artist Prince called this the "Internal Source". Other artists call it "Source", "the Universe", "God". It is all about balance. Remain humble and keep using the system. Keep your mind learning, but at the same time, get out of your own way, out of your head, and let the magic flow through you. When you respect this process, your ego becomes even more removed from it. It becomes more about serving the art. It becomes more about being a channel for beauty to come through you. It isn't you creating it; you are an antenna receiving it. Your role is to serve it to the world on behalf of something greater. You show up every day ready to receive the gems offered to you. The more you practice this with consistency, the easier it will feel.

GET OUT OF YOUR OWN WAY

Feel everything as it is right now in the present moment. This presence is the key to life. To move out of your own way requires you first to feel, to surrender, to let go. When you feel all, good or bad, with no judgment, all will dissipate into your awareness. Be present with all that is. This process requires acceptance, forgiveness, and unconditional love toward yourself and others. Place your awareness onto your body, and you will find that you can trust your instincts more and more. With freedom from the feelings holding you back, all thoughts attached to those feelings will lose their power. Thoughts will disappear. You will get lighter; the darkness will dissolve, leaving room for only your light to shine. This light is freedom. With this light shining, creativity becomes your natural state.

GENIUS

Genius will flow through you when you ask it to, when you allow it to. Move out of your way and let universal intelligence flow through you. Access to all answers will be there.

ACTION STEPS

PART VII: TRANSCENDENCE - ACTION STEPS	
ACTION STEP ONE	KEEP USING THE POLYMATH PRODUCER SYSTEM UNTIL IT BECOMES A PART OF YOU THINK FOR YOURSELF, FEEL FOR YOURSELF USE THE ROAD MAP TO REFERENCE YOUR JOURNEY DOWNLOAD A PRINT VERSION OF THE ROAD MAP AT WWW.POLYMATHPRODUCER.COM/RESOURCES
ACTION STEP TWO	USE THE SYSTEM, THEN TRANSCEND IT FUSE YOUR RATIONAL MIND WITH THE INTUITIVE SOURCE WITHIN YOU BECOME AUTHENTICALLY YOU BECOME A POLYMATH PRODUCER
ACTION STEP THREE	CREATE YOUR VISION. HAVE FUN AND LET THE GENIUS FLOW THROUGH.

We are Polymath Producers.
We learn and master the language of music production.
We analyze the greatest music of all time.
We stand on the shoulders of giants to be great ourselves.
We transcend genre and create our original sounds.
We value authenticity and trust the inner source.
We make our positive impact on the future of music.
I am a Polymath Producer.

MY GIFTS TO YOU

Congratulations, you've now learned the entire Polymath Producer System. As promised at the start, you now have a step-by-step system that you can use to master the language of music production.

I love it when books provide summaries at the end. So I have given you a few gifts at the end of this book.

1. **The Road Map:** Take this road map; it is an overview of the Polymath Producer System. This system repeats for life while you are achieving your goals. It will give you a clear step-by-step map of what to do to master the language of music production.

2. **Additional Resources For Faster Success:** Here, you'll find out more about the Polymath Producer community, video content, program and newsletter.

3. **Appendix I - Summary of Action Steps:** Use these action steps to master the language of music production. All in one place for your convenience.

4. **Appendix II - Polymath Producer Glossary:** You can use this section to recall the Polymath Producer terms and concepts.

Use those gifts to remember the key concepts and do the action steps for results.

THE ROAD MAP

I – Techniques: Read songs like a book.
Analyze one classic track and one modern track a day.
Find one technique at a time during music production analysis.

II – Resource Mining: Resource mine YouTube videos, books, mentors, and other resources. Find one technique at a time within these resources.

III – Core Principles of Arranging: While analyzing tracks, find the Ten Core Principles of Arranging within them. How were the principles used? Find patterns. Create your music with this principle-based framework. Master the principles of arranging.

IV – Stems Thinking: Get some stem files of tracks you love. Using the technique and principle frameworks, find out what each stem is doing. Use Stems Thinking while producing your own music. Master layering music.

V – Sonics: Do ear training until you have golden ears. Treat and calibrate your room, speakers, and headphones to hear the truth. Use the steps to industry standard to master sonics.

VI – Technique Library: Place every technique you learn from the previous five steps into your technique library.

VII – Catalog of Music: Use your technique library to build your catalog of music. Draw upon and cross-pollinate your technique building blocks. Use the Techniques, Principles, Stems thinking, and Sonic frameworks to create your own music.

VIII – Feedback and Iteration: Get feedback from your invisible checklist, analysis, the market, and believable mentors. Iterate your process until you get less feedback and more praise. This is the system. Watch as your skills and your tracks become masterful.

IX – Original Sound: Keep going further to create your own original sound. Cross-pollinate sounds and genres with other sounds and genres within your technique library. Collaborate with artists, producers, and songwriters to create original sounds and combine their strengths with yours. Find your golden thread teams.

X – Transcendence: Integrate these mental models and frameworks into your mind so that you become a Polymath Producer. Then, do it automatically. Open yourself up to receive the answers from the internal source. Feel your way to genius. Achieve mastery.

Repeat This and Get on an Upward Spiral of Success

You are now a Polymath Producer and part of the *Polymath Producer Movement*. Take this road map, and go and achieve your vision!

#	STEP	THE ROAD MAP
1	TECHNIQUES	Read songs like a book. Analyze one classic track and one modern track a day. Find one technique at a time during music production analysis.
2	RESOURCE MINING	Resource mine Youtube videos, books, mentors, and other resources. Find one technique at a time within these resources.
3	CORE PRINCIPLES OF ARRANGING	While analyzing tracks, find the Ten Core Principles of Arranging within them. How were the principles used? Find patterns. Create your music with this principle-based framework. Master the principles of arranging.
4	STEMS THINKING	Get some stem files of tracks you love. Using the technique and principle frameworks, find out what each stem is doing. Use Stems Thinking while producing your own music. Master layering music.
5	SONICS	Do ear training until you have golden ears. Treat and calibrate your room, speakers, and headphones to hear the truth. Use the steps to industry standard to master sonics.
6	TECHNIQUE LIBRARY	Place every technique you learn from the previous five steps into your Technique Library.
7	CATALOG OF MUSIC	Use your technique library to build your catalog of music. Draw upon and cross pollinate your technique building blocks. Use the Techniques, Principles, Stems Thinking, and Sonic frameworks to create your own music.
8	FEEDBACK AND ITERATION	Get feedback from your invisible checklist, analysis, the market, and believable mentors. Iterate your process until you get less feedback and more praise. This is the system. Watch as your skills and your tracks become masterful.
9	ORIGINAL SOUND	Keep going further to create your own original sound. Cross-pollinate sounds and genres with other sounds and genres within your technique library. Collaborate with artists, producers, and songwriters to create original sounds and combine their strengths with yours. Find your golden thread teams.
10	TRANSCENDENCE	Integrate these mental models and frameworks into your mind so that you become a Polymath Producer. Then, do it automatically. Open yourself up to receive the answers from the internal source. Feel your way to genius. Achieve mastery.

Additional Resources For Faster Success

You now have the road map to evolve into your true potential as a music producer. You can reference this book whenever you need while mastering the language of music production. The journey has only just begun.

But before you go...

I suggest you join myself and other Polymath Producers from around the world in the *Polymath Producer Community*.

The Polymath Producer Community (Free)

Inside you get the following:

- Complementary video content for the book.
- Downloadable PDFs of the diagrams and exercises from the book.
- Community of Polymath Producers from all around the world.
- Exclusive newsletter: the latest and best findings from me.

You can join at www.polymathproducer.com/resources or use the QR code below.

SHARE YOUR SUCCESS STORY

I'd love to hear from you about how this book changed your life. When you have taken action on the frameworks in this book and gained amazing results, send me screenshots, writing, photos, and/or videos of your success to jon@polymathproducer.com

List the form, whether it is an external achievement or an internal transformation you've achieved.

External Achievements:

Achievements are external successes. They are an external validation that shows you are growing during your journey.

Use the following external success markers:
- When you have bought the book.
- When you have finished the book and acted on the insights.
- When you have achieved business successes from applying the concepts in the book. (e.g., more clients, dream clients, more money)
- When you have achieved collaborations or placements.
- When you have achieved chart success.
- When you have achieved gold, platinum and diamond records.
- When you have won a music award.
- Something you value that I haven't stated.

Internal Transformations:

Transformations are internal successes. These are the people we become along the way and how we positively impact the world.

Use the following internal success markers:
- When you have achieved creative success by taking action on the steps from the book (could be insights, or music making becoming way easier).
- When you have produced the exact sound you've always wanted to make but couldn't until now.
- When you have produced the exact sound a client was looking for and they give you raving feedback.
- When you have positively impacted your life and the lives of those around you by implementing what you've learned in this book.
- When you feel like you will never struggle again at music production and feel a level of confidence and relaxation you've longed for.
- What you feel when you can support yourself and loved ones through your success as a music producer.
- What you feel when you feel creatively free.
- Something you value that I haven't stated.

Success stories will be placed in the Polymath Producer Hall of Fame on www.polymathproducer.com.

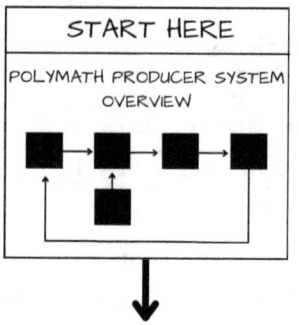

START HERE
POLYMATH PRODUCER SYSTEM OVERVIEW

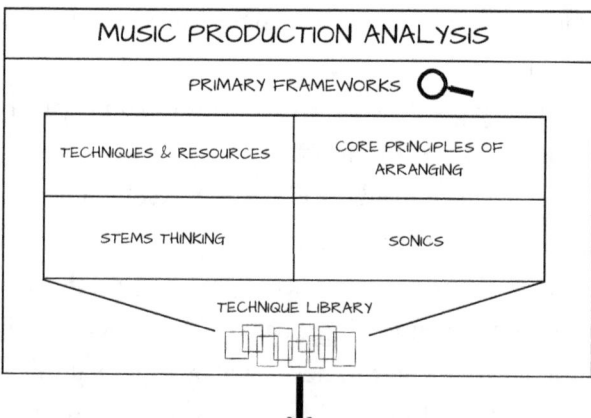

MUSIC PRODUCTION ANALYSIS
PRIMARY FRAMEWORKS

- TECHNIQUES & RESOURCES
- CORE PRINCIPLES OF ARRANGING
- STEMS THINKING
- SONICS

TECHNIQUE LIBRARY

MUSIC CREATION
CREATE MUSIC & ORIGINAL SOUND

FEEDBACK & ITERATION

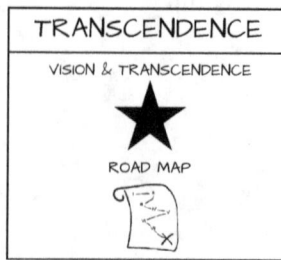

TRANSCENDENCE
VISION & TRANSCENDENCE

ROAD MAP

APPENDIX I:
Summary Of Action Steps

PART I: THE POLYMATH PRODUCER SYSTEM - ACTION STEPS

Action Step One: Memorize the Polymath Producer Philosophy and System. Find a glossary of Polymath Producer terms in Appendix II.

Action Step Two: Download free printable PDFs of the diagrams to pin up on your wall at www.polymathproducer.com/resources

Action Step Three: Join the Polymath Producer Community.

PART II: TECHNIQUES - ACTION STEPS

Summary of the Technique Framework:
- Listen to a track. Scan the stereo field. Frequency field: lows, mids, highs. Panning: left, center, right.
- Choose a specific instrument.
- Find out what technique(s) the instrument is doing. How is the instrument relating to other instruments? Why does it work in this track? How is it relating to other music you have analyzed?
- Write down what the technique is.
- Give the technique a name.
- Write *what* the technique is, *why* you would use it, *how* to use it and the *reference* where you found it. Place the technique in your technique library master document.

Summary of the Resource Mining Framework:
- Analyze music resources. These can include YouTube videos, books, mentors, articles, anything else with valuable techniques.
- As you consume the resource, look for one technique at a time the producer mentions.
- Write a name for the technique. Then write *what* the technique is, *why* you would use it, *how* to use it, and the *reference* of where you found it.
- Then place each technique into your technique library.

Action Step One: Gather your materials and set up the system. Including:
1. Streaming service.
2. Music in a playlist you want to analyze.
3. List of resources you want to analyze, including YouTube videos, books, mentors, etc.
4. Good headphones so you can hear the entire stereo field.
5. Music production analysis document.
6. Resource mining document.
7. Technique library master document.

Download print versions of the documents at www.polymathproducer.com/resources.

Action Step Two: Plot the tasks to do daily in your calendar. Schedule time for music production analysis, resource mining, and music creation.

Action Step Three: Take action daily, building your technique library. You can do this in only an hour a day.

Action Step Four: While creating music, use and implement the techniques you are learning in context.

PART III: CORE PRINCIPLES OF ARRANGING - ACTION STEPS

Action Step One: Print out the Core Principles of Arranging diagram. Stick it in your studio where you can see it. These principles are everything.

Action Step Two: Restudy this part until you have memorized and understand the Ten Core Principles of Arranging.

Core Principles of Arranging:
- Core structure principle
- Core harmonic structure principle
- Core rhythm principle
- Counter rhythm principle
- Spatial principle
- Foreground and background principle
- Energy principle
- Call and response principle
- Repurposing principle
- Synergy principle

Listen to all the references provided. Full playlist of music references available at www.polymathproducer.com/resources.

Action Step Three:
- While doing your regular music production analysis, bring attention to each core principle using the information within this book.

- Find one technique at a time within the Core Principles of Arranging.

Action Step Four: Use the Ten Core Principles of Arranging framework while creating your own music.

PART IV: STEMS THINKING - ACTION STEPS

Summary of the Stems Thinking Framework:
- Choose which world-class stem files to analyze.
- Put the stem files into your DAW on new tracks.
- Once the stems are all on the DAW, look at them through the lenses of the core principles of arranging and sonics.
- Stack them into the recommended group types: core rhythm drums, core rhythm instruments, counter rhythms, spatial principle, foreground and background hooks.
- Analyze the three types of layering in the stems.
  Type One: Analyze individual stems first.
  Type Two: Analyze the stems within the groups you have made.
  Type Three: Analyze how the groups of stems connect with the other groups of stems.
- Analyze the stem files through the lenses of all core principles of arranging and sonics. Also, look for all the layering decisions the producer has made. Then, find one technique at a time and place it in your technique library.

Action Step One: Apply the stems thinking analysis steps to stem files. Download stem files at www.polymathproducer.com/resources.

Action Step Two: Apply stems thinking to your own music creations by thinking in the three layering types.

Action Step Three: Apply the final test to your own music stems by asking, "Do these stems sound world-class?"

PART V: SONICS - ACTION STEPS

Action Steps One: Ear Training, Hear the Truth, Know the Sonic Principles and Sonic Tools
- Get a SoundGym membership. (If not SoundGym, use a similar ear training website that includes the REPS method.)
- Do one hour per day. Follow the masters and EQ first strategy.
- Reach golden ears in frequencies. Master volume, panning, saturation, compression, and FX games.
- Use software to calibrate your headphones to hear a flat frequency response while training and producing.
- If you want to treat your room and speakers, head to www.polymathproducer.com/resources for recommended resources.
- Know the Core Principles of Sonics, sonic tools, and your DAW.

Action Step Two: Repeat the Steps to Industry Standard Sonics
- Analysis (Reference matching). Use scientific method to reference match your track with your reference's sonics in recording, editing, mixing, and mastering. Document the techniques into your technique library.
- Produce your sonics. Make every part of the production chain the best it can be. Use the pro mixing and mastering workflow. Expose all problems in your production chain. Use tools to fix problems you face and achieve goals to reach industry standard sonics.
- Iterate to industry standard. Use additional resource mining and feedback from mentors if necessary to fill in holes in your technique library. Keep going around the steps to industry standard until you reach it.

PART VI: ORIGINAL SOUND - ACTION STEPS

Action Step One: Build your catalog of music - this is the number one priority. Use the four primary frameworks and your technique library to create your music. Use feedback and iteration until you achieve your goal.

Action Step Two: Think about the three times - they are past, present, and future. Draw techniques from them all. Aim to create perennial sellers.

Action Step Three:
- Find your golden thread teams.
- Become a songwriter.
- Collaborate and fuse technique libraries with your dream team.
- Join the Polymath Producer Community at www.polymathproducer.com/resources.

Action Step Four: Aim the system at the goal you want to achieve. Analyze influences you want to. Cross-pollinate the technique library you build to create your original sound.

PART VII: TRANSCENDENCE - ACTION STEPS

Action Step One:
- Keep using the Polymath Producer System until it becomes a part of you.
- Think for yourself, feel for yourself.
- Use the road map to reference your journey. Download a print version of the road map at www.polymathproducer.com/resources

Action Step Two:
- Use the system, then transcend it.
- Fuse your rational mind with the intuitive source within you.
- Become authentically you.
- Become a Polymath Producer.

Action Step Three: Create your vision. Have fun and let the genius flow through.

APPENDIX II:
Polymath Producer Glossary

WHILE ANALYZING music production, I developed a system to make the process of mastery as efficient as possible. I turned music production into a language. So I created a new set of terms to understand what I was finding. The following are some of the main terms in this book.

Polymath Producer: A person who understands the language of music production. Can complete the entire music production chain. Able to create music as a universal language and transcend genre.

The Polymath Producer Philosophy: The language of music production in the form of mental models and frameworks. Mastering the language of music production by analyzing the great music of all time.

The Polymath Producer System: A systematic approach to learning and mastering the language of music production. Includes music production analysis, resource mining, technique library, music catalog, iteration, and feedback.

The Language of Music Production: The four levels of music production – Techniques (words), Principles (grammar), Stems Thinking (full works) and Sonics (pronunciation).

Technique: Each decision a producer has made is a technique building block. Anything a producer has done in a track. Find techniques one at a time.

Music Production Analysis: When you listen to the history of recorded music and find actionable information. When you discover the techniques producers have used one at a time. When you view music through the lenses of the four primary frameworks: Techniques, Principles, Stems Thinking and Sonics.

Educated Decisions: All music production is decision-making. When you use music production analysis on the great tracks of all time you discover educated decisions. Educated decisions are decisions that you know have worked in the past. You also develop educated decisions by creating your own music.

Technique Framework: When you chunk music production into building blocks by finding one technique at a time. The "words" of the language of music production.

Resource Mining: Finding techniques in resources other than music production analysis. This includes books, YouTube videos, programs, mentors, articles, and any other form of people or media.

Technique Miner Mindset: When you program your reticular activating system to always be on the lookout for one technique at a time.

Technique Library: Every person has a technique library inside their mind. Picture a library; each book in that library is a song or resource you have analyzed. Inside that book are all the techniques you found from analyzing that song or resource. You draw upon this information when you produce your own music.

The Three Documents – Technique Filing: A tangible document form of your technique library. Includes the music production analysis document, the resource mining document, and the technique library master document. File the techniques you find into these documents.

The Ten Core Principles of Arranging Framework: Doing music production analysis by looking at how the music has used the ten core principles of arranging. Creating your own music with the ten core principles of arranging. The "grammar" of the language of music production.

Core Structure Principle: The structure where the entire arrangement can occur. Every track will have a form the music follows from start to finish. There are two types: macro-level and micro-level structures. The macro level is a traditional form like verse, chorus, verse, chorus. Micro-level structures are sub-forms built on top of the macro-level structure.

Core Harmonic Structure Principle: The harmonic structure of the entire arrangement. The harmony changes as the structure changes. The most straightforward way to understand this principle is chord progression. On a macro level, this means the key of the track and the chord progressions. On a micro level, this means chord couplets.

Core Rhythm Principle: The primary rhythm in which most of the instruments in the arrangement gravitate around. By gravitate this could mean in its entirety or as a complement to the core rhythm. It is the rhythm the listener generally grasps onto, also known as the groove.

Core Harmonic Rhythmic Driver: The primary harmonic instrument that flows with the core rhythm. It will act as the core rhythm if there are no drums. It will flow with the drums when there are drums.

Point of Difference: Using the isolated instruments that flow with the core rhythm to make a difference compared to the core rhythm drums.

Core Rhythm Highlighters: When you use layers of different instruments to accent parts of the core rhythm.

Counter Rhythm Principle: The secondary rhythm structures where the rest of the arrangement can occur. Instruments in the arrangement that play opposing rhythms to the core rhythm. This effect creates musical interest and energy.

Spatial Principle: The "stereo field" or "stage" where all the instruments in an arrangement occur. This is where the music is played. The rectangle prism in your mind's eye of the stage. This stage is where you place instruments within the stereo field. These instruments play music, which is made up of patterns and notes (hooks). You can place the instruments on the panning and frequency spectrum where you want to.

Foreground and Background Principle: The 3-D part of the stereo field (the stage). As you arrange, you will place some instruments closer to the front of the stage and others further back. You do this by creating using the three hook levels: primary, secondary and hidden hooks. You can also use sonics processing for depth.

Primary Hook: The primary focal point at any given time during the arrangement. There is usually only one primary focal point at any given time. Humans can only really focus on one thing at a time.

Secondary Hooks: Hooks that support the primary hooks and are generally audible to the average listener. Secondary hooks are more in the background. Can also be used as fills and act temporarily as a primary hook.

Hidden Hooks: Hooks that aren't obvious to the average listener unless you focus on them. These hooks are mostly in the background.

Energy Principle: The musical energy (hooks) the instruments play in an arrangement and when they play. How many instruments are playing at any given time. How those instruments layer on a bar-to-bar basis. The development of energy over the core structure using techniques, principles and stems thinking.

Call and Response Principle: The relationship between each instrument and the parts they play. One instrument plays a hook, which is a call. Then, the next instrument plays a hook: the response to that call. This continues between all instruments in the arrangement from start to finish.

Repurposing Principle: Repurposes the three hook levels into an entire arrangement. You invent the parts using the three hook levels (foreground and background principle). You then can create variations on those hooks to create new parts with repurposing.

Synergy Principle: The whole arrangement works as one single system. This principle links all Ten Core Principles of Arranging together as one. Every instrument in the arrangement has a purpose. The arrangement works as a team to create synergy.

Stems Thinking Framework: Layering tracks using the three layering types. Layering techniques (words) and principles (grammar) to create full musical works.

Layering Type One: The individual stem is solo or layered with other instruments, doubles, or textures.

Layering Type Two: A group of stems playing similar, following, or variations of ideas to each other.

Layering Type Three: Groups of stems relating to, following, or playing something similar or opposing to another group.

Sonics Framework: Mastering sonics using ear training, hearing the truth, and music production analysis of sonics. The pronunciation of the language of music production.

Sonics Chain: The parts of the music production chain that revolve around sonics. Including recording, editing, mixing, and mastering. The song and arrangement also play a role in sonics, by setting the foundation.

Sonics Principles: Within recording, editing, mixing, and mastering there are principles. These principles are the primary focus while analyzing and creating your own music. Everything branches out from these principles.

Hearing the Truth: Hearing accurate sonic information by treating and calibrating your room, speakers, and headphones. Creating a flat frequency response to hear true sonic sound.

Steps to Industry Standard Sonics: The three-step analysis framework to master Level Four - Sonics.

Reference Matching: Using an industry standard reference track to match your sonics to their same standard. Use the three-steps to industry standard sonics to successfully match the reference.

Sonic Tools: Use sonic tools to fix problems and achieve goals within the sonics framework. Tools used within the sonic principles.

Pro Mixing and Mastering Workflow: Mastering your rough mix to reveal all the flaws in your production chain. Then mixing and mastering your production with that data. You can also arrange, re-record and edit any parts needed also.

Original Sound: Created when you cross-pollinate techniques from your technique library together with your intuition. A sound that is unique to you.

Feedback and Iteration: You will need feedback and iteration to grow your skills as you create music. You can also get feedback from music production analysis and resource mining. You can get feedback from the market directly. You can also get this feedback through mentors: triangulate opinions with three-to-five people. You then iterate your music until you reach the standard you are after.

Catalog of Music: The catalog of music you will create over your entire career. Your own music creations.

The Lost Art: When you are immersed in the language of music production from the ground up with an in-person mentor. This process gives you a mindset transfer. This art is becoming rarer in the modern day. Music production analysis using the four primary frameworks can emulate this process.

Frameworks as Lenses: When you view music through the four primary frameworks – Techniques, Principles, Stems Thinking, and Sonics – you see music through different lenses. It is like using magnifying glasses to find information.

Cross-Pollination of Sound: Using techniques from any genre you want while creating your music. This process creates original sounds and new genres.

Polymath Producer Feedback Loop: Analyzing the great music of all time, you learn techniques from the masters of music production. You then start to think like a master yourself. Your music then becomes masterful.

Invisible Checklist: After analyzing the great music of all time, you begin to form a checklist in your mind of what needs to be done to create great music. This checklist becomes a world-class standard.

The Myth of Genre: Genre is created before it is defined. Genre is a cross-pollination of the building blocks from past genres. This evolution has taken place since music began.

The Golden Thread: When a producer teams up with an artist and songwriter(s)/producer(s) to create a unique sound around hit songs they write.

Polymath Producer Community: A place online for Polymath Producers to learn and master the language of music production together. It is also home to the Polymath Producer video/audio program version of this book.

Notes

In this section you will find the following:

- All *citations* mentioned in the book.
- All *music references* mentioned in the book.

If I have missed anything please let me know and I will update it.

PART I:

Part I Citations List

1. Ferriss, Tim. "Rick Rubin Interview". *The Tim Ferriss Show*. Podcast audio, October 29, 2015. https://www.youtube.com/watch?v=4AlZGl1o89s&t=1856s

2. Charlie Munger, Peter D. Kaufman, *Poor Charlies Almanack Expanded Hardcover*, 3rd Edition. The Donning Company Publishers, Jan 1, 2005.

3. Ferrier, Jonathan. "Client Interviews". Polymath Producer. *YouTube* videos. October 2018 - July 2024.

4. Ferriss, Tim. "Rick Rubin Interview". *The Tim Ferriss Show*. Podcast audio, October 29, 2015. https://www.youtube.com/watch?v=4AlZGl1o89s&t=1856s

5. Charlie Munger, Peter D. Kaufman, *Poor Charlies Almanack Expanded Hardcover*, 3rd Edition. The Donning Company Publishers, Jan 1, 2005.

6. "Law of the Instrument." *Wikipedia*. https://en.wikipedia.org/wiki/law_of_the_instrument

7. Orwell, George. "George Orwell, Quotes, Quotable Quote". *Goodreads*. 2024. https://www.goodreads.com/quotes/6145-who-controls-the-past-controls-the-future-who-controls-the

8. Daniel Coyle, *The Little Book of Talent: 52 Tips to Improve Your Skills*. Bantam, Aug 21, 2012.

PART II:

Part II Citations List

9. Gabriel Wyner, *Fluent Forever: How to Learn Any Language Fast and Never Forget It*. Harmony, Aug 5, 2014.

10. Alan Walker & Mood Melodies, "Alan Walker & Mood Melodies on Creating Alone - The Track," *YouTube*, May 30, 2017. https://www.youtube.com/watch?v=VwCdRqTVvBs

11. Ibid

Part II Music List

- Bowie, David. Heroes. RCA, 1977.
- Sheeran, Ed. Shape of You. Asylum - Atlantic, 2017.
- Ronettes, The. Be My Baby. Philles, 1963.
- Chainsmokers, The. Roses. Disrupter - Columbia - Sony, 2015.
- Weeknd, The & Punk, Daft. Starboy. XO - Republic, 2016.

PART III:

Part III Citations List

12. Pedler, Dominic. *Songwriting Secrets of the Beatles*. Omnibus Press, May 25 2010.

13. *The Great American Songbook*

Part III Music List

- Franklin, Aretha. Respect. Volt, 1965.
- Mitchell, Joni. Big Yellow Taxi. Reprise, 1970.
- Five, Maroon feat. B, Cardi. Girls Like You. 222 - Interscope, 2018.
- Swift, Taylor. Shake it Off. Big Machine, 2014.
- Mars, Bruno. Locked Out of Heaven. Atlantic, 2012.
- Flamingos, The. I Only Have Eyes for You. End. 1959.
- Warwick, Dionne. What the World Needs Now. Imperial Records, 1965.
- Outkast. Hey Ya. Arista, BMG, 2003.
- Knack, The. My Sharona. Capitol, 1979.
- Guess Who, The. American Woman. RCA Victor, 1970.
- Jackson, Michael. Rock With You. Epic, 1979.
- Notorious B.I.G. Mo Money Mo Problems. Bad Boy - Arista, 1997.
- Cruz, Taio. Dynamite. Island, 2009.
- Queen. We Will Rock You. EMI, Elektra, 1977.
- Vega, Suzanne, DNA. Tom's Diner (Remix). A&M, 1981.
- Survivor. Eye of the Tiger. EMI, Scotti Brothers, 1982.

Polymath Producer

- Weeknd, The. Can't Feel My Face. XO, Republic, 2015.
- Richman, Tommy. Million Dollar Baby. ISO Supremacy, Pulse, Concord, Universal, 2024.
- Golden, 24k, Dior, Iann. Mood. Columbia, 2020.
- Lazar, Major, DJ Snake, Mø. Lean On. Mad Decent, 2015.
- Sia. Cheap Thrills. Inertia, Monkey Puzzle, RCA, 2015.
- Maroon 5. Moves Like Jagger. A&M Octone, 2011.
- Mars, Bruno. Just The Way You Are. Elektra, Atlantic, 2010.
- Kesha. Tik Tok. RCA, 2009.
- Gaga, Lady. Just Dance. Streamline, KonLive, CherryTree, Interscope, 2008.
- Nelly. Hot in Herre. Universal, Fo' Reel, 2002.
- Cent, 50. In da Club. Aftermath, Shady, Interscope, 2003.
- Santana, Thomas, Rob. Smooth. Arista, BMG, 1999.
- House of Pain. Jump Around. Tommy Boy, XL, 1992.
- Queen. Another One Bites the Dust. EMI, Elektra, 1980.
- Morrison, Van. Moondance. A&R Studios, 1970.
- Cream. Sunshine of Your Love. Reaction/Polydor, Atco, 1967.
- Stones, Rolling. (I Can't Get No) Satisfaction. RCA, 1965.
- Sinatra, Frank. I've Got You Under My Skin. Capitol, 1956.
- Vivaldi. Concerto No. 4 Op 8. RV297 Winter 1. Allegro. 1725.
- Richie, Lionel, Ross, Diana. Endless Love. Motown, 1981.
- Simon & Garfunkel. Bridge Over Troubled Water. Columbia, 1970.
- Mars, Bruno. When I Was Your Man. Atlantic, 2013.
- Beatles, The. Yesterday. Capitol, Parlophone, 1965.
- Mars, Bruno. Treasure. Atlantic, 2013.
- Eminem. Lose Yourself. Shady, Interscope, 2002.
- Warwick, Dionne. Walk on By. Scepter, 1964.
- Jackson, Michael. Wanna Be Startin' Something. Epic, 1983.
- Rodrigo, Olivia. Driver's License. Geffen, Interscope, 2020.
- Sonic, Silk. Fly as Me. Aftermath, Atlantic, 2021.
- Lizzo. About Damn Time. Nice Life, Atlantic, 2022.
- Perry, Katy. Firework. Capitol, 2010.
- Medley, Bill, Warnes, Jennifer. Time of My Life. RCA, 1987.
- Big, Mr. To Be With You. Atlantic, 1991.
- Eminem, The Real Slim Shady, Aftermath, Interscope, Web, 2000.
- Sergei Rachmaninoff, 14 Romances, Op. 34: No. 14, Vocalize in C-Sharp Minor. 1915.
- Harris, Calvin - Lipa, Dua. One Kiss. Columbia, Sony, 2018.
- Harris, Calvin - Rihanna. We Found Love. Def Jam, SRP, 2011.
- Harris, Calvin - Rihanna. This is What You Came For. Westbury Road, Columbia, 2016.
- Thomas, B.J. Raindrops Keep Falling on my Head. Scepter, 1969.
- Disclosure, Smith, Sam. Latch. PMR, Cherrytree, Interscope, 2012.
- Cooke, Sam. You Send Me. Keen, 1957.
- Eagles, The. Hotel California. Asylum, 1977.
- Temptations, The. My Girl. Gordy, 1964.
- Lipa, Dua. Don't Start Now. Warner, 2019.
- J, Jessie. Bang Bang. Lava, Republic, 2014.

- Major Lazar, Lean On. Mad Decent, 2015.
- Marley, Bob, Wailers, The. Is This Love. Tuff Gong, Island, 1978.
- Perry, Katy. Teenage Dream. Capitol, 2010.
- Ace of Base. All That She Wants. Mega, London, Arista, 1992.
- INXS. Need You Tonight. WEA, 1987.
- Wonder, Stevie. Superstition. Motown, 1972.
- Carnes, Kim, Bette Davis Eyes. EMI, 1981.
- The Bee Gees, Staying Alive. RSO, 1977.
- The Police, Every Breath You Take. A&M, 1983.
- Timberlake, Justin. What Goes Around Comes Around. Jive, Zomba, 2006.
- Houston, Whitney. I Will Always Love You. Arista, 1992.
- Spears, Britney. Baby One More Time. Jive, 1998.
- Diamond, Neil. Sweet Caroline. Uni/MCA, 1969.
- John, Elton. Tiny Dancer. Uni, DJM, 1971.
- Prince. Kiss. Paisley Park, Warner, 1986.
- Crowded House. Don't Dream It's Over. Capitol, 1986.
- Mars, Bruno. When I Was Your Man. Atlantic, 2013.
- Lorde. Royals. Universal, 2013.
- Journey. Don't Stop Believing. Columbia, 1981.
- The Righteous Brothers. You've Lost That Loving Feeling. Philles, 1964.
- Patti LaBelle and LaBelle. Lady Marmalade. Epic, 1974.
- Drake. One Dance. Young Money, Cash Money, Republic, 2016.
- Commodores, The. Easy. Motown, 1977.
- Beyonce and Jay-Z. Crazy In Love. Columbia, 2003.
- Jackson, Michael. Billie Jean. Epic, 1983.
- ABBA. Dancing Queen. Polar, Epic, Atlantic, 1976.
- Ronson, Mark, Mars, Bruno. Uptown Funk. Columbia, Sony, RCA, 2014.
- Players, Ohio. Fire. Mercury, 1974.
- Sinatra, Frank, Basie, Count. Fly Me to The Moon. Reprise, 1964.
- Bieber, Justin. What Do You Mean? Def Jam, 2015.
- Foreigner. I Want To Know What Love Is. Atlantic, 1984.
- Mac, Fleetwood. Dreams. Warner, 1977.
- Symphony number 5, Beethoven. 1808.
- The Beatles. She Loves You. Parlophone, Swan, 1963.
- TLC. Waterfalls. LaFace, Arista, 1995.
- Seal. Kiss from a Rose. ZTT, Sire, Warner, 1994.
- Blondie. The Tide is High. Chrysalis, 1980.
- Franklin, Aretha. Say a Little Prayer for You. Atlantic, 1968.
- Redding, Otis. Sittin' on the Dock of the Bay. Volt, Atco, 1968.
- Queen. Bohemian Rhapsody. EMI, 1975.
- Orbison, Roy. Oh, Pretty Woman. Monument, 1964.
- Seasons, The Four. December 1963. Warner, Curb, 1975.
- Hanson. MMMBop. Mercury, 1997.
- Zimmer, Hans. Time. Reprise, 2010.

PART IV:

Part IV Music List
- Jackson, Michael, Thriller (Album). Epic, 1982.
- Rhienne, Rachelle. Orange Tree. 3 Sparks, 2023.
- Mars, Bruno. Treasure. Atlantic, 2013.

PART V:

Part V Citations List

14. The Wachowskis, Directors. *The Matrix*. Warner, 1999. 136 minutes. https://www.amazon.com/Matrix-Keanu-Reeves/dp/B000GJPL1S

15. Ferriss, Timothy. *The 4-Hour Chef: The Simple Path to Cooking Like a Pro, Learning Any Skill & Living a Good Life*. New Harvest, October 19 2012.

16. Adams, Scott. "What is a Talent Stack.?" *Sloww*. 2024. https://www.sloww.co/talent-stack/

17. Gudwin, Josh. Electricity, Silk City ft. Dua Lipa. *Mix with the Masters*. 2024. https://mixwiththemasters.com/videos/josh-gudwin-silk-city-ft-dua-lipa-electricity

18. Joshua, Jaycen, Pensado, Dave. Advanced Mix Techniques. *Mix with the Masters*. 2024. https://mixwiththemasters.com/videos/jaycen-joshua-advanced-mix-techniques

19. Merrill, Randy. Mastering in the Digital Domain. *Mix with the Masters*. 2024. https://mixwiththemasters.com/videos/randy-merrill-various-artists-mastering-in-the-digital-domain

20. Everitt, Shawn. Slow Burn, Kacey Musgraves. *Mix with the Masters*. 2024. https://mixwiththemasters.com/videos/shawn-everett-kacey-musgraves-slowburn

21. La Grange, Blake. *Mastering Accelerator*. 2024.

22. Wilcken, Hugo. Quotable Quote. *Goodreads*. 2024. https://www.goodreads.com/quotes/6903322-one-of-the-methods-that-he-and-bowie-used-on

Part V Music List
- Jones, Norah. Come Away With Me. Blue Note, 2002.
- Rhienne, Rachelle. Just Like Me. 3 Sparks, 2024.
- Rhienne, Rachelle. Late to the Party. 3 Sparks, 2024.
- Cabello, Camila. Havana. Epic, Syco, 2017.

PART VI:

Part VI Citations List

23. Avildsen, John G, director. *The Karate Kid*. Columbia Pictures, 1984. 127 minutes. https://www.amazon.com/Karate-Kid-Ralph-Macchio/dp/B000OLROWC

24. Csikszentmihalyi, Mihaly. *Flow*. Harper Perennial Modern Classics, July 1 2008.

25. Cialdini, Robert. *Influence: The Psychology of Persuasion*. Harper Business, December 26, 2006.

26. Dalio, Ray. *Principles*. Avid Reader Press/ Simon & Schuster, September 19 2017.

27. Feynman, Richard. "Richard P. Feynman Quotes." *AZ Quotes*. 2024. https://www.azquotes.com/quote/1070806

28. Justin Timberlake. *FutureSex/LoveShow: Live from Madison Square Garden, DVD*. Jive, Zomba, 2007.

29. Greene, Robert. *Laws of Human Nature*. Viking, Oct. 23 2018.

30. Holiday, Ryan. *Perennial Seller*. Portfolio, July 18, 2017.

31. Jobs, Steve. "Quotable Quote." *Goodreads*. 2024. https://www.goodreads.com/quotes/988332-some-people-say-give-the-customers-what-they-want-but

32. Tudahl, Duane. *Prince and the Purple Era Studio Sessions*. Rowman & Littlefield Publishers, Nov 17 2017.

33. Tedder, Ryan. The Art of Hit-Making. *Studio*. 2022. https://studio.com/classes/ryan-tedder/art-of-hitmaking

34. Gehringer, Chris. Mastering in the Digital Domain. *Mix with the Masters*. https://mixwiththemasters.com/videos/chris-gehringer-various-artists-mastering-in-the-digital-domain

35. Run-DMC/Aerosmith Version. *Wikipedia*. 2024. https://en.wikipedia.org/wiki/Walk_This_Way

36. Schopenhauer, Arhur. *Oxford Reference*. 2024. https://www.oxfordreference.com/display/10.1093/acref/9780191866692.001.0001/q-oro-ed6-00009189#:~:text=The%20man%20of%20talent%20is,they%20cannot%20even%20see%20to.

Part VI Music List

- Prince. Purple Rain (Album). Warner Bros., 1984.
- Prince. Around the World in a Day (Album). Warner Bros., 1985.
- Springfield, Dusty. The Look of Love. Colgems, 1967.
- Run-DMC, Aerosmith. Profile, Geffen, 1986.

PART VII:

Part VII Music List

- Rhienne, Rachelle. Sometimes I Think About You. 3 Sparks. 2021.

Part VII Citations List

37. Ferriss, Tim. "Rick Rubin Interview". *The Tim Ferriss Show*. Podcast audio, October 29, 2015. https://www.youtube.com/watch?v=4AlZGl1o89s&t=1856s

38. Robert Greene. *Mastery*. Penguin Books, Oct 29 2013.

39. Osho. "Osho: Books I Have Loved". *Osho International YouTube*, September 8, 2009. URL: https://www.youtube.com/watch?v=j1h8-WvzexY

40. David R. Hawkins. *Letting go: The Pathway of Surrender*. Hay House, Jan 15, 2014.

Acknowledgements

I STARTED CREATING the contents within this book in 2016. It has been almost a decade of work. Although there are seeds of its content decades earlier too.

Through it all, my parents have supported me. I want to start by thanking my parents, Christine and Ian. If it weren't for your unconditional support, this book wouldn't exist. The invention of new ideas requires time. To be able to have time requires an unconditional support system. You offered that to me and for that I am forever grateful. I love you.

Marina, you were with me from the start of this book and saw me through the daily ups and downs of creating the book. Thanks for your unconditional support and keeping my spirits high. LoML, LoMS.

Nick and Jack, the master men, thanks for being a support system while I kept periodically abandoning this project every year since 2016 and coming back to it. I finally got there in the end. Time to blast "Time" on the beach in victory.

Thanks to Rachelle for having faith that these methods work and letting me experiment these findings on the music we've created with 3 Sparks. Thanks also for supporting the use of the music as references for the book.

Thank you to Brenda for letting me stay at your home while I wrote the manuscript overseas. It was deeply appreciated.

Thank you Leonard for raising my standards when it comes to book creation and guiding me to think like a major publisher. "Come back when you're serious." Our conversations got me taking this book writing thing seriously.

Thanks to Larry Butler for editing the manuscript and for sharing your experiences in the music industry as a legend in your own right. You're a true gentleman.

Thanks to Lisa for answering all my questions about formatting. You helped relax my restless mind.

Thanks to all my mentors from music, books, programs, and the Internet from my entire life up to now. There are too many to name, but know you helped me become the person I am today.

Thanks to all the members of the Polymath Producer community for having faith in my ideas from the start. Thanks to all the community members who were beta readers. Vlad Freimann, Aron Foris, Abbey Hussein, Richard Davis, Rosan Sharma, Darren Michaels, Justin Gress, and Wesley L. Your feedback was deeply appreciated.

Thanks to all readers, clients and customers of my work, past, present and future. Your support of these ideas means the world to me.

Lastly, thank you God for guiding me through this all.

About The Author

Jonathan William Ferrier is what the music industry calls a "100%er". He is a songwriter and music producer with the skills to complete an entire production alone – a *Polymath Producer*. He can write a full song, create the arrangement, record, edit, and mix and master.

However, he specializes in songwriting and arranging within the music production chain. He works mainly with pop artists who want catchy songs with a unique sound. He currently goes by the producer name Jon Will.

"I aim to create songs and music productions that will stand the test of time."
– Jonathan William Ferrier

While learning and mastering music production, Jonathan began music production analysis. He then developed the Polymath Producer System between 2016 and 2024. This turned music production into a language. In January 2019, he decided to share this new language. He first shared it in a program called The Polymath Producer System. Clients got amazing and fast results. He then refined the ideas over the years and turned the program into this book for the public.

Sign up to Jon's newsletter for all future work at: www.polymathproducer.com

Here are what artists say about working with Jon:

"Jonathan is the man to find your sound. He worked with me to find the best sound that suited my brand and my voice and it has developed into something really special that I'm proud to release as my music. It's different and it's exciting and I couldn't have done it without him. Along with his independent expansive skills in production and songwriting, Jon has the ability to take on a personal and professional approach with whomever he collaborates, making it fun and highly productive. Jon is a wizard and he has diamond ears."– Rachelle Rhienne

"Jonathan is a fantastic producer and songwriter with an elevated approach to song creation. He uses his sharp instincts for writing memorable hooks and his unique and creative approach to production/arrangement as he draws on a wide background of musical inspirations to create phenomenal songs that stay in your head after first listen. He is an idea machine and we can always count on Jonathan to capture the essence of a hit song in an effortless, impactful way." – Marina Bennett

POLYMATH PRODUCER

polymathproducer.com

www.ingramcontent.com/pod-product-compliance
Lightning Source LLC
Chambersburg PA
CBHW060048230426
43661CB00004B/705